T0387933

VISIONS AND VICTIMS

VISIONS AND VICTIMS

Art Melodrama in the Films of Carl Th. Dreyer

Amanda Doxtater

THE UNIVERSITY OF WISCONSIN PRESS

Supported by the Society for the Advancement of Scandinavian Study and the Barbro Osher Endowed Chair of Swedish Studies at the University of Washington.

The University of Wisconsin Press
728 State Street, Suite 443
Madison, Wisconsin 53706
uwpress.wisc.edu

Printed in the United States of America
This book may be available in a digital edition.

Library of Congress Cataloging-in-Publication Data

Names: Doxtater, Amanda Elaine, author.
Title: Visions and victims : art melodrama in the films of Carl Th. Dreyer / Amanda Doxtater.
Description: Madison, Wisconsin : The University of Wisconsin Press, 2024. | Includes bibliographical references and index.
Identifiers: LCCN 2023046529 | ISBN 9780299347505 (cloth)
Subjects: LCSH: Dreyer, Carl Theodor, 1889–1968—Criticism and interpretation.
Classification: LCC PN1998.3.D74 D69 2024 | DDC 791.4302/33092 [B]—dc23/eng/20231108
LC record available at https://lccn.loc.gov/2023046529

For Jeanne

Contents

Illustrations

Preface

Carl Th. Dreyer once described filmmaking as his only great passion. I came to appreciate this passion not through his films alone but also through encounters that were fortuitous, contingent, and steeped in an archival experience of the director and his process.

The central and persistent strain of scholarship on Carl Th. Dreyer has claimed for itself a dispassionate position, one posited as *objective*. None of the scholarly work I seek to emulate, whether for its academic rigor, style, or approach, aspires to dispassionate objectivity. To the contrary, I believe that claims of value-neutral positivism and normative notions of scholarly objectivity and reproducibility have systematically repressed Dreyer's fascinations with embodied experience. More pointedly, the feminist heart of my project revolves exactly around critiquing the authority of this seemingly neutral voice as also inherently ideological. The position of purported nonpositionality reproduces patriarchal hierarchies that subordinate emotion (gendered feminine) to rationality and dispassion (gendered masculine). Scholarly voices performing objective authority have occluded the creative, embodied, and affective work of scholarly collection and recollection. In its choice to adopt feminist reading practices, *Visions and Victims* doesn't dismiss canonical Dreyer scholarship that has largely neglected popular culture, emotion, sensation, and corporeality as either inartistic or unworthy of real scholarship—it intentionally engages with and critiques it. My ambition for *Visions and Victims* is neither to applaud nor condemn Dreyer as a director but rather to explore the conflicted beauty and complexity of his film practice as art melodrama.

∼

I first visited the Dreyer Collection at the Danish Film Institute (DFI) as a graduate student and research assistant working with James Schamus on his book *Carl Theodor Dreyer's Gertrud: The Moving Word* (2008). I went not as an expert on Dreyer but as a Scandinavianist with a concentration in film studies and the language skills to read relevant sources in Swedish and Danish. Retrospectively, this was my first encounter with the pleasurable complexities of archival research. Three days in the collection on the second floor of the DFI also afforded an intriguing glimpse into Dreyer's own passion for research. The "Gertrud" file contained envelope upon envelope of his meticulous notes, both handwritten and typed, as well as newspaper clippings and lists of library books he had checked out. Dreyer had already located many of the secondary sources that I was tasked with consulting. I was moved by the care with which he organized his notes, labeling each envelope, as if intently engaging in a process of self-archiving. *Gertrud* (1964) was the last feature film Dreyer made before he died, and his handwriting reflected the way his hand shook as he wrote. It felt at once like a voyeuristic peek into Dreyer's private world—in addition to production materials, his files contained ephemera such as unpublished letters and receipts for chocolates he had bought for his wife—and at the same time, an intimately collaborative invitation into this world, as if this man had deliberately left these traces for future researchers to consult and consume.

I was hooked, and I returned to the archives as soon as I could. All told, I spent two years in Copenhagen working with the Dreyer and Nordisk Films collections at the DFI.

Before that initial encounter with the Dreyer collection, my image of the director had been varied. I had heard anecdotes about *La Passion de Jeanne d'Arc* being one of the best films ever made, an extraordinary modernistic, perceptual experimentation with formalism, and also one of the best performances ever captured on film, so much so that Maria Falconetti was thought to have been tortured by this sadistic director. The first film of Dreyer's I watched was *Prästänkan* (*The Parson's Widow*, 1920) in Mark Sandberg's seminar on early Scandinavian cinema at Berkeley. With this film's depiction of multiple generations, young and old, interacting in playful and ultimately mortal conflict, Dreyer's reputation grew more nuanced. *Prästänkan* showed the uncompromising Danish auteur to be an artist with humility and humor as well as an intriguing and perplexing desire for filmic authenticity. Instead of building sets, he insisted on using a centuries-old farmhouse at the Maihaugen heritage museum in Norway, a preference that caused terrible problems for lighting and production. *Jeanne d'Arc*, shot in chronological order, compresses the entire drama of the trial and immolation into a single day, while *Prästänkan* allows institutions and architectural spaces to foreground the way that new and old coexist and inform one another rather than replace each other neatly, in teleological succession. Retrospectively, I can see how those early discussions about nonlinear temporality, performance, and inhabitation in *Jeanne d'Arc* and *Prästänkan* informed my argument in this book.

Given that I conducted research in ways that sometimes felt like inhabiting the Dreyer and Nordisk collections, I experienced the temporality of Dreyer's career in a similar way. The early scripts that Dreyer wrote inhabited the same physical space of his "mature" films like *Gertrud*. Thus, when I treat Dreyer's oeuvre holistically in this book—reading his early work in relation to his late—it's because encountering them together opened interesting connections between them. Having the luxury of an extended period of time to interact with these materials meant that I could both ask specific questions of them but also let research questions emerge out of them. The Dreyer collection became a space of serious research play for me, opening up creative, performative, affective, and experiential ways of knowing.

∼

Dreyer's films also produced a peculiar response of attraction and repulsion in me as a spectator. I delighted in absorbing their breathtaking beauty and contemplating their conceptual paradoxes. They exhibit the uneasy coexistence of a stylized, restrained, minimalist aesthetic of estrangement and what I perceived as effusive scenes of heightened emotional expressivity, intense suffering, and violent physical discomfort. In *La Passion de Jeanne d'Arc*: Jeanne's glassy, resplendent eyes as she glances skyward, endless tears tracing ruts down her gritty, unadorned cheeks. In *Ordet*: the wild flush of desire at Inger's voracious embrace of life as she opens her mouth wide to bite her husband's chin. In *Day of Wrath*: Herlofs-Marthe's intense fury and humiliation as she is stripped to be tortured by yet another long slate of leering church patriarchs. And in *Gertrud*: the eponymous heroine and icy queen of love who, overcome by heartbreak, collapses in an agonizingly elegant swoon. Dreyer adamantly rejected accusations that the scenes of torture in his films were gratuitous, and the assertion that they might be irked him. Writing this book and working with these images through my burgeoning practice of videographic criticism has meant contending with my own perverse attraction to feminine suffering in Dreyer's films as well as my urge to critique it.

To my mind, most of the scholarly approaches to Dreyer's art cinema— whether passionate formalism; the great man narratives; the meticulous historical accounts about Dreyer's work performed with encyclopedic authority; the quasi-mystical, transcendental, or spiritual readings; the Lacanian; or the titillating psychobiographical—either occlude or underplay the intensely moving images of suffering in his work. These are often absorbed, rather unproblematically, as part of Dreyer's artistic ambition to elevate film from entertainment to take its proper place as a high art. My long-standing interest in melodrama studies, with its tendency to privilege both suffering and style—an interest that received a shot in the arm from working with Linda Williams—provided an obvious lens through which to consider Dreyer's images of white, largely feminine suffering and a series of accompanying research questions. Why haven't emotion and suffering been understood as central to Dreyer's innovation of art cinema? Must suffering be labeled tragic for us to appreciate Dreyer as an auteur? Why does the category of melodrama, albeit in some postmodern or ironic iteration, seem to stick to a character like Lars von Trier (who models himself as Dreyer's heir apparent) or to Nordisk Films Kompagni (the rip-roaring Danish silent era studio where Dreyer learned everything about filmmaking) and yet slide so persistently off Dreyer? In much Dreyer scholarship, the term "melodrama" is employed to describe what Dreyer had left behind, or what he was not doing, or an easy form that he boldly resisted rather than anything that might persist, whether passionately or conflictedly, in his "mature" films. Was Dreyer ashamed to be associated with melodrama or any of its substitute terms, including "popular culture" and "low culture"?

While decades of melodrama scholarship have recuperated the term as a positive category in film studies, in the context of Dreyer's work and Danish cinema history, its stigmatizing association with feminized or feminizing low culture remains significant. Reading Dreyer's filmmaking as melodramatic still raises eyebrows. This study seeks to change that, showing how Dreyer's art melodrama archive unsettles the standard teleological trajectory of his development from a practitioner of popular culture to an art cinema auteur. As I elaborate in the chapters to follow, this feminist approach reimagines the archive of the auteur and the kinds of truths it purports to tell.

Acknowledgments

I would like to gratefully acknowledge the people who have engaged with this project in its many iterations and helped me improve it. My work has benefited immensely from the generous attention paid to it by writing groups and colleagues: Anna Jörngården and Dean Krouk in IDEA; Karin Emmerich, Lanie Millar, Leah Middlebrook, Fabienne Moore, Casey Shoop, and Marc Schachter of SOCE; Mal Ahern, Jennifer Bean, and Leigh Mercer of WTF; Olivia Gunn, Scott Magelssen, Jasmine Mahmoud, Daniela Rosner, Adair Rounthwaite, and Ellwood Wiggins of PSWG, who introduced me to performance studies; and Ben Bigalow, Arne Lunde, Benjamin Mier-Cruz, and Liina-Ly Roos of SSAWA. Being able to share my writing on a regular basis with such brilliant scholars has been a privilege and a delight. An inspiring two weeks at Middlebury's videographic workshop, Scholarship in Sound & Image, in 2019 blew my chapter on *Gertrud* into new archival territory, for which I am grateful. I would like to thank Christian Keathley for encouraging me to create bravely, dig into my past failures, and not shy away from the personal. To my rockstar cohort from FSP bootcamp: Lynnette Arnold, Andra Chastain, and Danielle Filipiak, without whom this project would simply not be, I send solidarity, love, and gratitude. Many thanks also to Anna Mrozewicz for being a sounding board for all kinds of ideas about Nordic cinema and Dreyer. Thank you to Tom Smith for introducing me to Dreyer's eccentric work so many years ago.

I am grateful to my wonderful colleagues in the Department of Scandinavian Studies at the University of Washington for their support and collegiality. Special thanks to Andy Nestingen for his tenacious support, and to Olivia Gunn for being such a voracious intellectual; I treasure your friendship and sense of humor. Thank you to Maxine Savage for the stimulating Dreyer-related conversations surrounding the *Mikaël* commentary track. I would also like to thank the Department of Scandinavian at University of California, Berkeley, where this project began. My work benefited greatly from the generous mentorship of Mark Sandberg, whose endless patience, curiosity, and insight guided my early research on Dreyer. His scholarship on early Danish cinema serves as an endless source of inspiration. Thank you also to Linda Williams for spending so many hours reading drafts of chapters and for scrawling a tiny "wow" in pencil at the end of the one I wrote on melodrama. I will cherish it always. And *ett stort tack* to Linda Rugg for modeling what an affective and rigorous deep dive into an auteur one admires can look like.

My work over the past several years has been supported by generous grants from the Walter Chapin Simpson Center for the Humanities at the University of Washington, including a timely First Book Fellowship. I am deeply indebted to Kathleen Woodward and the staff of the Simpson Center for all the work they do as tireless champions of the humanities who sustain a vivacious intellectual community at the University of Washington. My research also continues to benefit from the generosity of Barbro Osher, who established an endowed chair of Swedish Studies at the University of Washington that I have the privilege and responsibility of holding.

I'm grateful for the profound generosity and kindness of the staff of the Danish Film Institute who facilitated my delightful and formative experiences in the Dreyer Archive. Thank you to Thomas Christensen, Lisbeth Richter Larsen, and Lars Ølgaard. *Tusind tak* also to Casper Tybjerg for helping with early institutional affiliation at the University of Copenhagen during initial phases of my research. His extensive scholarship on Dreyer continues to impress and overwhelm. I'm also grateful to Morten Egholm and Isak Thorsen for delightful conversations in Copenhagen about Dreyer and Danish cinema.

Visions and Victims reflects the assistance of several talented editors who I would like to thank: Humanities First for helping me polish the book proposal, Amy Benson Brown for helping develop the manuscript for review, and coach and editor Elizabeth DeNoma for stepping in at the last with a burst of energy, expertise, and enthusiasm to help me across the finish line. Last, but certainly not least, I would like to thank the University of Wisconsin Press and Amber Cederström for their expertise, generosity, and patience in helping me see my first monograph into the world.

I would never have even undertaken this project, let alone finished it, without the loving support of my family and friends. Thank you, Mom, for your steady encouragement, Dad, for sharing with me your delight of academic work—I've yet to meet anyone who loves it more—and my brilliant sister Rachel for all her love, Saturday walks on Alki, and her work raising S. I aspire every day to heed his wise counsel to "Be more cat." Thank you, Shannon, for being such a loving presence in my life for so long. Thank you, Sonja, for your inspiring sense of beauty, dynamism, and friendship. I miss you. To my dear friends in Eugene, from Crest Drive to Germany, thank you. Last but not least, a heartfelt thank-you to Sarita and Ethan, who helped me on my journey in unexpected and enlightening ways.

VISIONS AND VICTIMS

Introduction

The poet H.D. opens her review of Carl Th. Dreyer's *La Passion de Jeanne d'Arc* (1928) by calling it a film "that has caused me more unrest, more spiritual forebodings, more intellectual rackings, more emotional torment than any I have yet seen."[1] She excoriates the film's remorseless, hard lines and Dreyer's refusal to grant this saint any blossoming sensuousness or heavenly comfort that might temper the suffering of martyrdom. At the same time, she finds the cinematic suffering of the young Jeanne, portrayed by Maria Falconetti, intellectually and affectively compelling. "Heart and head are given over to inevitable surrender."[2] For H.D., a queer, female critic and spectator, the film raises a flurry of unsettling questions. "I know in my mind that this is a great tour de force, perhaps one of the greatest. But I am left wary, a little defiant. Again why and why and why and just, just why? Why am I defiant before one of the most exquisite and consistent works of screen art and perfected craft that it has been our immeasurable privilege to witness?"[3] H.D.'s question, her repeated "Why?" is inextricable from her admiration for "Carl Dreyer, a Dane," whom she describes as "one of the most superb of the magnificently growing list of directors" and also "responsible for this odd two-edged sort of feeling."[4] H.D.'s profound and persistent *why*—part surrender, part defiance, part cool, intellectual racking, part furious emotional and physical torment, part head, and part heart—resonates with my impetus for writing this book about the films of Carl Th. Dreyer. That "two-edged sort of feeling" runs not only through *La Passion de Jeanne d'Arc* but also through Dreyer's long career and beyond. It also animates a film genre and critical category that I call *art melodrama*.

Art melodrama is an iteration of the melodramatic mode informed by art cinema. It explicitly combines melodrama's privileging of the expressive potential of the suffering human body, emotion, and spectacle, on the one hand, with art cinema's claims to ambiguity, aesthetic distance, media consciousness, reflexivity, authorial subjectivity, and formal experimentation, on the other. Art melodrama heightens and dramatizes the interrelationship of expressivity and reflexivity, feeling and thought, more overtly than other generic iterations of the melodramatic mode, such as the domestic family melodrama or the action film, often resulting in films that engage with themes of sadism and masochism. That is, art melodrama often features bodies in extremis, framed in such overt ways that the viewer reflects on the ways the film generates corresponding forms of extremis in her own body as well. Essentially hybrid and "impure," art melodrama marries sensibilities commonly deemed antithetical to one another: popular and elite; mainstream and independent; obvious and ambiguous; feminine and masculine; passive and active.[5] Art melodrama's reflexivity is often medium-reflexive and intermedial; it examines cinema by juxtaposing it with theater, the pictorial arts, music, literature, and print media, among other forms of aesthetic representation. It articulates the discursive space of high culture within low, and low culture within high.[6] As such, art melodrama calls presumed aesthetic binaries into question by marking, dramatizing, and exploiting the tensions between them. *Visions and Victims* opens up new possibilities for reading mass culture and high culture as intimately, if contentiously, interrelated.[7] Perhaps most importantly, art melodrama allows us to reconceptualize the gendered expectations associated with being a spectator of either art cinema or melodrama. Art melodrama expands critical, cinematic reflexivity to include the extreme affects typically associated with feminized and infantilized bodies: embodied awareness and sympathy for others conveyed through shock, pain, and emotional intensities such as anger, grief, confusion, and elation.

Art melodrama is a subset of melodrama. Sometimes functioning as a genre, sometimes as a mode in and of itself, art melodrama partakes fundamentally in melodrama as a popular mode, modality, or sensibility that informs innumerable discrete genres, such as the domestic melodrama, the soap opera, the musical, or the action film.[8] That said, the term "melodrama" also has been used to articulate practices not immediately associated with popular culture. Since popular culture became a legitimate object of academic study in the 1960s and 1970s, critics have seen its potential to also be artistic, stylized, and sophisticated. This shift dates back to Peter Brooks's canonical work *The Melodramatic Imagination: Balzac, Henry James, Melodrama, and the Mode of Excess* (1976), which made it possible to talk about expressionist drama, or the historical avantgarde, or a stylist like Henry James as deeply invested in and influenced by popular culture.[9] In film studies, Thomas Elsaesser's equally canonical "Tales of Sound and Fury: Observations on the Family Melodrama" from 1972 established Hollywood melodrama as serious fare; Douglas Sirk's retrospective rereading of the five films he made while employed at Universal from 1952 to 1959 as critical of the ideologies undergirding bourgeois, postwar American life allowed critics to embrace film melodrama by reading it against the grain, as ironic and even subversive ideological critique.[10] Importantly, as Linda Williams and Christine Gledhill argue, this elevation of Sirkian melodrama to art simultaneously delegitimized other forms of melodrama that were made for and consumed by female spectators as uncritical or unironic.[11] As a genre, art melodrama helps identify elements of art cinema reflexivity in these melodramatic texts as well.

"Art melodrama," as I engage the term, returns in part to this foundational melodrama scholarship in the 1970s and 1980s by reconsidering and rereading some of its forgotten nuances: Brooks's distinction between primary and secondary melodrama, and the consequent implications for understanding how melodrama develops; Elsaesser's call to explore the genealogies of melodrama; and Gledhill's elaboration of the complex array of identification strategies operating in melodrama and popular culture. The term "art melodrama" also provides conceptual unity for more recent scholarship that traces the melodramatic mode outside Hollywood, reading art cinema auteurs like Pedro Almodóvar, Michael Haneke, Wong Kar-wai, and Lars von Trier as melodrama auteurs.[12]

Art melodrama also enlivens the relatively undertheorized category of art cinema by analyzing its imbrication with melodrama's expressivities and embodiments. Theorization of art cinema enjoyed its heyday as film studies came into being as a scholarly field in the 1960s and 1970s, going hand in hand with auteur and genre studies. In contrast to scholarship on melodrama, which has continued to explode in subsequent decades, interest in art cinema as a critical category has subsided, in part due to a fatigue with centering white, male European auteur filmmaking in the post–World War II era and its related privileging of modernist, masculinized modes of spectatorship and formal experimentation. But the pseudo-Brechtian ambition of art cinema to speak to a critical spectator only partly describes the experience of consuming art cinema; art cinema's emotional and affective import has been systematically underestimated from the start. Some recent work has reconsidered art cinema's utility as a critical category in part by grappling with its embodiments. Rosalind Galt and Karl Schoonover, whose revisionist work in *Global Art Cinema: New Theories and Histories* (2010) defines art cinema precisely in terms of the impure discursive spaces it opens up, describe embodiment as one aspect of art cinema's inherent impurity. Part of this involves troubling understood notions about art cinema's demand for aesthetic distance, or the intellectual capacity to resist overidentifying with a fictional text. In Galt and Schoonover's words, "Aesthetic distance is called for, but the rigor of distanciation is constantly crossed with an emotive bodily response and a virtual engagement with the other."[13] Art melodrama, as I employ the category, explicitly names that space of distance and intimacy within art cinema's larger impurities—the space in which cerebral pleasures and perplexity intertwine with a broad spectrum of bodily sensations, from melancholy, delight, fear, anger, and unease to overwhelming, lingering feelings of dread and pathos. Art melodrama marks the kind of spectatorial experience that Barbara Klinger articulates in her work on *The Piano* (Jane Campion, 1993) and that John David Rhodes explores when he reads art cinema in relation to affective labor.[14] *Visions and Victims* contributes to those renewed discussions of art cinema that generate new personal and institutional histories, conceptualizations of cinema spectatorship, questions about national versus international film cultures, and interest in film form around the world.[15]

The exploration of art melodrama in *Visions and Victims* also brings to light unexpected similarities in the way melodrama and art cinema have been theorized. For one thing, defining each term can be vexing; existing work on melodrama and art cinema encompasses almost every theoretical and methodological approach imaginable, ranging from the close reading of film texts to analyses of reception, production, and institutions. Beyond that, each term sometimes refers to a mode and sometimes to a genre. Despite melodrama and art cinema often standing in for low and high culture, respectively, a binary that continues to be operative in this study, each category has been defined—and also lauded—as *the* antithetical other to mainstream (Hollywood) cinema and its regime of continuity editing, whether by being too ambiguous (art film) or too emotionally excessive (melodrama). Scholars have reclaimed the otherness both of melodrama and art cinema. Linda Williams has shown melodrama to be not in excess of "classical" Hollywood narrative but rather integral to it, thereby redeeming popular culture. David Andrews, working from the other direction, redeems art cinema's need to define itself as exclusive by making that exclusivity global, and popular. In defining art cinema, he writes, "What we need is a fully relative, multigeneric approach that casts a wide net in gathering examples of cinematic exclusiveness."[16] Similarly, melodrama and art cinema each share an ambiguous relationship as other to both the normative mainstream and the avant-garde; each sometimes occupies the space of the "middle brow."[17] Art cinema is both more narrative and also more accessible—both in terms of its formal attributes and its distribution channels—than its avant-garde kin. In contrast to other forms of popular cinema, such as the early slapstick of Charlie Chaplin and Buster Keaton, melodrama has generally not been appropriated or admired by the avant-garde.[18] Seen especially through the lens of art melodrama that I propose here, melodrama and art cinema, which have been considered diametrically opposed, share compelling similarities. Each draws viewers in and out of fictional worlds, establishes and thwarts identification, demonstrates media consciousness, and engages with spectatorship by alternating between direct and indirect modes of address. Crucially, the thrill of reading melodramatic bodies can very much involve reading for maximum ambiguity—art cinema's quintessential demand, as David Bordwell defines it.[19] Art melodrama expands what reflexivity and medium-consciousness look like and helps name an array of traditionally feminized elements operating in a traditionally masculinized form and vice versa.

When John Mercer and Martin Shingler identify art cinema as a prime location for future work on film melodrama in *Melodrama: Genre, Style, Sensibility*, it is Scandinavian art cinema that exemplifies this new scholarly frontier in cinema outside mainstream Hollywood. What Mercer and Shingler gesture toward as a general horizon of possibility, I bring into focus as *art melodrama*.

> The work of Ingmar Bergman for example, usually categorised outside of the mainstream of popular cinema as "art-house," frequently deals with thematic concerns and demonstrates a stylistic aesthetic that might be understood as articulating a melodramatic sensibility. Films like *Persona* (1966) with its theme of muteness, or the claustrophobic atmosphere evoked in *Cries and Whispers* (1972), both featuring female protagonists, are especially good examples of the ways in which Bergman's cinema could be read as melodrama. Equally the films of the Dogme 95 movement such as *Festen* (Thomas Vinterberg, 1998) and, especially, *Breaking the Waves* (1996), *The Idiots* (1998) and *Dancer in the Dark* (2000) (all directed by Lars von Trier) whilst utilising a scrupulously realist aesthetic, deal with highly-charged emotional states and situations, seemingly pushing the boundaries of realism to its limits in ways that can provoke extreme discomfort in audiences.[20]

Employing Scandinavian art-house cinema in this context is a tribute to the outsized role that this relatively small region of the world historically has played, and continues to play, in defining art cinema. The other side of this coin is a perceived incongruity between Scandinavian cinema and melodrama. For Mercer and Shingler, Scandinavian art cinema serves as an ultimate melodramatic outlier, the place one would least expect to find "films that challenge audience expectations and have the ability to elicit strong emotional responses through their charged dramatic register."[21] At some level, despite decades of recuperative scholarship, melodrama's low culture stigma persists in their account above in fundamental and subtle ways: melodrama is not supposed to "provoke extreme discomfort in audiences," and art cinema is not supposed to "elicit strong emotional responses." With its reputation for cool, reserved frigidity, Scandinavian art cinema is perhaps an outlier among outliers. As Steve Neale puts it in "Art Cinema as Institution," Scandinavian art film—epitomized by Carl Th. Dreyer and Ingmar Bergman—is a particularly "austere" form of art cinema, in contrast to "the plush visual spectacles of Bertolucci and Chabrol" or the "romantic humanism of Truffaut," to give just two examples.[22] Conspicuously present in Neale's detailed list of art cinema auteurs, and conspicuously absent from Mercer and Shingler's potentially melodramatic Scandinavian art-house auteurs, is Denmark's most distinguished and arguably most austere director, Carl Th. Dreyer (1889–1968). It's a curious omission.

Although Dreyer made relatively few films—just fourteen features and eight shorts—over the course of his long career, several contribute significantly to the emergence of European art cinema.[23] He began working in cinema in his early twenties in the Danish studios of the silent era, where he learned the craft of filmmaking and eventually directed his first two feature films, *The President* (*Præsidenten*, 1919) and *Leaves from Satan's Book* (*Blade af Satans Bog*, 1921). Between 1920 and 1930 Dreyer directed seven films in five different countries: Denmark, France, Germany, Norway, and Sweden. His Danish production of the film *Master of the House* (*Du skal Ære din Hustru*, 1925) was his first clear critical and financial success in French markets. With that breakthrough he was invited to France under contract with Société Générale des Films. While living in Paris with his family from 1926 to around 1931, Dreyer directed *La Passion de Jeanne d'Arc* (1928), pulling together a film crew experienced with avant-garde movements in France and Germany. In 1930 Dreyer established his own production company to direct *Vampyr* (1932), his first sound film, over which he exerted perhaps the greatest degree of artistic control but which also was a resounding financial failure. The experience threw him into a depression and for several years afterward he worked as a journalist to support himself and his family. It wasn't until 1942 that he began directing again in Denmark, making short public service films and then *Day of Wrath* (*Vredens dag*, 1943), his Danish comeback.[24] Despite mixed critical reception from contemporary reviewers, *Day of Wrath* is considered one of his major works of art cinema, along with *Jeanne d'Arc* and the final two feature films that Dreyer directed, *Ordet* (1955) and *Gertrud* (1964). *Ordet* won the Golden Lion at the Venice Film Festival, situating Dreyer within the burgeoning European film festival circuit that came into being with European postwar art film, such as Italian neorealism, and securing his position as Denmark's most distinguished auteur film director. In an iconic image from the *Gertrud* premiere in Paris, four years before his death,

Dreyer stands chatting with the luminaries of the French New Wave, Jean-Luc Godard and Anna Karina, projecting the sense of his status as a grandfatherly patriarch of European art cinema.

The category of art melodrama helps make legible the peculiar array of spectatorial pleasures and discomforts that Dreyer's film work, both early and late, elicits—his variable combinations of hot, passionate tears and icy, stylized cinematic estrangements.[25] Neither melodrama nor art cinema alone suffice to articulate the territory his films inhabit between avant-garde, art film, and "classical" Hollywood; Dreyer's films elicit searing combinations of emotional identification and critical distance. *La Passion de Jeanne d'Arc*, which combines a profusion of suffering with radical experiments with rapid montage, wild camera angles and movement, and the close-up, has been read as *narrative* avant-garde (my emphasis).[26] Meanwhile, Dreyer's other major films—*Day of Wrath*, *Ordet*, and *Gertrud*—present moving narratives of domestic conflict through long takes and hyperbolic stylization, the duration of which unsettles the spectator by another formal extreme. Dreyer's innovation of cinema as an art is varied and unconventional; his stylized, modernist, and evocatively stagy films are strangely novel and conservative at the same time.[27] The experimentation with spare cinematic form, to which Dreyer's reputation for austerity is bound, has also overshadowed his interest in affect, feeling, emotion, and the body. *Visions and Victims* contends explicitly with Dreyer's use of affective spectacle—whether tears caught in an effusive barrage of close-ups in *La Passion de Jeanne d'Arc*, or a woman stripped of her clothing and interrogated as a witch in *Day of Wrath*, or the elegant, heartbreaking swoon of Gertrud, the uncompromising heroine in Dreyer's last feature—as art cinema inflected by the mode of melodrama, that is, *art melodrama*.

A Master of Melodramatic Suffering:
From the Woman's Film to Corporeal Spectacle

Dreyer's mastery of the melodramatic mode is as undeniable as it is underestimated. The most obvious—but certainly not the only—evidence of that underestimation is that the film work he produced over the course of his long career (1912–64) demonstrates a sustained engagement with a central preoccupation of melodrama: suffering. As Linda Williams writes, "Sympathy for another grounded in the manifestation of that person's suffering is arguably a key feature of all melodrama."[28] I use suffering and pathos interchangeably to refer to a wide range of experiences in Dreyer's oeuvre, encompassing physical and psychological pain, emotional intensity, and duress. Suffering, in Dreyer's oeuvre, often revolves around highly aestheticized representations of female self-sacrifice and persecuted innocence—narrative tropes that have been instrumental in theorizing melodrama as a genre, and as more or less synonymous with the "the woman's film." Ebbe Neergaard, a film scholar and Dreyer's contemporary, writes that the theme of "a woman's lonely suffering in an evil world" runs as a pervasive current through the director's oeuvre, from beginning to end.[29] *Visions and Victims* brings into focus the slow burn of thwarted desires, betrayed lovers, sacrificial mothers, emotionally manipulated victim-heroines, love triangles, intergenerational conflict in the domestic sphere, and tearful, swooning, hysterical characters throughout Dreyer's oeuvre, putting them in conversation with the various traditionally feminized genres: the woman's film, maternal melodrama, and domestic melodrama—informed by melodrama as a mode.

In addition to that variety of film melodrama, Dreyer was also a master of corporeal spectacle, a hyperrealist manifestation of the melodramatic mode that runs adjacent to performance traditions like avant-garde performance art, circus sideshow spectacle, and religious ritual, whereby performer-participants subject themselves to intense experience and bodily harm to elicit shock, thrill, and transformation in themselves and in spectators.[30] Suffering, in other words, is not exclusively psychological or desirous, nor is it limited to the domestic sphere in Dreyer's work; it is also visceral, violent, spectacular, and public. Laura Mulvey and Mary Ann Doane, among others, have used the word "spectacle" to refer to the particular evacuation of female agency and objectification of female figures accomplished by the "masculine" gaze in mainstream cinema.[31] In this project, spectacle refers to sensational performance situations more reminiscent of classic melodrama or early sensational film melodrama in which bodies risk incurring harm.

I expand this idea of spectacle to include sensational subject matter in Dreyer's films, like corpses rising from the dead and human beings burned alive, fainting, or experiencing strong emotion. This spectacle relies on the materiality of bodies, by objectifying them in some way to produce shock, emotion, concern, or pathos but need not, in my analysis, entail a specifically gendered objectification by cinematic apparatus. The term "spectacle," as I employ it, integrates melodrama with what Mark Sandberg calls "effigy culture" in *Living Pictures, Missing Persons: Mannequins, Museums, and Modernity*, his book tracing the body in-turn-of-the-century Scandinavian display, performance, and recording practices that flourished there as a consequence of the region's belated and rapid industrialization. Effigy culture combined hypermaterial, graphic representations of the body with modern technologies of representation like radio and film. Scenes of physical harm and graphic pain—of tortured, bound, vampire-like, possessed, burned, and naked bodies—constitute a key melodramatic throughline in Dreyer's work that can be traced back to his early career working with a melodramatic imagination inflected by the dramatic potential of differentiating the live body from effigy. As a fundamentally expressionistic mode, melodrama has long privileged the body as a site for negotiating meaning, whether narratively, by suturing morality and virtue to figures of persecuted innocence, or as a central aspect of mise-en-scène that conveys visually what cannot be expressed in dialogue.[32] Corporeal spectacle exploits human flesh to slightly different ends, eliciting both titillation and thrill but also a radical form of empathy. Imagine a representation of harm so lifelike that it produces the impulse in a spectator to stop the performance to save a character or the actor performing the character from experiencing any harm. By heightening the chances that spectators care more about the bodies of actors than characters, corporeal spectacle threatens the coherence of the diegetic world depicted. The violent pathos of bodies in extremis can startle the spectator into a critical awareness of the narrative fiction she is consuming.

This streak of visceral realism that runs through Dreyer's oeuvre has remained largely undertheorized, except when it emerges in moments where Dreyer is portrayed as a "sadistic" director willing to go to any lengths to extract a "realistic" performance from his actors.[33] As many scholars have now shown, realism is not the antithesis of melodrama, but that dichotomy has long held sway in the standard reception of Dreyer's work. Consequently, moments of extreme pathos in his oeuvre have been read in one of three ways: unproblematically, as evidence that he was making tragedy; that his filmmaking transcends the material world to realize the spiritual; or that Dreyer was working through the psychobiographical trauma of a biological mother who gave him up for adoption and later died trying to abort another child.[34] Scholars have largely interpreted Dreyer's uncompromising demand for realism and authenticity, in particular, as proof of the seriousness of his aesthetic aspirations. By contrast, *Visions and Victims* articulates how nuanced realism and authenticity form a key element of Dreyer's melodramatic practice.[35] Pathos may not be the exclusive domain of melodrama, but the reverse is also true: serious, realistic images of meaningful, moving, and violent physical and psychological suffering are hardly the exclusive domain of tragedy or high art. The prevalence and the rhetorical power of the term "melodrama" in Danish cinema history and the connections between Danish cinema history and melodrama scholarship are compelling and vibrant to me, so I read this genealogy as melodrama rather than as popular tragedy. One could, however, write an interesting study arguing that Nordisk was making popular tragedy given the prevalence of that genre designation in early cinema. Seeing Dreyer's work described as tragedy rather than melodrama signals to me that melodrama's low culture stigma still operates and, by the same token, that tragedy functions rhetorically as shorthand to designate high art.[36] Theorizing Dreyer's imagination of the victimized, affective body of women's suffering is critical to understanding how his work invokes and contributes to a long history of representing suffering and melo- drama under the auspices of humanism.

Again, Dreyer makes an interesting case study. In contrast to the films of di- rectors like Douglas Sirk or Lars von Trier, it is exceedingly difficult to read Dreyer's depictions of pathos ironically or as unconscionably fetishized suffer- ing. Dreyer's films exude a sincerity that is continually reinforced by his public persona as a modest and reserved, but intense, filmmaker who earnestly be- lieved film to be an art capable of addressing crucial issues, such as the injustice and persecution of patriarchy. While it is important to remain skeptical of universalizing claims of humanism, there is also space to acknowledge Dreyer's lifelong devotion to melodrama as part of cinema's capacity to elicit com- passion.[37] As he wrote in 1943, "In all art, it is the human being that is most crucial."[38]

Attraction-Repulsion:
Art Melodrama, Feminism, Queer Theory

Art melodrama, returning to H.D.'s review, elicits an unsettling, "two-edged" feeling. It can be unnervingly beautiful: both difficult to watch and difficult not to. As perhaps Dreyer's most powerful and formally experimental depic- tion of suffering, *Jeanne d'Arc* elicits in H.D. a strong, somatic identification that is inextricable from a lingering awareness of cruelty. She remarks that long after leaving the theater her hands still clench of their own accord at the mem- ory of the striking images of a young woman's persecution and martyrdom. "Also why must my very hands feel that they are numb and raw and bleeding, clenched fists tightened, bleeding as if beating at those very impregnable me- diæval church doors?" she asks.[39] H.D. documents the other audience mem- bers' responses to the film's exquisite brutality as also visceral and graphic: "We are left pinned like some senseless animal impaled as she is impaled by agony."[40] Importantly, formal experimentation and heightened affect go hand in hand. H.D. describes the film's violent pathos as coming about through an aware- ness and appreciation of its formal eccentricities, not in spite of them. "Do I *have* to be cut into slices by this inevitable pan-movement of the camera, these suave lines to left, up, to the right, back, all rhythmical with the remorseless rhythm of a scimitar?"[41] At once impaled by, and taking distanced pleasure in, Dreyer's editing choices, H.D. gestures toward art cinema's undertheorized emasculation and potential queering of the spectator. Throughout *Visions and Victims*, I employ the term "queer," as a critical category to signal difference from or resistance to norms, particularly in ways that oppose the gendered pro- scriptions and binary oppositions of patriarchal heterosexism. Queering the spectator here refers to the loss of control, the effusive or ecstatic undoing of a bounded or rational sense of self. Queer also functions in this study as an umbrella category that refers to "an inclusive, amorphous, and ambiguous contraheterosexuality," under which H.D., who experienced lesbian and heterosexual relationships in her life, could be included.[42]

What H.D. shows us is that whether represented on screen or sitting in a theater, the feminized, affected body on which the melodramatic mode relies is entirely commensurate with the attentive, reflective body that art cinema imagines as its ideal spectator. To the extent that art cinema aims to elicit feelings of confusion in its spectators, whether by the use of stark imagery or denying narrative closure, the imagined body of an art cinema spectator is intentionally unsettled. Art cinema has traditionally been conceptualized as masculine, rational, critical; but one can interpret the modes of receptivity it encourages as also being both conventionally feminine and feminizing. Art melodrama, then, makes evident the ways that art cinema and melodrama each spark an awareness of the boundaries of the spectator's subjectivity and also enlist identification in ways that involve relinquishing mastery over those same boundaries.

Critical to art melodrama's potential as a feminist reading practice is the work of making evident the way it elicits antagonism in spectators, combining emotion and thought. As a compelled, critical, queer, modernist, and female spectator, H.D. admires the striking representations of female suffering that she feels in her flesh, while at the same time she critically contemplates whether she really *must* endure them. H.D.'s response situates her within a line of feminist thinking around these images that Linda Williams will call an "attraction-repulsion to the pathos of virtuous suffering."[43] Williams is describing the reaction of the predominantly white, second-wave feminist film scholars in the 1970s to watching films like *Stella Dallas* (King Vidor, 1937). Feminist scholar-spectators had mixed feelings about what it meant to consume the depictions of sacrificial, passive female suffering that were so prevalent in the woman's film, a genre that purported to represent women's concerns and was marketed to female spectators. Feminist film scholars faced the delicate task of critiquing the sexism underlying depictions of female suffering in the woman's film as a product of Hollywood's inherently patriarchal and exploitive capitalist structures, while also reclaiming it as a legitimate—if neglected—object of cultural and artistic expression. At the time, the assumed "proper" feminist response to such representations of passivity and pathos was to disavow them in the name of promoting gender equity. The most improper response was to cry or empathize with the suffering of those female protagonists.[44] And yet, as Williams goes on to argue, the fact that 1970s feminist film scholars kept returning to such representations in their work in order to reject and critique them again and again, belied the power of attraction that melodrama's pathos wielded as well as its usefulness to feminist scholarship.[45] Consuming and examining representations of pathos can now be appreciated as an acceptable scholarly endeavor; being moved by or being vulnerable to strong images of pathos signals a complex indication of humanity, whatever one's positionality.

Dreyer's films can clearly elicit quandaries for spectators about what the "proper" ethical response to consuming them might be. There is no question that the passive, idealized suffering of female protagonists is overrepresented in Dreyer's oeuvre, and for this, his work deserves to be interrogated at least as insistently as the female characters he depicts.[46] There can be no doubt that images of predominantly white, feminized victimization dominate Dreyer's films. Here, I enlist the magnetism of melodrama's pathos—revolving as it does around predominantly white femininity—to critique a historical canon of art cinema that alternately ignores or idealizes the suffering of these bodies. This is a canon in which white, male, and European directors are also overrepresented—especially during the period when Dreyer's star ascended in the 1940s, 1950s, and 1960s.[47] *Visions and Victims* also considers how Dreyer's return to images of female suffering again and again indicates that he, too, was both attracted to and repulsed by these moments.[48] Although his film work suggests a distinct attraction to extreme experience and pain, it is often tempered with an equally forceful repulsion to the act of unduly causing harm. As I have demonstrated elsewhere, Dreyer's unpublished thoughts on the perilous beauty of the bullfight suggest that he very consciously grappled with the ethical quandaries that arise around aestheticized suffering or pushing actors to their emotional and physical limits on set.[49] Dreyer believed film to be an art worthy of substantial personal sacrifice by everyone involved. He was drawn toward the potential of using suffering to say something about the human condition.[50]

Williams's subsequent scholarship on melodrama expanded its reach from a genre designation—with a limited scope and marginalized position in Hollywood, given its association with the woman's film—to a mode that made its presence legible in a wide variety of genres often gendered masculine, such as the action film. This effectively centered melodrama as integral to—rather than in excess of—the dominant strain of "classical" Hollywood narrative. Williams's revisionist reading of D. W. Griffith as both melodramatic and founding narrative cinema positioned melodrama as central rather than peripheral to this dominant tradition. In one sense, this queers the canon, by drawing attention to what gets excluded from its normative discourse. In another sense, this move initiated, or furthered, a process of mainstreaming melodrama to the extent that some would argue that the mode now represents its own kind of norm. As Matthew Buckley provocatively asserts, it no longer makes sense to ask "What is melodrama?" but rather "What isn't melodrama?" suggesting that melodrama constitutes a dominant rather than a marginalized discourse of modernity.[51] *Visions and Victims* owes a great debt to this scholarship and aspires to contribute to it. Much like Williams reads Griffith's art cinema, I read Dreyer's as foundationally melodramatic. This book is inspired by the conviction that the standard reception of Dreyer's work over the years has reproduced patriarchal hierarchies that subordinate emotion (gendered feminine) to rationality and dispassion (gendered masculine) in order to establish Dreyer as a great filmmaker and master of art cinema. *Visions and Victims* thus aligns with a feminist project of asserting melodrama, emotion, and the body as central in Dreyer's work rather than peripheral to what makes his films great. Reading Dreyer's art melodrama also queers the canon, opening his work up for future scholarship that embraces the full intersectional reach of melodrama studies, which includes queer studies, camp and sincerity studies, disability studies, feminisms, discussions of vulnerability and victimhood, and critical race and whiteness studies.

Visions and Victims reconsiders Williams's early formulation of attraction-repulsion in light of conversations in queer studies that enlist negative affect as a strategy for disrupting a heterosexual or heteronormative status quo. Melodrama impacts Dreyer's career not exclusively as a positive force to be recuperated but also as an alluring, excessive, potentially abject other to the normative trajectory of cinematic development as an art that he had internalized and promoted. It wasn't an allegiance to feminism that compelled Dreyer to disavow melodrama during his lifetime; rather, it was melodrama's, or Nordisk's, association with mass culture. Although committed to depicting complex female characters, openly embracing this work as melodrama was definitely not a position available to Dreyer during his lifetime. Dreyer aspired to elevate film from entertainment to a legitimate art form. In contrast to Peter Brooks's reading of Henry James as a consummate stylist who also avidly admired the intensities of Honoré de Balzac's melodramatic worldview, Dreyer distanced himself from popular culture. Although he did express the ambition to make artistic films that would speak to broad audiences, the gendered hierarchies of high and low art, and the collective scholarly disparagement of mass culture and melodrama as primitive or commercial, were acutely present to him. Dreyer's career provides an interesting case study for the workings of art melodrama in that his innovation of the form is spurred—somewhat paradoxically—by the denial and disavowal of one of its key constitutive elements.

Dreyer's disavowal of melodrama, or of what he more commonly referred to as past forms of cinema, could be quite performative and dramatic. Here

Eve Sedgwick's theorization of shame and queer performativity—also theorized around the work of Henry James—comes into play.[52] Seen from a queer studies perspective, Dreyer's attraction-repulsion to Nordisk melodrama encompasses aspects of shame and desire in its unleashing of a creative impulse to change, disguise, and transform what cannot be overtly emulated or embraced. To distance himself from his melodramatic past, Dreyer looks back at his former self and his earlier work in a gesture that resembles James, who around 1907 wrote new prefaces to his earlier writing as part of the New York edition of his collected works. As Sedgwick theorizes, the endeavor of looking back to engage with his earlier work was steeped in feelings of shame revolving around the failure of the New York edition to sell or be recognized by his readership. At the same time, shame importantly opens up the "rich landscape of relational positionalities" of queer performativity.[53] James dramatizes the perilous and productive circuit of narcissism/shame that connects the speaker to his own past and figures "his relation to the past as the intensely charged relationship between the author of the prefaces and the often much younger man who wrote the novels and stories to which the prefaces are appended—or between either of these men and a yet younger figure who represents the fiction itself."[54] The queer performativity I see operating in Dreyer surrounds his dramatizing again and again the self-discipline needed to contend with a cinematic inheritance from the silent era in order to bring film into the future. Contending with this past, however, also involves performative, dramatic resurrections of it. Each of my readings of five of Dreyer's most well-known films in the chapters to follow investigates the rich landscape of relational, art melodramatic positionalities that his early work initiates.

Art Melodrama as Archive

Throughout *Visions and Victims*, I use the word "archive" in multiple, interrelated ways. The term refers in part to the textual traces of Dreyer's filmmaking process and work housed in the Dreyer collection at the Danish Film Institute, which includes boxes of papers, notes, and newspaper clippings, many of which he himself labeled and organized. In this sense it also encompasses a fairly conventional understanding of the archive as a state's authoritative collection of historical documents that preserve and construct its history. The DFI, where both the Nordisk collection and Dreyer's collection are housed, is one instance of this. The considerable time spent with Dreyer's materials suggests to me that archival research, self-archivization, and also the affective relationship to a film's textual traces (pre- and postproduction) are all important aspects of Dreyer's filmmaking practice. This comes through in his films as well. Dreyer's Nordisk scripts refer to using such institutional archives for research that can be used to make films. His script for "Ned med Vaabnene!" (Lay down your arms) cites newspaper sources in which the director might find photographic images of soldiers returning from the Balkans to realize a scene of railroad platforms full of wounded soldiers. Dreyer will also represent such archives cinematically for authoritative and dramatic effect, for instance, at the beginning of *La Passion de Jeanne d'Arc*, when a disembodied hand turns the pages of the trial manuscript. And as I return to in chapter 6 on *Gertrud*, he will create an entire film about love and love of the research archive, imbuing the film with the affective and performative potentialities of academic research. *Gertrud* performs an archival sensibility in the broadest sense of the term, both in its reference to Dreyer's early career and the creative access to the past. In its the most expansive sense, archive encompasses both traces and the animation of traces through researcher performance.

I also use the term "archive" to gesture toward the repository of visual and textual materials as well as recurring themes and ideas with which Dreyer engaged to make films, whether or not they were published or filmed. To a certain degree, archive, art melodrama, and art melodrama archive are sometimes interchangeable in that they all gesture toward the way I read Dreyer's collected film work (published and unpublished, filmed and not filmed), as akin to what Barbara Klinger calls a "reservoir of past textual encounters that cut across aesthetic boundaries, any of which can be activated in the process of viewing."[55] Klinger's point is that the customary divide between high and low culture comes undone when spectators read art cinema or modernist texts through the vast collection of popular culture references they have accumulated. Art melodrama as archive attempts to be a critical category—important in Dreyer's context—by which high and low are read together as producing tensions as well as hybridities. When Dreyer viewed art cinema through melodrama, it was in part through a stigma that engendered aesthetic friction. In Dreyer's career, low and high correspond to early and late, past and present. By enlisting the term "archive," I also enlist the archive's temporal complexities, for instance, the way in which it purports to preserve the past while, at the same time, inevitably gesturing toward a future moment.

Visions and Victims seeks to contribute a melodramatic perspective, as it were, to ongoing discussions that figure the archive as a multitemporal space of performance and reenactment. This archival impulse will be particularly overt in the chapters bookending *Visions and Victims*. My first chapter, "Reading Dreyer's Early Archive," offers another look at Dreyer's early work at Nordisk through a brief history of the company that traces how the studio came to be equated with, and stigmatized by, the term "melodrama." I use this history to argue that Nordisk melodrama was inflected by what Mark Sandberg calls "effigy culture," prevalent in Scandinavia at the turn of the century, which retrospectively reads as proto–art melodrama. The second half of the chapter outlines my practice of reading Dreyer's art melodrama archivally. The final chapter of this book, "*Gertrud*: Melodramatic Refusal and the Art Melodrama Archive," analyzes Dreyer's last film, *Gertrud*, as Dreyer's performative reenactment of the research archive that illuminates his emotional, embodied practices of art melodrama. All the chapters draw connections across the supposed break between Dreyer's career at Nordisk and his post-Nordisk work. Chapter 2 reads *La Passion de Jeanne d'Arc* as reimagining—and purifying, stripping—the interactive space of the *varieté* theater and the performing body of the *varieté* starlet. Chapter 3 reads *Vampyr* as Dreyer's reexamination of Nordisk's volitional melodrama and its ambivalent victimizations. The analysis of *Day of Wrath* in chapter 4 shows how Dreyer's late work is bound to early work through imagery of needlework and questions of an inherited past, and chapter 5 reads *Ordet* as an effusive and miraculous fantasy that resolves all tension between art cinema and melodrama. In addition to demonstrating compelling continuities and discontinuities with Dreyer's early work, each chapter illuminates the mechanisms of art melodrama's constitutive hybridity and reflexivity. Each chapter articulates how Dreyer's film stages its own hybrid status as art melodrama via his attraction and repulsion to the mode of melodrama—as a performative revisiting and reworking of the archive of his earlier work at Nordisk, along the lines of what Rebecca Schneider theorizes as the "inter(in)animation" of the archive.[56]

Dreyer's films demonstrate a persistent interest in representing the past, or rather, the recurrence or reenactment of past bodies and experience. Dreyer's conflicted relation to his past, and by extension a film-historical past, resonates also with Heather Love's formulation of "feeling backward," by which personal feelings have implications for larger historical narratives.[57] Reading art melodrama archivally in *Visions and Victims* also resonates with queer historiography, which troubles teleological understandings of history, in this case a standard narrative of cinema's historical development. This queer reading of Dreyer's career also reimagines a developmental narrative away from melodrama as, instead, a genealogy of art melodrama in which Dreyer is an invested practitioner. Dreyer scholarship has unnecessarily extracted him from a genealogy of Danish art melodrama stretching from the early cinema to the "smart" or postmodern melodrama of Lars von Trier.[58] In the context of Dreyer's career, art melodrama functions not as a category symbolic of the heights to which melodrama can aspire to become but rather as the potential emerging through a queer encounter with the past. Neither is art melodrama simply the process of transforming or disguising melodramatic subject matter into formally estranging art cinema, although it can encompass that; rather, it's a by-product of the productive tensions between high and low art.

Dreyer's career maps onto a long tradition in film scholarship of separating art cinema and melodrama as high and low art, respectively. This separation often takes place when scholars reiterate an evolutionary history in which narrative cinema begins melodramatically, as a primitive, childlike, superficial, overly gestural silent-era form with uncomfortable ties to the theater. In this progression, the cinema then evolves into the antithesis of melodrama—namely, a self-reflexive, experimental, and psychologically invested art cinema. As David Bordwell puts it in his monograph on Dreyer, "Even before we study the films, Dreyer invites an unusual interest. For one thing, his career spans the mature development of the cinema from 1912 to 1968, from (to put it melodramatically) *Musketeers of Pig Alley* to *La Chinoise*."[59] Dreyer's personal development as a director is even more closely aligned with the story of Denmark's development as small-nation cinema maturing to compete artistically on the world scene. The two come of age together, so to speak. For Dreyer this happens by performing a decisive break from Nordisk, where he began his career. *Visions and Victims* queers this developmental trajectory by which the future for cinema is perceived as more mature, artistic, and developed by appreciating Nordisk as deserving of another look, as already practicing vibrant, diverse, and intriguing variations of art melodrama. *Visions and Victims* pays attention to Dreyer's largely unexplored early script work at the studio, beyond his extant films, as failing, beautifully, to develop in conventional ways. Versions of all the major artistic concerns of Dreyer's later work can be found operating at Nordisk: pathos, volition, psychological interiority and its expression on bodily surfaces, media reflexivity, authenticity, performance, art, love, betrayal, will, loss, sacrifice, and corporeality. Moral ambiguity, formal experimentation, and a fascination with representing psychological nuance on film is not what differentiates Dreyer's late work from his early work—it's what links them together. This book traces surprising continuities between key feature films in Dreyer's oeuvre and his early work at Nordisk. Analyzing Dreyer's archive in this way brings the kinds of reward that Jack Halberstam theorizes as the queer art of failure, which "allows us to escape the punishing norms that discipline behavior and manage human development with the goal of delivering us from unruly childhoods to orderly and predictable adulthoods. Failure preserves some of the wonderous anarchy of childhood and disturbs the supposedly clean boundaries between adults and children, winners and losers."[60]

In the story *Visions and Victims* tells, Nordisk embodies a kind of pleasurable anarchy of attraction that continues to flourish in Dreyer's work even after he purports to have transcended it. These are moments of queer undoing and remaking that contribute to histories of both art cinema and Danish cin-ema. Tracing the tears as they melt through the frost of Dreyer's films is one thing, but the revisionary power of his art melodrama can also *tear* through the fabric of a certain narrative about Danish film history. Dreyer's art melo-drama archive is constituted by multiple temporalities. Reading Dreyer art-melodramatically has implications for queering the canon of European art cinema—a canon not typically constructed via melodrama—given that Dreyer is one of the white, male, cis-gender European directors at its center. As *Visions and Victims* moves chronologically through Dreyer's oeuvre, exploring five of his most well-known feature films, it also queers this normative trajectory. Each film stages Dreyer's more conflicted temporality: the attraction-repulsion to his past as he attempts to move cinema forward as an art. It is toward this past, Dreyer's early archive and Nordisk art melodrama, that we now turn.

Reading Dreyer's Early Archive

Nordisk Scripts and Art Melodrama

In 1916, while employed at Nordisk Films Kompagni, Dreyer worked on a script titled "Rovedderkoppen," later filmed by director August Blom and distributed in English as *The Spider's Prey*.[1] The film's eponymous protagonist is a devious criminal mastermind, Mrs. Valentine Kempel (Rita Sacchetto), who seduces male victims and extorts money from them. Her gang has also kidnapped Ada, the fiancée of Einar, who has hired the intrepid Police Inspector Krag to avenge the death of his brother, who committed suicide after falling victim to Valentine's charms. In one exciting scene, Inspector Krag disguises himself to gain entrance to Valentine's ornate boudoir. Once inside, he rips off his fake beard and draws a gun on her. After a failed attempt to stab him with a dagger hidden in a bouquet of flowers, she reclines back in an armchair, seemingly in submission. A cutaway shot reveals a close-up of Valentine's delicate hand sliding onto the chair's armrest, a carved head of what appears to be a Chinese dragon. Slowly, her lithe finger presses its eye, triggering a secret alarm and alerting her gang.[2] Seeing their ringleader in duress on a secret surveillance screen, the gang surprises Krag, ties him up, and flees with Valentine. Fortunately for Krag, they forget the dagger on the floor, allowing him to free himself and take off in hot pursuit.

At first glance, "Rovedderkoppen" embodies the kind of superficial, pulp entertainment that Dreyer and others would associate with Nordisk—and yet Dreyer's script may invite us to take another, closer look. The description of Valentine's boudoir reads: "Luxuriously decorated in an oriental style. Many of its objects seem to be the bizarre whims of an eccentric and spoiled woman. In reality, there is a hidden intention to everything."[3] The fundamental conceit of the scene, full of trickery, disguise, and ornate layering of patterns and textures, is precisely that superficiality is not what it seems. Surfaces must be pleasurably interrogated—that's the name of the game. Similarly, Nordisk's reputation for superficiality in fact belies a wealth of creativity, while Dreyer's work at the company reveals him to be an accomplished, creative—and engaging—practitioner of melodrama.

Dreyer explored an exciting array of melodramatic embodiments operating at Nordisk during its first decades: wronged lovers, prodigal sons, criminals, aerial acrobatics, car crashes, devious divas, recently bankrupt nobility, orphans, thieves, deceived lovers, circus performers, *varieté* spectacles, revolvers, fires, explosions, car chases, tightrope walks, dance numbers, drowning victims, love triangles, hypnotists, long and passionate kisses, and the machinations of so-called white slave traders. And he almost certainly wrote many more scripts than the approximately twenty-five with which he is credited in the Danish national filmography. Dreyer's scripts are interesting because they grant insight into his creative personality; although many Nordisk scripts (particularly the early ones) are barebones, functional descriptions of action for shooting with scant reference to dialogue, character description, or anything that might eventually be included on an intertitle, Dreyer's scripts contain not only suggestions for camera setups, notes on shot scale, prop choice, visual effects, and mise-en-scène but also extended literary passages and descriptions. Dreyer was not a lone creative wolf at Nordisk but rather one of many talented stylists there. At their best, Dreyer's scripts resemble the top work of Nordisk's other talented writers and directors, such as Harriet Bloch, Paul Sarauw, and Robert Dinesen, whose dramatic, spectacular scripts also display the personal traces of conscious stylists working creatively with studio conventions.[4] Most of Dreyer's Nordisk films are no longer extant, but their archival traces show that the film factory production model allowed Dreyer to express himself cinematically, in written form. Nordisk also wasn't exactly the anonymous scene that Dreyer often contended it was. Authorial designations can often be seen on scripts that bear Dreyer's signature on their front covers. He and other writers were sometimes even granted the mark of authorship to advertise a film: both *Gillekop* (August Blom, 1919) and *Grevindens Ære* (*Lace*, August Blom, 1919) give Dreyer a writer's credit on the cover of the film's published program.

This chapter introduces readers who may not be familiar with Dreyer's early scripts at Nordisk to their prevalent thematic concerns, the scope of their aesthetic ambitions, and the extent to which they are marked by Dreyer's personal artistic vision. Dreyer, I argue, begins amassing his art melodrama archive at Nordisk. His work there incorporates the kind of melodramatic, gestural, embodied interiority that we continue to see in his later work under the name of art cinema. After offering a brief history of Dreyer's early career at the studio, tracing how his personal development as a director will become imbricated with historical accounts of the nation's film industry, I look closely at how the term "melodrama" functioned in discourse surrounding Nordisk. Despite the superfluity of genre designations that the company employed to market its films, in general, the studio came to be most closely associated with melodrama. Using the term "melodrama" is thus a fascinating rhetorical tool that worked as a source of shame or, at the very least, chagrin for Dreyer both during his career and in work published after his death. Thus, the first part of this chapter tells the story of how *Rovedderkoppen* was billed as a "crime novel in 3 acts and 50 scenes" in its day but came to bear the designation "erotic melodrama" in the national database of Danish film.[5] In Dreyer's history with Nordisk, melodrama often functions rhetorically as shorthand for mass culture, low culture, Nordisk, and even Danish early cinema. It also sometimes occupies the position of primitive, excessive, childish, exoticized, or otherwise unwieldly forms of cinema that in turn stands in contrast to "mature," artistic cinema. I use the term "artistic cinema" interchangeably with art cinema, here, to refer to the future that Dreyer imagined for film as an art. The general narrative by which Danish cinema or Dreyer is said to leave melodrama behind in order to grow up is intertwined with the rhetoric of restraining, simplifying, purifying, and disciplining, which also deserves closer scrutiny. Understanding the way melodrama has been publicly shamed in the Danish context helps us understand Dreyer's deeply felt need to distance himself from his early archive. At the same time, the stigma of Nordisk as a producer of melodrama has also occluded what Dreyer was attracted to at the studio. Nordisk was inflected both by Scandinavian naturalist and realist theater and by the hypermateriality and temporal discontinuities inherent in the cultural zeitgeist of late nineteenth-century Scandinavian display, recording, and performance practices that Mark Sandberg calls "effigy culture."[6] If Dreyer's art melodrama displays moral ambiguity, it is in part because Nordisk's melodramatic imagination showed intriguing variations from standard conceptions of early film melodrama either as Manichean, intent on clarifying good and evil, or as lacking psychological interiority.

The final section of this chapter lays out the methodological groundwork I employ to read Dreyer's pre- and post-Nordisk career together as a performative archive of art melodramatic experimentation. This chapter introduces ways of connecting Dreyer's film work and formulations of queer historiography, performance, reenactment, and a kind of embodied archive that subsequent chapters will continue to tease out. This is the story of Valentine's body. Returning to "Rovedderkoppen," as her fingers slip into the dragon's eye sockets, electricity courses through her, completing a circuit. Invisible yet powerful, this charge becomes a metaphor for her seductive agency, her potential. As Dreyer's script reads, "The Predator Spider stands up. She literally radiates with energy. Now is the time to act."[7] Valentine's fingers are compelling here because they hold the energy of female bodies in Dreyer's films to come.[8] Her fingers are also Jeanne's short, grubby fingernails in *La Passion de Jeanne d'Arc* and the contorted twist of her arm as jailers pry off the ring that weds her to Christ. They question the binding of Herlofs-Marthe's hands to the ladder upon which she will career into the flames in *Day of Wrath*. And they carry the passion of Inger's exquisitely limp and trembling hands at the culmination of *Ordet*, when she rises from the dead and reaches out to stroke the face of her weeping husband. Valentine's fingers reverberate as Dreyer's art melodrama archive.

Dreyer's Past at Nordisk Films Kompagni

Standard accounts of Dreyer's artistic development cast his early years at Nordisk as his introduction to the craft of cinema. Nordisk provided the didactic environment where Dreyer tried his hand at all aspects of filmmaking. He began working part-time for Nordisk in 1912 writing intertitles at the age of twenty-three. By June 1913 he had signed a contract to work as a scenarist in the company's newly established story department, where he came to specialize in adapting literary and dramatic work for the screen. In 1915 Dreyer began working full-time for the studio.[9] Working at Nordisk afforded Dreyer the opportunity to learn the nuts and bolts of collective, fast-paced, efficient filmmaking and editing.[10] The studio allotted little or no time for rehearsals. Directors at the company would shoot film after film during the light summer months, and then editors would assemble the footage during the dark winter months. This production model meant that a director did not necessarily provide artistic input on the final cut of the film. Although the company's system was designed to produce a great number of films quickly, it did allow its directors artistic input on some unexpected aspects of the production, including choosing sets, casting, determining props, and helping devise lighting schemes. In 1918 Dreyer was given the chance to try his hand at directing even as he continued scriptwriting. The only two feature films Dreyer directed at Nordisk were *The President* (1919), a film based on Karl Emil Franzoz's novel *Präsidenten* (for which Dreyer had earlier acquired the rights), and *Leaves from Satan's Book* (1921). Disputes with the company over funding and artistic differences during the production of *Leaves from Satan's Book* prompted Dreyer to leave Nordisk and seek funding opportunities abroad. Working outside the studio's constraints would purportedly allow him to exert full creative control over his films. In Dreyer's post-Nordisk career, he developed a reputation for being detail oriented and uncompromising as well as making relatively few films, practices that Nordisk's production schedule supposedly inhibited.

Nordisk has dominated national film histories such that it has become virtually synonymous with early Danish cinema. Ole Olsen, the innovative and charismatic entrepreneur who founded the company in 1905, developed a system for producing films with a broad, international appeal. Between 1911 and 1916, the company mass produced feature-length genre films; only the French companies Pathé Frères and Gaumont surpassed Nordisk's production.[11] Nordisk made around two thousand features and early short films of varying aesthetic quality during its Golden Age, roughly 1910–20. Eventually, Nordisk's focus on *kunstfilm* (art films), as multireel features were called, would play a key role in the studio's phenomenal successes in the 1910s. In contrast to the one-reel films, the longer format allowed Nordisk to develop characters and experiment with more complex narrative structures. The company's artistic aspirations were also evident in its development of professionalized scriptwriters and moves to adapt literary works for the screen.[12] The multireel art film would lay the groundwork for Nordisk's combination of humanistic stories, psychologically interesting drama, and sensational spectacles. The studio established its reputation by producing a steady stream of what were consumed as quality films with high production values and dramatic plots, advertising that "1. elegant acting, 2. good plots, 3. superb cinematography" set its product apart.[13] Nordisk films sold well abroad in part because they were set in non-Scandinavian, ambiguously continental locations and featured characters with British, German, or American names.[14] Around World War I, however, the company lost its dominant position in the world market. Critics in the 1920s associated the company's financial downturn with its failure to move beyond the generic formulas and melodrama upon which its fortunes had been made. Subsequent scholarship has also attributed the company's downfall to Nordisk's loss during World War I of large sections of its extensive distribution network and its problematic alliances with Germany, where the company had established strong distribution channels. That, combined with competition from the newly formed Universum Film-Aktien Gesellschaft (UFA) in Germany and an influx of films from Hollywood, signaled the end of the Danish Golden Age, although the company still operates today.[15]

Many accounts of Dreyer's career often dramatize his genius in relation to a dramatic departure from Nordisk after filming *Leaves from Satan's Book*. The film becomes emblematic of his purportedly decisive break with mass culture and melodrama. Dreyer's uncompromising artistic ambitions for film, the story goes, were incompatible with what he was asked to do at Nordisk. Inspired by D. W. Griffith's epic film *Intolerance*, Dreyer sought to increase his budget for *Leaves from Satan's Book* from 150,000 to 230,000 kronor after production had begun. A blunt refusal from Nordisk prompted Dreyer to write a letter to the studio's director, W. Stæhr, in March 1919, in which he threatened to take the project to Sweden. Nordisk stood its ground on Dreyer's contractual obligations and Dreyer eventually "crawled to the cross," as Edvin Kau puts it, to complete the project.[16] Rhetorically, however, the conflict helped cement Dreyer's reputation as an intense and uncompromising artist, a reputation that came to vastly overshadow the fact that he concurrently mastered Nordisk's commercially successful popular-culture fare.[17] Understanding Dreyer's practice of art melodrama involves first understanding how Nordisk came to be stigmatized as melodramatic, such that it became a source of shame for him.

Becoming Melodrama, Tracing the Stigma

The connection between early Danish cinema and melodrama is largely accepted out of hand in Danish cinema history. Writing for the Danish Film History on the DFI's website, Peter Schepelern refers to 1910–20 as the "Golden Age" of Danish cinema and also the "age of the melodrama," citing melodrama with erotic themes to be dominant at the time.[18] Rhetorically, melodrama becomes interchangeable with early cinema, standing in for a childhood of cinema that will mature and be superseded by more restrained and nuanced forms of artistic expression (this progress narrative also diminishes film production in Denmark that will continue to make melodrama in the 1930s and 1940s, largely for domestic consumption). As Matthew Buckley writes, melodrama's associations with immaturity entailed its long-term disparagement as primitive and inartistic: "Until about a half-century ago, melodrama was generally understood to be a crude, excessive, irrational, naïve, superficial, marginal, and finally insignificant type of modern drama—a 'minor' form, best exemplified by a handful of cheap, primitive, and ephemeral genres of the popular stage and screen, that had long since been superseded, on the modern stage as on the modern screen, by the more complex, controlled, rational, reflexive, substantive, and historically significant forms of realism and modernist aesthetics."[19]

Dreyer's friend Ebbe Neergaard seems to have been the first film historian to associate Nordisk with melodrama and in doing so align the development of Denmark's film industry, at least in part, with the schema that Buckley outlines. In his influential work, *Historien om dansk film* (*The Story of Danish Film*, 1956), the first book of its kind in Denmark, Neergaard attributes Nordisk's fate—and by extension the Danish film industry's—to the success of a form that has been translated as the "long 'social' melodrama."[20] Neergaard uses the category of social melodrama less as a genre marker than as a broader description of popular entertainment that depicted class difference, offering glimpses into the lifestyles of the upper class as well as those living on the fringes of society. Social melodrama provided "a distinctive impression of that interesting, raw, and wild life, presumably led in spheres that they [cinema-goers] had likely heard of but never encountered: among thieves, apaches [*sic*], demimondes, entertainers, circus carnies, actors and other artists."[21] As the casual inclusion of the term "apaches" in this list suggests, the nonnormative Other that melodrama symbolized was marked by race as well as class difference.[22]

The function of the term "melodrama" in Dreyer reception was not exclusively negative. Neergaard also praised Nordisk melodrama, for instance, for drawing on talented actors from the theater to develop a more nuanced acting style appropriate for the cinema and for using the close-up, evocative lighting, and composition in innovative ways. Neergaard also commends the studio for its ability to elicit emotion in audiences, and films like *Evangeliemandens Liv* (*The Candle and the Moth*, Holger-Madsen, 1915), which he regards as a quintessential social melodrama, for intricately combining artistic and affective strengths:[23] "The light creates a mood, composition of the image places the actor: emotion was the point of the production, ranging from the compellingly sentimental to forcefully shocking to authentically pathetic."[24] As we will see in the next chapter, melodrama will come to embody inauthentic pathos in the discourse surrounding *La Passion de Jeanne d'Arc*. Neergaard also praises Benjamin Christensen for making "good melodrama," exemplified by *Det hemmelighedsfulde X* (*The Mysterious X*, 1914) and *Hævnens Nat* (*Blind Justice*, 1916): "Through camera positioning and editing Benjamin Christensen lifts the melodrama in both of these aged films up to be a narrative relevant to us, the people and things come alive."[25] While applauding the aspiration to elicit emotion as a legitimate one for film as an art, this backhanded compliment also establishes melodrama as a deficient, irrelevant, and ultimately "aged" form in need of uplift: paradoxically childlike but also old, as if in arrested development. Often Nordisk melodrama is linked, rhetorically, to old-fashioned subject matter but acknowledged at the same time for its advances in filmic technique, which are presented as modernizing and innovating. When Dreyer dismisses *The President* as inartistic, he remarks in the same breath that at least it allowed him to experiment with the flashback. In a similar vein, David Bordwell has drawn attention to the company's innovation of what he calls a tableau aesthetic, or creative use of long takes, deep focus, and blocking, all of which distinguish it formally from Hollywood filmmaking at the time.

Some scholarship has read Nordisk films as more psychologically nuanced than American melodrama of the period. In his study of contemporary reception of early Danish cinema in the American press, Ron Mottram argues that early Danish cinema between 1910 and 1914 looked more psychological and relied less on action and spectacle than American cinema at the time because of the former's affinities to Scandinavian literary culture of the period.[26] Mottram attributes this to the influence of Henrik Ibsen's naturalist theater, which he refers to as materialist, socially critical, and psychologically inspired. Interestingly, naturalist or realist (and eventually modernist) theater by figures like Ibsen and August Strindberg are often enlisted to exemplify a broader cultural move away from melodrama. Answering a call by Danish university professor Georg Brandes in a series of lectures beginning in 1871, Ibsen and other cultural figures of the Scandinavian Modern Breakthrough shifted the emphasis on cultural production from images of idealized, often mythological subjects to work that reflected contemporary social debates. E. Deidre Pribram enlists Ibsen as emblematic of a broad developmental trajectory and cultural shift away from melodramatic aesthetics and toward psychological interiority in the twentieth century. By this logic, melodrama's sociocultural aesthetics of emotional expressionism were understood as gradually being supplanted by a more critically privileged aesthetics of deep interiority and psychology, focusing on the truth of individual experience.

Dreyer will similarly invoke the discourse of psychological interiority to describe what differentiates his late work from his early work. Ibsen's realist theater becomes emblematic of that new way of telling stories about the invention of the psychic subject that privileges psychological depth as a source of truth in the twentieth century, when "the prevailing notions of high art win over melodrama and emotion."[27] Importantly, Pribram undoes this developmental trajectory away from melodrama and toward psychological interiority, reimagining melodrama's commitment to emotionality as a key cultural value that persists in future cultural production rather than disappears—an argument that parallels my argument about art melodrama. Additionally, psychological depth in this naturalist/realist moment remains fully consistent with embodied melodramatic expression. Ibsen, Strindberg, and other writers of the Scandinavian Modern Breakthrough, including Herman Bang, author of the 1902 novel *Mikaël* (Michael), which Dreyer adapted for film in 1924, engaged in quite spectacular, expressive explorations of exteriorizing interior experience. Indeed, many canonical Scandinavian authors from this period have been read as melodramatic.[28] The influence of Scandinavian "high art" on Nordisk, in other words, manifested itself as an interest in interiority that was also spectacularly embodied and performative.[29] While Nordisk melodrama may have been retrospectively understood as employing psychological complexity, for Dreyer, the studio symbolized the dearth of psychological interiority associated with artistic nuance.

By and large, however, critique of Nordisk melodrama for its *lack* of artistic merit significantly overshadows praise of it. Nordisk's talent for eliciting a range of affect, from shock to pathos, rarely comes through in accounts of the company's melodramatic production. It is similarly downplayed in accounts of the expertise Dreyer gained while at the company. Returning to Neergaard's history, melodrama's commercial success eventually counted against it, and the connection between Nordisk's Golden Age output and artistic expression would become increasingly tenuous. Moreover, as the company's fortunes declined at the time of World War I, Nordisk became a kind of scapegoat in public discourse that epitomized the general ineptitude of a Danish film industry to adapt to changing times. As melodrama's low culture stigma grew stronger, rhetorically, it became inextricable from Nordisk's successes as well as its failures. Neergaard chalks the company's rise and fall up to Ole Olsen's failure either to recognize or relinquish melodrama for the "primitive" form that it was: "One might ask how the production fairytale could have such a sad ending, but one would be hard-pressed to find an answer. It is likely nothing more than the fact that Ole Olsen was a strong and dominating man, who effectively inspired and initiated as long as it was a matter of a fairly conventional, quite primitive product like the 'social' melodrama, but that he didn't understand how to facilitate the freedom and encouragement that creates great artists."[30] The lesson to be learned from Nordisk was that remaining attached to melodrama hindered artistic advancement; great artists didn't make either mass culture or melodrama. Neergaard characterizes Dreyer's directorial debut at Nordisk in similar terms: "*The President*, which premiered on February 9, 1920, was characterized by Nordisk Film's particular fondness for the melodrama. . . . What first and foremost leads us to see *The President* as still belonging to the old 'Nordisk' style, the strongly melodramatic, is the film's fable and the actors' performances in the big emotional scenes."[31] Nordisk functions as the placeholder for evoking primitive, past, and exaggerated kinds of representation, and using melodrama to signal artistic stagnation or the failure to develop would have lasting effects on the way Dreyer's early career is conceived.

Compounding the downturn in the Danish film industry during World War I was the rise of a new, competing Swedish production model adopted around 1917 after the success of *Terje Vigen* (*A Man There Was*, Victor Sjöström, 1917). If Denmark represented cinema past, Sweden represented its future development as an art. The Swedish studio Svenska Bio made fewer, more expensive, more artistic films, frequently based on literary adaptations, a model that exacerbated the dichotomy between Danish and Swedish national cinemas after World War I.[32] One key moment when Dreyer distanced himself from early Danish cinema in no uncertain terms and contributed to the reification of Nordisk's lowbrow stigma was a 1920 newspaper article he wrote titled "Swedish Film." Here Dreyer disparages the Danish film industry for manufacturing what he calls "Count and Countess" films.[33] In 1913 director Urban Gad alluded to Nordisk as "the film factory" (*filmfabriken*), referring to specialization the company had undergone starting in 1910–11, and the name stuck.[34] Dreyer reiterates this rhetoric, writing that Denmark, where "films have always been *manufactured*," will never claim any significant place in film history. "On the road that traces the evolution of film, there is no landmark that reminds us that *here* Danish film culture cut new paths."[35] Adopting a linear understanding of cinema's development, Dreyer extols the advancements made by Swedish directors Victor Sjöström and Mauritz Stiller. Their soulful films convey their artistic vision and contribute to film's cultural prestige. Dreyer even refers to Sjöström as "the father of the Swedish art film."[36] Nordisk's outdated sensationalism, according to Dreyer, had little to do with film's real calling, namely, to be "a medium for true and genuine human representation."[37] Again, elevating artistic film and dismissing popular cinema are two sides of the same coin:

> The flood of bad films that came out of Danish film factories during this period drowned the chances that Danish film had had. Favorable circumstances had created a world market for Danish film, capital existed in abundance, the only thing missing was that a man with the authority that taste and culture give should raise film to a higher sphere. But he did not turn up. A doubtful odor still hung over Danish film and frightened away the intelligentsia—an odor so persistent that the public in our more fastidious neighboring countries still hold their noses at the sight of a poster for a Danish film.[38]

The energy that Dreyer devotes to disparaging Nordisk as a smelly, mass-produced object, implicitly the stuff of lower spheres of culture, is a remarkable testament both to the studio's stigma and to his perceived need to publicly distance himself from it.

Dreyer scholarship has reiterated Dreyer's public rejection of Nordisk as the particular renunciation of melodrama. In the first English-language monograph on Dreyer, David Bordwell echoes the rhetoric in the "Swedish Film" article, adding the phrase "melodramatic devices" to describe Dreyer's view that by 1920 all Danish film production had become cliché and sensational.[39] A description of silent-era Danish cinema in *Nordic National Cinemas* from 1998, written by Tytti Soila, Astrid Söderbergh-Widding, and Gunnar Iversen, attests to the persistence of this tradition of flagellating Nordisk and early Danish cinema as mass-produced, sensationalistic, and profitable popular culture melodrama: "The melodramatic subjects, the spectacular plots, the bold erotics and the descriptions of crime provoked a debate in wide circles, not only in Denmark. In Sweden many of these films were totally banned, and

'Danishness' became an abusive word referring to all films that were considered offensive to good taste."[40] While the studio distributed internationally inflected films all over the world, it also came to be synonymous with Danishness.

Film historians from Edvin Kau to Casper Tybjerg have continued to enlist the term "melodrama" to discuss early Danish cinema in ways that associate Nordisk with melodrama without overtly disparaging it or delving too deeply into it.[41] Marguerite Engberg's work is most important for theorizing the prevalence and popularity of what she calls "the erotic melodrama" at Nordisk, a form made possible with the advent of the multireel *kunst* film.[42] Engberg first introduces the term in her influential 1977 study on the development of Danish silent cinema from 1896 to 1914, in which she identifies erotic melodrama as one of many thematic subgenres of the melodramatic mode operating at Nordisk, including sensation, circus, war, and literary films. Engberg enlists a schematic definition of melodrama as a form involving an "exaggerated appeal to the emotional" that may or may not culminate in a happy ending.[43] Erotic melodrama at Nordisk often revolved around love triangles and incorporated daringly long kisses, titillating erotic material, and violent superficial effects. These films could feature vamp-like female figures who demonstrated a sexual agency that was equally threatening and alluring. She notes that the studio didn't call those "erotic melodramas" melodrama(s) but rather *kærlighedsfilm* (love films).[44]

Dreyer's personal development and success as a director became entangled in the ups and downs of the early days of the Danish film industry in complicated ways.[45] Soon after leaving Nordisk, he made a series of films abroad, a move that is often cast as indicative of his tenuous relationship and ultimate break with the Danish film industry. In some respects, Dreyer's career constitutes the Danish film industry as a kind of structuring absence; Denmark's provincial, small-nation cinema away from the metropolitan cultural centers of Europe is painted as being everything that Dreyer is not. As Danish filmmaker Henning Carlsen wrote in his 1968 obituary for Dreyer, "Carl Th. Dreyer's importance as a film artist was international, and his stature must be measured by a yardstick we have not really got in this country."[46] Or referring to *La Passion de Jeanne d'Arc* (made in France), Neergaard wrote, "It was created in other words, outside of a Denmark in which film art had no home at that time, and it gave a Dane worldwide recognition as an outrageously single-minded director whose strength was and continues to be made of an uncompromising will to artistic autonomy and professional independence."[47] Statements like this are typical of the pervasive tendency in Dreyer scholarship to cast his early career in Danish cinema as too provincial, too commercial, or too artistically constrictive to have contributed to the formation of his artistic genius. In addition to being figured as an international auteur swan in a pond of Danish ducklings, Dreyer often also embodies and epitomizes a particularly austere kind of Danishness.

The story of how Dreyer came to hold such a prominent position in Danish film history is intertwined, I argue, with the history of how melodrama has been employed as a rhetorical tool to write it. The history of melodrama's stigmatization in early Danish cinema and Nordisk Films Kompagni, in turn, helps us understand how looking back at his early work might have instilled Dreyer with feelings of shame. But this is only part of the story. Reading Dreyer's Nordisk scripts together with his recognized masterpieces reveals that the binary distinctions between primitive and advanced, childlike and mature, melodrama and art cinema, past and future, old-fashioned and modern blur across Dreyer's archive. Further, these binary distinctions were already being negotiated at Nordisk in ways that rumple the narrative of Dreyer's development as an auteur. All of this, I think, continued to draw Dreyer to return to material in these Nordisk scripts. The remainder of this chapter will turn away from Dreyer's repulsion to Nordisk to take a closer look at what attracted him.

Effigy Culture at Nordisk:
History, Performance, Inheritance

On the front page of his "Esther" script (*Den hvide Djævel/The Devil's Protegé*, Holger-Madsen, 1916), adapted from the first part of Honoré de Balzac's novel *Splendeurs et misères des courtisanes, Esther Happy* (*Esther heureuse*, 1838), Dreyer signed a modest note to Nordisk producers with suggestions about how to situate the film in time: "Permit me humbly to suggest that the director entirely avoid telephones, automobiles, and such inventions that would guide one to think of modern times. Perhaps it would also benefit the film if all the interiors were given the sense of being 'old-fashioned,' in as much the film might be given *a certain* temporal hue, without making use of historical costuming. In any case, that would avoid modernizing the novel in such a way as to seem jarring. This is, however, only a suggestion."[48] Dreyer's interest in modernizing via a stylized, ambiguous sensibility of the past indicates that Nordisk allowed him to begin thinking about accomplishing the kind of "anachronistic modernity" that would characterize his feature films like *Ordet* and *Gertrud.*[49] Dreyer sustained a career-long interest in setting films in the past, to various ends. The note also suggests that Nordisk was grappling with questions of how to represent multiple time periods at once, even though Dreyer often equated Nordisk with cinema's silent era past in a way that unified and simplified it. He did this in 1943 when he wrote that for directors to imbue a film with their personality and artistic vision meant confronting the influence of two residual forces from the past: the silent cinema and the theater, or "the inheritance [*arv*] from the silent era—a legacy, that sound film has yet to shake off."[50] Looking back to the past, and also feeling the past within him, in order to eschew it will be a key way in which Dreyer performs his auteur personality. Nordisk will also provide him ample opportunity to negotiate the pleasures and anxieties of the historical past, broadly conceived, before Nordisk comes to represent Dreyer's own past.

Mark Sandberg argues as much in *Living Pictures, Missing Persons: Mannequins, Museums and Modernity*, which shows how Nordisk cinema was inflected by the radical social transformation that Scandinavia underwent beginning in the 1860s when it experienced rapid industrialization, well after other parts of Europe.[51] This belated experience of modernity and modern capitalism engendered fervent attempts to preserve and display the material traces of a rapidly disappearing past. While Scandinavia was, of course, not unique in having to deal with the temporal disorientations of modernity, the decision to establish several living history or folk museums where traditional historical buildings were preserved and reassembled in urban centers for the edification and entertainment of new publics does set the region apart from other cultural contexts. Alongside museum and display practices intent on preserving the physical remains of the past, Scandinavia also embraced new recording technologies such as the photograph, the phonograph, and the cinema. Sandberg enlists the term "effigy culture" to refer to the widespread negotiation of the past at the turn of the nineteenth century, in part through the display and preservation of material remains.[52] This cultural moment regularly integrated hypermaterial forms of representation with more ephemeral recording technologies like the photograph and cinema in a myriad of ways. Consequently, spectators were used to engaging with imbricated representational technologies, a play within a film, painting within a wax cabinet display, a photograph within a film. The various manifestations of effigy culture also manipulated the space in which spectators encountered representations, interlaying and alternating experiences of voyeurism and immersion. Consumers of effigy culture, in other words, regularly encountered interlayered historical sensibilities, intertwined experiences of mobility and space, and multiple kinds of media. Sandberg doesn't associate effigy culture at Nordisk specifically with melodrama, but his work establishes a baseline of media reflexivity and temporal interplay at the studio that I see constituting art melodrama and, ultimately, contributing to the nonlinearity of Dreyer's archive.

Effigy culture, as the term implies, privileges the body as a key element of the mise-en-scène to be read. This provides another important connection with melodrama. Dreyer's entire career demonstrates an enduring fascination with negotiating effigy's hypermateriality and cinema's ephemerality to reflective, affective, and spectacular ends, whether as a slew of drowned corpses scattered across the beach in his early Nordisk script "Hotel Paradis" or a dead woman returned to life in *Ordet*.[53] Effigy culture and Dreyer's art melodrama each operate as a kind of cerebral body genre and performance that asks spectators to differentiate between shades of liveness and being: dead, performing, sleeping, hypnotized, seduced, enthralled, or shocked. Ontological questioning, spectacle, and entertainment go hand in hand. Many of Dreyer's earliest scripts show him exploring the possibilities of staging and filming danger using the human body in effigy—literally. *The Secret of the Bureau* from 1913, for instance, features a cliff scene that juxtaposes the spectacle of a character climbing the height of a tree—the actor was to wear spiked telephone boots—with the spectacle of that same character clinging onto a branch for dear life, this time conveyed by a mannequin/doll. Dreyer makes careful notes about these effects in the script. In other instances, Dreyer actually put his actors' bodies in harm's way to achieve the spectacle. In *Glomdalsbruden* (*The Bride of Glomdal*, 1926) the actor Einar Sissener supposedly almost drowned while filming a climactic action scene shot in river rapids. Such moments ask spectators to contemplate the status of bodies they're watching, to distinguish what appears on screen from what happens on set. Effigy culture, to put it melodramatically, exploits the tension between eliciting affect or thrill and reflecting on the material constraints of representing a scene of physical harm or risk. Dreyer continued to orchestrate spectacular, titillating, and emotional reflection on the media specificity of the body throughout his career, including his most well-known actor-to-mannequin substitution, the immolation sequence of *La Passion de Jeanne d'Arc*, in which he cuts between a shot of the actress, Maria Falconetti, surrounded by smoke and about to burn and shots of a mannequin that will eventually go up in flames. Dreyer exploits this as late as *Day of Wrath*, which also includes an immolation sequence. Across his archive, Dreyer sets up scenes that prompt spectators to take reflective distance and decipher layers of real and less-real. Such reflection goes hand in hand with the pleasures of immersing oneself in fiction.

It's fitting that Dreyer's note on the *Esther* script draws specific attention to historical costuming as key to his vision for conveying the film's ambiguous temporality. Effigy culture draws attention to the potential for costumed bodies to perform historical disjuncture. This entailed presenting the body in a wide range of mediations that overlaid present and past, from live actors in costume participating in plays, historical tableaux, or historical reenactment in folk museums to painted portraits, filmed bodies, mannequins, and wax figures in wax cabinets.[54] Actors, dressed in historically marked costumes within the mise-en-scène, contributed to the negotiation of a historical past within the present. *The Parson's Widow* (*Prästänkan*, 1921), the first film that Dreyer directed after leaving Nordisk, and which he filmed in a farmhouse in the Maihaugen living history museum, is an excellent example of this. In an essay on the film, Sandberg extends his thinking on effigy culture to read *The Parson's Widow* as invested as much in process or "project" as in the final product.[55] Often Dreyer deploys powerful older characters—often formidable matriarchs—to embody and symbolize the past in the present moment. They perform a substantial, corporeal, almost unmovable presence like an architectural structure.[56] *The Parson's Widow* explicitly stages the past generation as a hindrance to a future generation set to take its place. The widow Margarethe (Hildur Carlberg), as tradition has it, must marry the next pastor to hold the position, and Sofren (Einar Röd), a man much younger than she, arrives with Kari (Greta Almroth), posing as his sister but to whom he is actually engaged. *The Parson's Widow* ends ambiguously when the stolid Margarethe wills herself to die, allowing for the young couple to assume their place in the parsonage. The selfless action of the parson's widow secures her status as a sympathetic character, but she remains present in the solid architecture of the parsonage, an evocative symbol of the way that the past inevitably continues to impinge on future forms of (married) life. As Sandberg writes, "The plot problem all along has been that of *gjengangere* [ghosts, or dead who do not remain dead], of the dogged persistence of tradition, bodies and objects that do not make way for the new. . . . His [Dreyer's] further intellectual interest in the story was finding a way out of the simple repetition of the past."[57] This rings true broadly across Dreyer's archive.

We find evidence of Dreyer's interest in embodying the conflict between past and future as intergenerational conflict in one of his earliest Nordisk scripts, "Elskovs Opfindsomhed" (*Love's Ingenuity*, Sophus Wolder, 1913), in which two young lovers play tricks on a tough but sympathetic matriarch and property owner who has forbidden their marriage. Here the gag draws explicit attention to the performance and costuming of actors: the would-be groom enlists the help of his sister, a professional actress who dresses like a man to seduce the old proprietress into granting the couple's wish to be married. In contrast to the bittersweet ending of *A Parson's Widow*, Dreyer's 1913 script ends happily, with the matriarch's feelings smoothed over and the couple marrying—another symbolic reconciliation with the past, this time without necessitating a character's death.

In many ways, Sandberg's work on effigy culture prefigures key aspects of what Rebecca Schneider—working in performance studies—will engage with as historical reenactment in *Performing Remains: Art and War in Times of Theatrical Reenactment*. Both scholars address many of the key issues of performance,

Figure 1. The widow Margarethe remains a powerful reminder of the past even after her death. Frame capture, *The Parson's Widow*.

history, time, liveness, and the body that I want to engage as melodrama. Schneider draws specific attention to performance and the historiographic potentialities of the performing body itself. Reminiscent of the scene of Valentine's fingers with which I opened this chapter, the reenacting body, as Schneider conceives it, opens up "a relationship to history that partakes of the double negative: a reenactment *both* is *and* is not the acts of the Civil War. It is *not not* the Civil War. And, perhaps, through the cracks in the 'not not,' something cross-temporal, something affective, and something affirmative circulates. Something is touched."[58] Sandberg and Schneider each engage with questions of ontology, liveness, and performance in relation to recorded, material, archival traces of history. For each, the body can serve as a recording device of sorts and touch, as it were, other moments in time. Bringing their work together heightens the performative aspects of effigy culture and opens up readings of Dreyer's art melodrama as reenactment. The trial and immolation of Jeanne in the *La Passion de Jeanne d'Arc* project, for instance, is not the trial itself, but it is also *not, not* the trial.

Performing the *Not, Not* at Nordisk:
Dreyer's First Feature Films

The two films Dreyer directed at Nordisk, *The President* (1919) and *Leaves from Satan's Book* (1921), each illuminate the interest he shared with Nordisk in employing the performing body cross-temporally, engaging with the past to elicit pathos in media-savvy spectators. *Leaves from Satan's Book* (1921) reads like performance of historical reenactment across time as traced by the body of an actor-performer, played by Satan (Helge Nissen). Condemned to walk the earth, Satan must tempt humans toward evil but hopes each time that he will fail—only in this way will his sentence be reduced. Satan appears in four different epochs: the time of Jesus, the Spanish Inquisition, the French Revolution, and the Finnish Civil War, performing in costuming appropriate to the historical period in question. Nissen's body persists across time, a focal point for reading different layers of makeup and disguise within the diegesis. Nissen plays Satan, and Satan, in turn, performs someone of another time, both at the same time. Satan is both Satan and also not Satan. Like Dreyer's note, Satan is both of another era—and not. Actively differentiating between the physiognomic body of the actor and the several semiotic roles, he plays multiple historical moments legible at once. The ensuing media-reflexivity, for spectators, takes the form of enjoyable scenes of dramatic irony. Once they have recognized Nissen in his new temporal guise, spectators read him as Satan, while the characters he tempts remain oblivious to that fact. On one hand, time moves forward chronologically in the series of epochs that follow one after another. On the other hand, the past persists to be dragged across time and into a future moment, via the materiality of Nissen's body.

An entire corpus of historiographical inquiry about melodrama and queer studies can help situate the historical allegory in *Leaves from Satan's Book* as both melodrama and, interestingly, queer. Russian formalist Sergei Balukhatyi offers a particularly corporeal analogy for the development of "classical" French melodrama in his *Poetics of Melodrama* (1926), where he describes melodrama's core mechanisms as a skeleton that constantly develops new fleshly iterations or disguises over time.

> In its "pure" aspect, melodrama acts directly through its constructional and emotional forms, but melodrama can also be found in many other types of drama in which its "pure, primordial" principles are masked, weakened, and complicated by other aspects, such as realistic portrayal, psychological motivation, or ideological dialectics. . . . It is possible for a melodramatic skeleton to become covered with the solid flesh of realistic material and concealed beneath an elegant

Figure 2. Helge Nissen performs the role of Satan performing the role of Grand Inquisitor. Frame capture, *Leaves from Satan's Book.*

layer of psychology and ethical, social, or philosophical content. We thereby lose the feeling of melodramatic style and accept the play as a "higher" genre.[59]

Balukhatyi's melodramatic skeleton echoes a reference that Ebbe Neergaard once made to Nordisk's erotic melodrama being "the backbone" of the Danish film industry during the silent era.[60] Christine Gledhill analyzes how melodrama moves through time, off the Victorian stage and into film and television, by reading bodies' development of celebrity persona within the star system. The star system, Gledhill argues, extends melodramatic costuming practices that juxtaposed character type with the real-life body of the star beneath, reminiscent of the kind of semiotic and phenomenological tracking of Satan's body in *Leaves from Satan's Book.*[61] Dreyer's film also evokes something of the temporal disjuncture of the time-traveling Orlando in Virginia Woolf's novel by the same name, whom Elizabeth Freeman reads in *Time Binds: Queer Temporalities, Queer Histories.*[62] For Freeman, queer historical texts represent nonsequential forms of time and bring past and present together to counter political and affective ends. Such corporeal engagements with history open up ways of experiencing historical knowledge as embodied experience—like the *touch* of history. Connecting effigy culture, Nordisk, Dreyer, Balukhyati, melodrama, and queer historiography, I suggest that each draws upon the body to reimagine old and new, high and low, across historical time. Whether looking through disguise and makeup to imagine a body beneath or stripping flesh and muscle to imagine Nordisk's backbone—each body reads cross-temporally. Dreyer's fascinations with the particularities of effigy, its realness, purity, and "authenticity," and the privileging of liveness emerge for him in relation to curiosities already prevalent in his work at Nordisk, not only after he'd left.

The President similarly presents characters who exist in the present moment but whose actions and bodies contend with past actions. Here again, history is both embodied by generations but also repeated. The past is ambiguously figured within the individual as embodied inheritance. If *Leaves from Satan's Book* focuses on peeling away external layers, embodied inheritance raises questions about the past as interiority, emanating from within or made visible by coming to recognize patterns of behavior. If *Leaves from Satan*'s book follows Satan's performing body chronologically forward in time and expressively outward, Dreyer's 1919 directorial premiere, *The President*, looks backward and inward, employing the flashback to find the past embodied in the present. The protagonist of *The President*, Karl Victor von Sendlingen (Halvard Hoff), also succeeds in breaking the devious pattern of three generations of aristocratic men who seduce and abandon their lower-class lovers and the children resulting from these couplings. Dreyer uses flashbacks in this film to visualize Karl Victor's interior conflict, when he must break a vow that he makes to his father to marry in his class in order to rid himself of the burden of perpetuating the wrongs of the patriarchs who have come before him. We can also read *The President* as exploring shame, not in terms of Karl Victor's former self but in terms of his forefathers'. Embodied inheritance involves reading the ambiguity of self, revolving around the question of how an individual character comes to know or feel the influence of the past within them. A character's interiority or psychology is portrayed as contingent on understanding how the past manifests itself on and within their bodies, as a combination of interior experience—thought, doubt, distress, fascination—and physical traits, symptoms, and interpersonal relationships. This is a common mechanism in Ibsen's plays from the time, which reflect tensions between the present and what has come before. Often the past manifests itself as an unsavory, haunting presence, the usually undesirable repetition of the past in the present. Dreyer's archive is replete with instances of embodied inheritance, when the body becomes a key site to rework the problems and potential of an inherited past. In the latter part of his career, his protagonist Anne in *Day of Wrath* (1943) grapples with the seductive possibility that she has inherited powers from her deceased mother that allow her, effectively, to undertake a literal form of what Ibsen in *Rosmer-sholm* calls "soul murder." During his time at Nordisk, Dreyer was already exploring whether a younger generation might break the cycle of generational "sin" and bad behavior. His script "Hotel Paradis," like *The President*, ends with the happy interruption of the pattern. In "Hotel Paradis," a young man and woman share a bond of love so strong that it can right horrific wrongs committed in the past; many years earlier, her parents killed his father during a robbery.

As I read them, the first two films that Dreyer directed were deeply engaged with feelings of temporal disjuncture in the body; he was contending with his Nordisk past even before it was the past, reworking it in the present to imagine what he perceived as the future of cinema: artistic cinema. Tom Milne's assessment of Dreyer's early directing attempts is interesting in this context: "Dreyer's first two films, after a five-year apprenticeship as titlewriter, scriptwriter and editor with Nordisk films, were pretty much what one might expect of a tyro film-maker who had just seen Griffith's *Intolerance* and was determined to lift the Danish cinema into dignity by the scruff of its neck: ambitious, literary, technically deficient, and with a clumsily passionate seriousness which makes them look almost like cruel parodies of *Day of Wrath* or *Ordet*."[63]

At first, Milne appears to reiterate a familiar story about *The President* and *Leaves from Satan's Book* as encapsulating all that is ridiculous and immature about Dreyer's work at Nordisk, particularly in comparison with his "mature" feature films. But other, more interesting, perspectives emerge here as well. Milne articulates the pressure that Dreyer felt to save Denmark's film industry. The passage also implicitly suggests that Nordisk's film factory environment didn't squelch Dreyer's artistic expression but rather fostered artistic practices that in many instances would take their fullest form only years afterward. Early Danish cinema even has a body, complete with neck scruff. And crucially, Milne's expression, "cruel parody," queers the linear historical trajectory he tries to assert. *Day of Wrath* and *Ordet*, of course, were made after *The President* and *Leaves from Satan's Book*, but Milne reads Dreyer's late films, anachronistically, as being the precedent for his earlier ones. His impulse troubles the linear chronology teleology in a splendidly performative, and queer, way. Milne inadvertently makes my main point, namely, that Dreyer's archive, with its fascinating patterns and repetitions, actively resists the normative teleology by which we have come to understand his development as an auteur. *Ordet* is not exactly Nordisk art melodrama, and it is also not, not Nordisk art melodrama. Put another way, Milne approximates the temporal perplexities that animate Dreyer's art melodrama archive.

This chapter has shown that Dreyer's work at Nordisk is inextricable from his later work and argued that in Dreyer's art melodrama archive, past and present coexist and inform one another in evocative, nonchronological ways. This, in turn, lays a foundation for the argument undergirding all of *Visions and Victims*—namely, that Dreyer's art melodrama can queer normative understandings of cinema's development as an art. In the chapters to follow, we will see how Dreyer practices art melodrama by drawing on the archive, reenacting and renewing it in such a way as to dramatize the interaction of multiple historical moments. The ghosts of Nordisk melodrama refuse to stay dead.

La Passion de Jeanne d'Arc
Art Melodrama, "Authenticity," and Performance

La Passion de Jeanne d'Arc (1928) constitutes Dreyer's most visceral and corporeal attempt to grapple with his attraction-repulsion to melodrama. The film culminates with an immolation that is one of the most remarkable sequences of pathos to be captured on film. We witness in graphic detail the climactic results of Jeanne's (Maria Falconetti) trial as she is bound to the stake to burn. Sweetly compliant, she bends down to pick up the rope that has slipped down from her waist. As the flames rise, Jeanne's discomfort becomes palpable; she coughs and sputters, her nostrils flaring as she struggles not to breathe in the smoke. As she takes her last breath, her head falls limply to her chest and fire engulfs her body. A ravenous wall of flame melts away her flesh. Interspersed with shots of Jeanne's suffering are other graphic shots of onlookers moved by her suffering. A sympathetic Massieu (Antonin Artaud), whose empathy sets him apart from his fellow churchmen, implores her to be brave and holds out a crucifix for her to embrace for comfort. We catch glimpses of officials at the trial slowly realizing that their persecution of the young woman has backfired disastrously. Most vividly, the frenetic lamentation of spectators running in every direction is captured in Eisenstein-like montage and wild camera angles. Violent, almost manic editing combines pans of weeping peasants, the close-up of a baby startled from the breast, the glimpse of a child wailing over its dead mother—all of which convey a mass public on the verge of revolution. Jeanne d'Arc's martyrdom is proclaimed through exquisite pathos followed by an eruption of action, both portrayed with unbridled cinematic prowess.

Layer upon layer of successive film scholarship has established *Jeanne d'Arc*'s reputation as Dreyer's magnum opus, whether as avant-garde, modernist, historical, quasi-mystical or religious, or the ultimate instance of filmic realism. Dreyer's characterization of his film as embodying "realized mysticism" engendered an interpretive tradition revolving around the film's depiction of martyrdom as transcendental or spiritual. *Jeanne d'Arc* enjoys a unique status in the context of Dreyer's oeuvre as the most vibrant and sometimes confounding example of the director's experimentation with modernist cinematic form. In one early review of the film in the Danish newspaper *Politiken*, published shortly after its premiere in France, Ebbe Neergaard describes *Jeanne d'Arc* as one of the most peculiar films he has ever seen, citing Dreyer's emphatic and relentless use of the close-up as typical of the film's utterly untraditional status.[1] The film's erratic camera movements: its tilts, swish pans, erratic zooming; its interspersed high and low angle shots; its placement of action at the edge of the frame; its disjointed editing and montage; its abstraction of mise-en-scène, and percussive use of close-ups all contribute to Dreyer's reputation as a director first and foremost interested in experimenting with avant-garde cinema form.

The film's intriguing and unconventional production history, which includes testimonials from cast and crew attesting to Dreyer's insatiable artistic demands, also contributed to the film's canonical aura. Dreyer demanded that an extensive set be built to replicate Rouen, although the final cut of the film is almost entirely devoid of establishing shots depicting it. Set workers dug deep trenches to achieve the film's extreme low-angle shots. Production lasted around six months; every scene was shot five to ten times. In scripting the plot, Dreyer also compressed events from five months of Jeanne d'Arc's trial into a single day and shot the film more or less chronologically. All of this contributed to the production veering wildly overbudget. As a result of this extravagance, the production company, Le Société Générale de Films, broke its initial three-film contract with Dreyer. He took the matter to court, and although he prevailed, the ordeal exacted a significant personal toll on him.

Accounts of the extensive demands that Dreyer put on his actors are typically used as evidence of Dreyer's commitment to an extreme form of realism. All makeup was prohibited during the production, and Dreyer demanded that each actor be present and in costume every day regardless of whether that individual would be needed for the day's shooting. He purportedly also demanded that the tonsure of every actor playing a priest be shaved even if their costuming also included headwear that would cover it up and it wouldn't be visible to film spectators. Rumors about the intensity of Falconetti's experience while performing the role of Jeanne, which hinted at the possibility that Dreyer had violated ethical boundaries to achieve his vision for the film, also contributed to the film's cult and critical status. As David Bordwell remarks, "Indeed so intense were Dreyer's demands that some have accused him of immersing Falconetti *too* deeply in her role, of torturing her no less cruelly than the judges tortured Jeanne. It is hard to see how else Dreyer could have elicited

Figure 3. Jeanne d'Arc draws her last breath before burning at the stake. Frame capture, *La Passion de Jeanne d'Arc*.

from an actress celebrated for light comedies a performance of unequalled tragic power."[2] Accounts of Dreyer's misconduct in pursuit of authentic depictions of suffering went so far as to accuse him of sadism. Paul Moor's 1951 article, "The Tyrannical Dane," is a key example, suggesting that Dreyer had an unusual interest in filming anguish and horror and that he would pinch his actors to achieve the expression of pain that he desired. Moor writes, "When Maria Falconetti played 'Joan' for him, Dreyer ordered all her hair cut off; Falconetti pled, raged, and, finally, conceding, wept bitterly; Dreyer not only filmed her weeping, but there were among those present some who swear he derived an uncommon enjoyment from the spectacle."[3] The renunciation of makeup, the elaborate construction of inhabitable sets, and shooting in sequence in many ways exceeded what could be captured in the film's final cut. Both contemporary and subsequent critical discourse surrounding the film perpetuated the notion that whether because of its artistry or its intensity, *Jeanne d'Arc* was like nothing Dreyer had ever done before.

But let us flash back to "Lydia," a script that Dreyer wrote some ten years before *Jeanne d'Arc* while he was employed in Denmark at Nordisk Films Kompagni (discussed at length in chapter 1), which was eventually filmed as

Lydia by Holger-Madsen in 1918.[4] A heady tale of overlapping love triangles, forgery, murder, suicide, and scenes of debauched theater life, "Lydia," like *Jeanne d'Arc*, also culminates in a woman's spectacular death by fire. One fateful evening, Lydia is slated to perform the world premiere of her death-defying "fire dance" (*Ilddans*), described in the film's program as a ritualistic "adoration of fire" (*en Tilbedelse af Ilden*). As she dances, she steps into the flames to commit suicide onstage. Watching the spectacle in rapt attention from the audience, her lover, Fribert, eventually comprehends that her performance has become real and he lunges toward the stage to intercede, but his struggle to reach her through the chaos of a burning theater is in vain. Fribert reaches Lydia in time to carry her expiring body up to the roof of the theater, where she is revived for a brief moment, begs for his forgiveness, kisses him, and then dies. Distraught, Fribert throws himself off the roof. Moments later, his unwitting fiancée encounters his dead body on the sidewalk below.

At first take, the two immolations seem entirely incompatible, their audience address radically different. *Jeanne d'Arc*, one might argue, offers a serious,

Figure 4. Lydia performs her ritualistic fire dance. Production still from *Lydia* (Holger-Madsen, 1918), courtesy of Danish Film Institute.

Figure 5. Fribert (Valdemar Psilander) as a transfixed spectator watching Lydia perform. His unwitting fiancée (Zanny Petersen) sits to his right. Production still from *Lydia* (Holger-Madsen, 1918), courtesy of Danish Film Institute.

artistic, authentic depiction inspired by historical events, while *Lydia* demonstrates an overwrought film spectacle set in a theater, staged to elicit thrills. The pathos of *Jeanne d'Arc* is laced with reflection brought about through a barrage of estrangements and camera disorientations, while *Lydia*'s posturing affords only cheap thrills and overidentifications of the kind of popular culture at Nordisk that Dreyer himself disparaged as inartistic.[5] *Jeanne d'Arc* represents the future of the cinema's capacity for artistic, modernist, and realist representation, while *Lydia* displays the clunky, filmed-theater aesthetic of a primitive past that art cinema has long outgrown. Although Holger-Madsen's filmed version of Lydia's immolation no longer exists, production stills suggest that Fribert's deciphering of Lydia's performance was likely conveyed through frontal reaction shots: Fribert's point of view (POV) in the audience alternated with a shot of him from the POV of stage center. The sequence would have been a far cry from the masterful editing of *Jeanne d'Arc*'s pyrotechnic ending.

But a second look at the two scenes reveals intriguing parallels between Dreyer's work while at and after Nordisk. Each scene revolves around the spectacle of a female body being destroyed by fire in a space of performance—

the stage of a variety theater and a public execution—including diegetic spectators who watch and respond.[6] Both performance situations blur the boundaries between entertainment and ritual sacrifice. Fire, in both instances, forces spectators to confront the materiality of the body performing in front of them, impelling them to react. The depiction of suffering in each scene implicitly raises ethical questions about what it means to consume this kind of pathos. The spectacle of an actress's flesh in harm's way in each case prompts the spectator to feel empathy and at the same time reflect on, or become acutely aware of, the ontological conditions of mimesis, the boundary and vacillation between a female body acting and not acting.[7] Each asks spectators to distinguish "authentic" from feigned suffering. Fribert charges the stage when he understands that Lydia's flesh is actually going to burn and that the performance has become real. The shock of awareness is echoed by the shout from the frenzied crowd in *Jeanne d'Arc* proclaiming, "You've killed a saint!" In each sequence, characters in the fictional world witness suffering, which sparks action. Each scene dramatizes the transformation of spectator from passive consumer of spectacle to active participant, charging into the fray. In each film, the passivity of fourth-wall voyeurism gives way to an enlivened, articulated space of interaction alternating between the POV of various diegetic spectators and the POV of the performer.

"Lydia" and *Jeanne d'Arc* each pulse with what I call *varieté*, a topos or perhaps subgenre of art melodrama prevalent at Nordisk that explored pathos and spectacle engendered by live spaces of performance, the interactions of bodies within it, and the media reflexivity involved with filming them. My initial interest in the term *varieté* emerged from its prevalence in Nordisk scripts. *Varieté* complicates the claims of "authenticity" and "purity" that generations of critics have made about *Jeanne d'Arc*, including the way Dreyer dramatizes a break with Nordisk popular culture by claiming to strip the *varieté* star to reveal her "authentic" self and suffering. While Dreyer rhetorically promoted the discourse of purifying the film by eliminating low-culture melodrama and stripping away its inherent inauthenticity, *Jeanne d'Arc*, in actuality, accentuates the juxtaposition of artifice and truth already inherent in *varieté* as a form. Further, by tracing the performing bodies in *Jeanne d'Arc* alongside Dreyer's film *Michael* (1924) and through his earlier script "Esther," adapted from the first part of Honoré de Balzac's novel *Splendeurs et misères des courtisanes, Esther Happy* (*Esther heureuse*, 1838) and filmed as *Den hvide Djævel* (*The Devil's Protegé*, Holger-Madsen, 1916), I show the extent to which *Jeanne d'Arc* draws on the core thrills of the *varieté*: its spectacle, aesthetics, pathos, and preoccupation with liveness; its performative juxtapositions between "authenticity" and inauthenticity; and its preoccupation with the ontology of suffering. Rather than abolishing melodrama, from production to final cut, *Jeanne d'Arc* reimagines the space of the *varieté* and the body of the *varieté* star. Being sensitive to the low-culture stigma of Nordisk while remaining drawn to its mechanisms, Dreyer claims to make Nordisk melodrama more "authentic" by transforming *varieté* spectacle into show trial. The media reflexivity of Dreyer's experiment in artistic process and the pressure he puts on the bodies of his actors to perform Jeanne's trial imbues art melodrama with the vivacity of avant-garde performance art or historical reenactment. Dreyer's equally am-bitious experiment in "authentic" performance deserves to be considered alongside or as part of his experiment with cinematic form. Throughout this chapter, I keep the term "authentic" in quotation marks to gesture toward its rhetorical association with non-melodrama, even as the *Jeanne d'Arc* project helps articulate it more concretely *within* melodrama, as an iteration of art melodrama.

Art Melodrama of the *Varieté*

The art melodramatic mechanisms operative in both "Lydia" and *Jeanne d'Arc* revolve around the *varieté* as a topos of performance. The term resonates with the notion of theatricality that André Loiselle and Jeremy Maron trace in *Stages of Reality: Theatricality in Cinema*, namely, as film that involves repre-sentational spaces that center on the observation of performance and, as such, call attention to their status as representation. These filmed representational spaces deploy signs "within a space for the self-conscious purpose of being perceived, of being recognized by the spectator."[8] We can think of theatricality here as synonymous also to the representational practices prevalent in Scandi-navian effigy culture and wax museums at the turn of the century that I de-tailed in the previous chapter (to this point, *Jeanne d'Arc*'s immolation se-quence asks the cinema spectator to ponder in which shot Falconetti's body has been replaced by a wax mannequin that will actually burn). *Varieté* allows a film to exploit play-within-the-play situations and scenes of performance, both on and off the stage, to heighten the media reflexivity and the materiality of the "live" theatrical interactions represented. Diegetic theater spectators in these films, along with film spectators, experience the pleasure of recognizing the sign as sign, with a "sensuous acknowledgement that what is being ob-served is a construct."[9] The pleasurably ambiguous status of the performing body often lies at the heart of *varieté*'s sensuous acknowledgment.

Early forms of *varieté* were prevalent in Nordisk's melodramatic imagina-tion despite the fact, as we saw in the previous chapter, that neither Denmark nor the other Scandinavian countries could claim the same robust tradition of melodramatic boulevard theater as England or France. By the turn of the century, a version of theatrical melodrama had made its way into Copenhagen's cosmopolitan imagination in the new Vesterbro entertainment district, where its prime manifestations were the *varieté* stage and sensational circus spectacles.[10] At Nordisk, *varieté* took many forms in the diegesis: proscenium theaters such as literal variety theaters, fairground venues, and circuses that signaled exciting underworlds filled with seedy criminals, unscrupulous cads, burlesque-like dancers, circus-like sideshows, exotic dance numbers, and musical acts. As I employ it, the term also encompasses the depictions of equivalent theatrical spaces aligned to higher social strata, whether private spaces like *tableau vivant* performed in aristocratic salons or relatively elite cultural spaces, like the museum, opera, or national theater. *Varieté* also functions as shorthand to refer to situations that make use of embodied identities through performances of disguise and revelation, whether actor-characters who engage in the dramatic manipulation of makeup, costuming, and disguise before going onstage or private detectives and cunning criminals disguising themselves to various ends. *Varieté* delights in drawing attention to the embodied spectacle of diegetic characters engaged in a range of performative interactions: acting, nonacting, and spectating. Nonactor characters in the diegesis often become performer characters by being thrust onstage, setting multiple identities and identifications into play. The *varieté* at Nordisk offers a concentrated, early instance of art melodrama's intriguing commixture of forms: theatricality, performance, visual art, and film that delights in the overt exploitation of performing bodies to entertain and to elicit pathos. Part of the titillation of these scenes is their capacity to question reality by drawing attention to the means of representation. Spectators of melodrama are often mistakenly assumed to practice a kind of overidentification, but as Christine Gledhill has shown, melodramatic pathos relies on complex schemes of dramatic irony in depicting suffering.[11] *Varieté* accentuates these melodramatic and protomodernistic mechanisms—high and low sensibilities intermingle. We can call this art melodrama, too, both proto-modernist and fully melodramatic at the same time.[12]

Varieté is conceptually adjacent to Heide Schlüpmann's theorization of the intersection of theater and cinematic space in German cinema in the 1910s in *Unheimlichkeit des Blicks* (1990) (*The Uncanny Gaze*, 2010), in which she reads female spectatorship as enmeshed in the complexities of the public sphere, lived social space, aesthetic experience, and desire. Schlüpmann differentiates between melodrama (*Kino-Melodrama*) and social drama (*soziales Drama*) in pre–World War I German cinema. Melodrama, produced for female audiences, was essentially conservative and "produced the perfect illusion of looking at oneself on the screen," effectively reinstating gendered norms of heterosexual marriage and doing little for the cause of female emancipation.[13] The social drama, by contrast, was more complex. Intended for male as well as female audiences, this form emphasized sexual difference and changing gender roles in modern German society and propelled the development of a new aesthetic of film drama. Social drama, which Schlüpmann argues could share elements of melodrama, combined the spectacle of the cinema of attractions with narrative cinema in ways that opened up possibilities for female desire and spectatorship. Effectively, she draws upon what I would call *variété* to make her argument about the development in German cinema. In particular, her reading of the sensuality of Asta Nielsen's female body in the gaucho dance scene in *Afgrunden* (*The Abyss*, Urban Gad, 1910) in which her body is oriented toward the camera rather than toward the diegetic theater audience depicted, and thus awakens in the film spectator the longing for what she calls "the pleasures of the real, in opposition to those of illusion," resonates with the female performer characters I treat in this chapter, including Jeanne d'Arc, Lydia, and Esther.[14] Schlüpmann draws an interesting distinction between Nielsen's body as both performing the roll of an artiste, or star of the stage, and being a star of screen to argue that her body merges film and theater as two visual spaces on film, "the space the female artist shares with the stage and her audience, and the second space in which we, the film spectators, see stage as well as audience, but also get a glimpse of a slice of the bourgeois world beyond the performance."[15] I see the power of moments like Asta Nielsen's gaucho dance in *Afgrunden* (Gad, 1910) as not necessarily unique or specific to Nielsen but rather indicative of more pervasive art melodramatic or proto–art melodramatic practices in the interrelated Danish and German film industries.

Negating Melodrama in the Name of "Authenticity"

Dreyer's art melodrama emerges from his long-standing attraction-repulsion to the melodramatic mode. As established in the previous chapter, his elevation as a director of art cinema has been predicated explicitly on his renunciation of Nordisk and its popular culture pulp. To recap: citing artistic differences, Dreyer left Nordisk after completing his second and final feature there, *Leaves from Satan's Book* (1921). The rhetorical disparagement of melodrama as low culture was a significant force in the historical accounts of Dreyer's break with Nordisk. Melodrama's stigma effectively ensured that, during his lifetime, Dreyer would never openly embrace the mode.

Dreyer was acutely aware of the way his oeuvre was being incorporated into Danish cinema history as exemplifying the possibility that Danish cinema might overcome its more or less shameful, or childish, melodramatic past and bring about the future potential of the cinema as art. His friend, Ebbe Neergaard, introduced a key term to describe what made Dreyer's films artistic—authenticity—a term that Dreyer would also use to frame *Jeanne d'Arc* as melodrama's dialectical opposite. When he wrote the first authoritative book on Dreyer in 1940, Neergaard proclaimed: "Even by his first film [*The President*, 1919], Dreyer had achieved results that corrected exactly what would come to be Nordisk Films' weak point. Melodramatic style. Through his work with *milieu* as it is characterized through decor, minor characters, and extras, he sought to create the first foundation for filmic *authenticity*."[16] Neergaard's book on Dreyer, translated into English in 1950, was instrumental in establishing Dreyer as an international auteur who became so by transcending his early years at Nordisk.[17] Reviewing a reissued version of Neergaard's work in 1964, Danish author and critic Klaus Rifbjerg continued to echo this antimelodrama rhetoric that positioned it as antithetical to artistic film: "It can't be put in a more simple and banal way. The reality that Dreyer brought to film by cleaning up all the melodramatic hocus pocus, by stylizing and at the same time guiding *reality*, the authentic milieu, the 'actual' people, into film has brought the art from cheap sideshow performance (*gøgl*) to a point where today, it to some extent feels its most vital."[18] In this cultural climate—spanning most of Dreyer's lifetime—it would be difficult if not impossible for Dreyer ever to openly embrace either melodrama or his own work at Nordisk.

"Authenticity" (aligned with realism) was a self-evidently positive, if ultimately ambiguous, term used by Dreyer and his critics to describe his ambitions for untheatrical, artistic film. It signifies, among other things, the opposite of pretending, such as moments when acting is understood to be is suspended; the corporeal, visceral experiences of actors and spectators; and strong, sincere pathos. The rhetoric of "authenticity" reverberated through Dreyer's career, but it reached a fever pitch with the *Jeanne d'Arc* project. Distancing his work from the stigma of Nordisk, Dreyer embraced a similar rhetoric, proposing to strip *Jeanne d'Arc* of any trace of artifice and imagine the film as melodrama's dialectical opposite, "authentic" cinema. In his article "Realized Mysticism," published shortly after the film's release, Dreyer described his ambitions to present truth by breaking with previous film traditions, in part by banishing makeup, filming in sequence, and "renouncing methods of 'beautification.'"[19] Such rhetorical claims to purification and renunciation, combined with the many production accounts attesting to the film's austerity, more or less established the notion that in *Jeanne d'Arc*, Dreyer successfully purged any trace of what might be called melodramatic excess or theatricality to make a film of a completely different—higher—order.[20]

Dreyer reiterated the rhetoric of film as "authentic" and the theater, theatricality, and melodrama as "inauthentic" using ontological terms, that is, the extent to which each might be considered real. In his 1933 article, "The Real Talking Film," Dreyer aligns the theater with inauthentic, exaggerated representation at a distance, while the cinema becomes "authentic" through its proximity to the spectator and to reality. He wrote:

> A theatrical performance is a picture seen from a distance. For the overall effect to be lifelike, it has to be painted with a coarse brush—the paint has to be applied in thick dollops. All details have to be made coarse and enlarged—exaggerated. In the theater everything is inauthentic, and everything depends on bringing the inauthentic details into such an agreement with each other, that altogether it produces a colorful illusion of reality, while film presents reality itself in a rigorous black and white stylization. . . . The distance between theater and film amounts to the distance between *representing* and *being*.[21]

Dreyer's disparagement of the theater as inauthentic belies the fact that he continued to be attracted by it throughout his career. Intriguingly, *Jeanne d'Arc* opens with a prologue that explicitly invites the spectator to read the film as dramatizing and staging pathos: "We are witness to an amazing drama: a young, pious woman confronted by a group of orthodox theologians and powerful judges."

And while Dreyer may have sought to distance himself from melodrama and theatricality as low cultural forms, "authenticity" for him remained deeply entangled with situations of performance, or *varieté*, throughout his entire career. Dreyer's art melodrama archive includes a wealth of performing bodies and audiences of the kind linking *Jeanne d'Arc* to his Nordisk scripts. A cursory glance reveals his persistent fascination with filming the pathos, thrill, and negotiations of identity afforded by dramatic spectacles, plays-within-the-play, and performer characters. *Varieté* allowed Dreyer to explore suffering in female characters—a career-long preoccupation—in situations of dramatic irony. *Michael* (1924) features a very deliberate play-within-a play scene, when those embroiled in a love triangle attend the opera only to watch another love triangle perform in the ballet *Swan Lake*. Eponymous divas such as Lydia and Esther and concert musicians performing with cursed violins in "Guldets Gift" (*The Temptation of Mrs. Chestney*, Holger-Madsen, 1916) foreshadow the ensemble of performer characters in Dreyer's last film, *Gertrud* (1964). In Dreyer's script "Rovedderkoppen" (*The Spider's Prey*, August Blom, 1916), a dramatic urge animates the disguising and unmasking of arch criminals and detectives pursuing them. Another metatheatrical moment of questioned identities in "En Forbryders Liv og Levned" (*A Criminal's Diary*, Alexander Christian, 1916) features an escaped criminal elegantly stealing the prop-like paraphernalia of his criminal persona from a nearby museum after it had been put on display. Performing bodies in Dreyer's oeuvre could also be comical or farcical, as in one of his earliest surviving Nordisk scripts, "Elskovs Opfindsomhed" (*Love's Ingenuity*, Sofus Wolder, Denmark, 1913), in which a character who is a performer in the fiction cross-dresses as a young suitor to charm an older woman, or in "Hans rigtige Kone" (*Which Is Which?*, Holger-Madsen, 1917), a play of mistaken identities featuring another performer character. Dreyer's interest in the theater could also be straightforward, as demonstrated by the many play texts he adapted for the screen, including *Ordet* (1955) and *Gertrud* (1964), and the theater reviews he wrote for Copenhagen newspapers.[22] The notion that theatrical impulses in Dreyer's work might be purged as inauthentic misrepresents Dreyer's extensive experimentation with juxtaposing theater and performance in the fictional world of a film.

In fact, *Jeanne d'Arc* allows Dreyer to pursue even more ardently the questions of liveness that he begins working through conceptually at Nordisk. His extensive (and expensive) production experiment with *Jeanne d'Arc*, constructing a small city set of Rouen for actors to inhabit and shooting the film in sequence so that his cast could relive the trial, effectively turned the project into an immersive performance event—an extensive experiment in historical reenactment. The film's production demonstrates that Dreyer remained fascinated by (and dependent on) the material being of acting bodies—an actual presence taken for granted in the theater—to achieve cinematic stylization. The dramatic sensibilities that recur throughout Dreyer's oeuvre, from his early scriptwriting endeavors to his last feature films, are deeply—if not explicitly— engaged with performance. Dreyer's purported break with Nordisk is superficial and rhetorical; in practice, he continues to explore the performance of melodrama and *varieté* under the seemingly more legitimate guises of realism, formalism, tragedy, and "authenticity." Dreyer's vociferous repulsion of the *varieté* relies on an equally strong attraction and dedication to its core mechanisms of juxtaposition. As I argue in the following section, Dreyer eradicates melodrama in a melodramatic way, making its suffering more intense and more explicitly corporeal by heightening the media reflexivity and performativity of the *varieté*.

Jeanne d'Arc: Stripping, Galvanizing,
Disguising *Varieté* Performance Space

Although Dreyer overtly privileges film over theater, it would be more accurate to say that with *Jeanne d'Arc*, as with his art melodrama work at Nordisk,

Figure 6. Establishing Jeanne d'Arc's ecclesiastical courtroom as a performance space. Frame capture, *La Passion de Jeanne d'Arc*.

he actually continues reimagining the relationship between the two. With *Jeanne d'Arc*, Dreyer strips the *varieté* of its proscenium stage and reimagines it as a courtroom show trial. This veils the space of the *varieté* in naturalistic garb while continuing to cultivate and accentuate the drama of its live inter-actions. The opening shot of the interrogation, which employs an iris shot to reveal the courtroom, reads like a stage as the camera tracks the length of the audience of ecclesiastical spectators eagerly anticipating the performance about to commence. The camera's POV situates the film spectator as an audi-ence member amid the silhouetted rows of onlookers at the front of the house, a perspective frequently seen at Nordisk. In the illuminated performance space before them, stagehands scurry to arrange stools and props in preparation for the spectacle. In *Jeanne d'Arc*, particularly frenetic editing galvanizes *varieté* space to approximate a sense of bodies sharing a performance space and inter-acting in close proximity. The peculiarly fast editing, dramatic zooms, and erratic camera placements during the interrogation all work to collapse the distance between spectator and stage into a single phenomenological field. The spatial disorientation that Dreyer brings about by abandoning eyeline matches cinematically reimagines the space in Nordisk films between performers and audiences. Like *variété* spectator-characters, whose complete disregard of proscenium boundaries means they regularly find themselves onstage in the middle of the action, one judge suddenly appears onstage beside Jeanne, close enough to spit on her cheek. The cinematic virtuosity of the interrogation sequences utterly deflates any appeal to fourth-wall voyeurism in the diegetic realm of the film.

This editing also has the effect of intensifying melodramatic suffering by staging it at a micro level. Extreme close-ups in quick succession highlight the corporeality of performing actors: the twitch of a cheek, a tiny smirk, a raised eyebrow, the flare of nostrils, or the unsavory swabbing of an ear. Bodies fill the theater space and the film frame. The grotesque macro-physiognomy of the judges conveys an uncomfortably intimate sense of immersion. The dramatic space that emerges through this phenomenological attention reverberates with the emotions and reactions—felt and perceived—of those present to witness Jeanne's suffering. Thus, Dreyer presses on film to overcome its inevitable ontological absences, desiring to make film an experience comparable to what Erica Fischer-Lichte calls a performance event. Performance, in Fischer-Lichte's theorization, is predicated on the phenomenological feedback loop between performer and spectator.[23] Live performance, whether between individuals or on the scale of mass religious ritual, avant-garde performance art, or circus sideshow, has the potential to transform its participants.[24] It is this unmediated, transformative power of performance that Dreyer elicits via *Jeanne d'Arc's* intricately choreographed depiction of a chaotic flurry of micro perceptions.

Variété at Nordisk presented a vibrant space of liveness—on and through film—in ways that make *Jeanne d'Arc's* camera placement and editing look like a continuation of the studio's art melodrama techniques. Spatially, the *variété* exploited every inch of the house to generate encounters between performing coded as real life and performing coded as performance. Actors pulled audience members onstage; audience members could, in turn, dramatically interrupt a performance midscene with some real-life proclamation intended for an actor onstage. Offstage spaces also provided important opportunities for drama. Rivals challenged each other backstage, in the wings, or from the audience. The dramatic potential of the theater flowed in every direction. Filming this "live" space demonstrated Nordisk's media awareness of the different ontological and representative capacities of theater and film. The camera was positioned everywhere: in the balcony, on the stage to capture an audience reaction frontally, or obliquely from the orchestra pit. The cinematic space of the theater expanded to include the greenroom, with frequent shots of actors putting on makeup or disguises in mirrors and shots of the stage from the wings. The performance space of the theater could be opened up through shot-reverse-shot editing or through longer takes that exploited deep focus.[25] The alternations between, and imbrications of, "authenticity" and artifice at Nordisk produced thrills of immersion and reflection for diegetic audiences and cinema spectators alike.[26]

Made four years before *Jeanne d'Arc*, Dreyer's film *Michael* also exploits the dramatic, affective, and reflective impact of *varieté*, providing an interesting intertext between Dreyer's Nordisk scripts and *Jeanne d'Arc*. Based on a novel by Danish author Herman Bang, *Michael* is the tale of a heartbreak, the relationship of love and paternalism between two men, a master painter and his muse, that is destroyed when an alluring, impoverished Russian princess comes between them. *Michael* makes the narrative framing mechanism of the *varieté* space elaborate in a scene in which the protagonists go to the opera to see a ballet of *Swan Lake*. The cinematically constructed theater space is alive with the vibrant transmission of affect between bodies along with the dramatic play of glances. The opera sequence in *Michael* employs the play-within-a-play reflexivity of the *varieté* to invite the film spectator to contemplate how the onstage performance might illuminate the relationships between key spectators in the audience. Although *Michael* doesn't feature a performer character dancing onstage such as Lydia (or Esther, mentioned below), extensive shots of the ballet dancers ask the film spectator to imagine how the intrigues of Tchaikovsky's *Swan Lake*, with its devious enchantments, disguised identities, doomed love, and broken marriage vows, reflects the more naturalistically staged love triangles and entanglements of the diegetic spectators consuming the spectacle from their loges.

As with the show trial in *Jeanne d'Arc*, the opera scene creates the sensation of live, affective, interactive space through the interplay of gazes, camera placement, and shot variation. Dreyer ignores the fourth wall by placing the camera onstage, offering several POV shots from the perspective of the dancers, evoking the stills of naturalistic audience members watching Lydia's fire dance.[27] The articulation of space in *Michael* is more elaborate than in "Lydia"—by including a larger shot selection and a greater number of camera positions—but uses longer takes than *Jeanne d'Arc* and doesn't use extreme close-ups. Multiple shots of audience members in *Michael* that don't include any of the film's main characters anticipate the mass of highly individuated yet anonymous onlookers in *Jeanne d'Arc* who will watch Jeanne burn. Diegetic spectators applaud and mill about waiting for the curtain to go up and down. An usher claps for the performance where he stands by the exit, and the heads of anonymous spectators are silhouetted in a shot of the dancers from the balcony POV. The dancers onstage are also depicted as invested spectators, gazing out and inter-

Figure 7. The diegetic frame of the proscenium stage disappears in *Michael*. Frame capture, *Michael*.

Figure 8. Silhouetted spectators in the foreground accentuate the many audience perspectives in the depicted performance space. Frame capture, *Michael*.

acting with audience members. Shots with the camera positioned onstage distinctly demonstrate the POV of the dancers, who watch the audience filing out of the theater but then pausing to clap some more. The opera sequence in *Michael* also includes shots of dancers and audience members framed so tightly that the architectural frame of the proscenium stage disappears. In these shots, dancing bodies and rows of clapping spectators fill the entire film frame, graphically, in ways that subtly test the naturalism of the scene and gesture toward *Jeanne d'Arc*'s even more radical abstraction of *varieté* performance space.

The fact that we see similar approaches to constructing *varieté* in both *Michael* and *Jeanne d'Arc* makes sense given the genealogy of cinematographers linking the two films: Karl Freund was director of photography on *Michael* with Rudolf Maté serving as his assistant. Later, Maté worked as director of photography for Dreyer on *Jeanne d'Arc* and *Vampyr* (1932). In addition to a similar variety of camera placement, each film also demonstrates abrupt, zooming, extreme close-ups onto eyes. As if highlighting their shared interest in *varieté*, one year after making *Michael*, Freund would work on a film with exactly that title, *Varieté* (*Variety*, 1925), directed by Ewald Andre Dupont at UFA and staring Emil Jannings, Maly Delschaft, and Lya De Putti. Dupont's film offers a striking confirmation of the term's elasticity. A work of art melodrama, *Varieté* depicts a dramatic tale of love, betrayal, and revenge literally set among circus performers and sideshow acts of Berlin's Wintergarden. Critics praised the film's daring trapeze sequences, in which Freund's "unfastened camera" swung upside down multiple times over crowds to dizzying effect. Maté will similarly swing the camera upside down in the culminating sequence of *Jeanne d'Arc* as soldiers cast weapons from inside the castle. As in both *Michael* and *Jeanne d'Arc*, Freund's "unfastened camera" is regularly put in the service of an aesthetic of live performance that disregards conventions of continuity editing and imbues *Varieté*'s dramatic love triangles, plot twists, and daring spectacle with an avant-garde sensibility. This relates to Christophe Wall-Romana's argument about Jean Epstein, namely that French cinema in the 1920s and 1930s offered a precedent for intentionally combining high and low elements to create what he calls avant-garde, working-class melodrama.[28]

Dreyer could express a similar intentionality for his ambitions with *Jeanne d'Arc*, namely, to enlist formal experimentation to heighten the film's emotional impact and broaden its audience appeal. As he stated in his introductory remarks before a screening of *Jeanne d'Arc* at the Danish Film Museum in 1950, "My film about Jeanne d'Arc has unjustly been called an avant-garde film, which it absolutely is not. It is not a film intended for film theorists but rather a film of universally human content, intended for a broad audience and with a message for any open human mind."[29] Dreyer's art melodrama, in other words, encompasses an explicit, if sometimes underacknowledged, passion for pursuing intense affective sensibilities that could transcend—or at least unsettle—experimentation with cinematic technique. In an interview for *Cahiers du Cinema* in 1965, Dreyer would remark in French, "What interests me above all—more than the question of technique—is reproducing, as sincerely as possible, the most sincere feelings possible."[30] Here Dreyer casts his interest in authenticity as an ambition for emotional sincerity and positions experimenting with cinematic technique as a means to that end. Dreyer's art melodrama emerges through his interest in creating, finding, and disclosing a kind of "pure" pathos in the bodies of his actors and protagonists.

As we have seen, at other moments during Dreyer's career, the innovation of cinematic form functions rhetorically to excuse the persisting presence of melodrama, associated here with narrative content. Rob Edelman's encyclopedia entry on Dupont's film illustrates the persistence of this hierarchy of form versus content as well as the persistent force of melodrama's stigma almost a century after either *Jeanne d'Arc* or *Varieté* were made. Edelman describes Freund's camerawork in *Varieté*, including his use of the detached camera as a "technical tour de force," which transforms the ordinary subject matter, "a predictable melodrama, with characters who are more types than three-dimensional personalities," into something extraordinary.[31] In a rhetorical move also used to describe Dreyer's work, melodrama, in this equation, signals a shameful lack of complexity that must be overcome by technical means in order to convey interiority coded as authentic and sincere, or the antidote to pulp and artifice. "The camera becomes the conscience of the characters, who exist in a world of phony glamor, two-bit circuses and decadent music halls, and finally, in the case of Jannings, a cheerless prison," Edelman argues.[32] Dreyer's attraction-repulsion to melodrama can sometimes manifest itself in this way as employing formal innovation to reimagine recognizable genre conventions. As I discuss in the next chapter, Dreyer undertakes this with *Vampyr*, which reinvents the Nordisk *Offer* (victim) film. Like makeup or disguise, Dreyer's innovation with form gives artistic legitimacy to his attraction to popular culture.

As I discussed in chapter 1, Sergei Balukhatyi's *Poetics of Melodrama* (1926) offers a particularly fleshy take on melodrama's concealments and revelations in relation to high and low genres and form. His theory also raises questions about how "authenticity" relates to discourses of purity. Balukhatyi describes the skeleton as "pure" melodrama over which new, different flesh can be stretched to make it look artistic, like higher genres:

> In its "pure" aspect, melodrama acts directly through its constructional and emotional forms, but melodrama can also be found in many other types of

drama in which its "pure, primordial" principles are masked, weakened, and complicated by other aspects, such as realistic portrayal, psychological motivation, or ideological dialectics. . . . It is possible for a melodramatic skeleton to become covered with the solid flesh of realistic material and concealed beneath an elegant layer of psychology and ethical, social, or philosophical content. We thereby lose the feeling of melodramatic style and accept the play as a "higher" genre.[33]

It is important to address the claims of purity here and those that will reverberate around the *Jeanne d'Arc* project. The melodramatic skeleton that Dreyer would have encountered at Nordisk, crucially, was neither pure nor fixed but rather already hybrid. With *Jeanne d'Arc*, Dreyer stretches new cinematic flesh on a skeleton of proto–art melodrama that is already growing with moral ambiguity and reflexivity. And while the discourse of purity running through Balukhatyi's metaphor enacts a beautiful reversal of the process by which Dreyer and others will claim to purify film of its melodramatic excesses, the rhetoric of pure primordial principles or some pure skeleton of melodrama is still imprecise at best and problematic at worst. Although Dreyer's rhetorical claims to cinematic purity can be forceful and extensive, as I discuss in the next section, in practice his art melodrama texts remain decidedly impure, in the sense that Roselind Galt and Karl Schoonover define art cinema in *Global Art Cinema* as constitutionally impure.[34]

That said, Balukhatyi's bodily metaphor of skeleton and flesh also coincides in a provocative way with Dreyer's persistent experimentation with suffering female bodies—and corporeality in general—over the course of his career. Melodrama has always had a privileged claim on the body. Dreyer frames the *Jeanne d'Arc* project rhetorically, as stripping away inauthentic trappings in the search for purity, effectively reimagining the relationship of skin to flesh, and flesh to bone, and body to costuming. This intensification of the *varieté*'s alternations between "authenticity" and artifice, for Dreyer, coalesces particularly around the spectacle of a performing (female) body.

Varieté "Authenticity" in Dreyer's "Esther" Script: Deciphering the Performing Body

Disparaging Nordisk as exclusively producing artifice underestimates the extent to which beautifications and revelations at the studio depended structurally on establishing worlds and moments coded as more real, more "authentic." As we have seen in spectacularly corporeal moments such as the fire dance in "Lydia," Dreyer was practiced in exploiting the ontological variations he understood as differentiating performance from reality. Reading Dreyer's

"Esther" script, adapted from Honoré de Balzac's novel *Splendeurs et misères des courtisanes* (filmed as *Den hvide Djævel / The Devil's Protegé*, Holger-Madsen, 1916), offers another insightful lens through which to read the scenes of dramatic persecution in *Jeanne d'Arc* that revolve around Jeanne's insistence on wearing clothing coded as masculine. Dreyer's "Esther" script shows how in the *varieté*, performance added layers of signification to melodrama's core ambitions—recognizing authentic pathos in another and revealing goodness—through and because of embellishment, costuming, and makeup.[35] Interestingly, Dreyer changes Balzac's courtesan-with-a-heart-of-gold into a *varieté* starlet performing to support herself and her brother, Lucian. The orphan siblings struggle to make a better life for themselves in Paris but ultimately fall under the malign influence of escaped arch-criminal Jacques Cellin.

In the same way Dreyer will later stage *Jeanne d'Arc* as the persecution and revelation of her true heart, he sets his protagonist Esther up as a true-heart character enduring the adversity of a shoddy theatrical world. The costuming she is forced to wear epitomizes her plight. In naturalistic strokes, Dreyer's script conveys the discord between Esther's essential sincerity and the theatrical exterior she presents: "She is a young and healthy woman who has had to earn a livelihood for herself and her brother for a while now by performing in varietés on the outskirts of town. Despite being surrounded by vice for so long, it has in no way infected her. On the contrary, the impoverished, feigned elegance of her costuming betrays her profession. Her essence is absolutely sympathetic."[36] Of interest to Dreyer is the way that the artifice of the *varieté* milieu at once disguises this true heart and constitutes the precondition for the rich baron in the audience to see Esther's virtue in spite of her costuming, and then fall in love with her. Here, onstage artifice and offstage "authenticity" coexist and reinforce each other by means of juxtaposition.

The onstage performance and naturalistic, offstage realms could also reinforce one another and heighten the pathos by aligning. Dreyer writes a climactic spectacle for "Esther" in which she performs a scene titled "Marguerite and the Golden Calf" (*Marguerite paa Guldkalven*). Although Dreyer's script doesn't provide details about how the "Marguerite" scene was to be shot, Charles Gounod's opera *Faust* (1859) included an extravagant scene in which Marguerite is held in a prison for the murder of her child amid an orgiastic Walpurgis Night gathering of witches and courtesans. Mephistopheles tempts her with the promise of forgiveness, but she steadfastly refuses, opting instead to mount the scaffold and commit her fate to God. At the last moment, a chorus of angels triumphantly announces her salvation. Dreyer's scene sets up a parallel between the performed spectacle of Marguerite's virtuous rejection of temptation on the scaffold and Esther's "authentic" self-sacrifice performing in the *varieté* for her livelihood. Marguerite's endurance of torture on stage likely amplified the pathos of Esther's plight in life offstage. The rush of Marguerite's last-minute salvation onstage might have also accentuated the pathos of Esther's eventual suicide offstage, in real life, from which no chorus of angels saves her. Dreyer's script also draws connections between Esther's onstage temptation and a Faustian scene involving Lucian, in which he succumbs to temptation, selling his soul to Jacques for riches—in stark contrast to Esther. Here, theatrical spectacle and its more naturalistic counterpart coexist and inform each other. Interestingly, in Nordisk's filmed version, Dreyer's eponymous heroine and pillar of virtuously performed sacrifice has been deleted entirely. Program and stills reveal that Nordisk simplified Dreyer's love quadrangle, which culminated in a double brother and sister suicide, to a more conventional triangle of exploitation in which a destitute Lucian dies a fairly straightforward, passive, and pitiable victim-hero. In the case of "Esther," Dreyer's melodramatic imagination exceeded Nordisk's.

In contrast to the way that melodrama is normally understood to focus on designating innocence to differentiate good from evil, Nordisk's proto–art melodrama often valued the pleasures of deciphering performance—a practice of media reflexivity—over questions of declaring or restoring innocence. Esther is not a straightforwardly innocent character; she actually becomes complicit in the plot to swindle the baron. More interesting than the revelation of her questionable innocence is the fact that her innocence and suffering are put onstage to be experienced and deciphered by diegetic spectators like the baron, the audience, and, ultimately, the film spectator. *Varieté* derived as much pleasure from reading and deciphering the ironic misprisions made possible by staging innocence, guilt, or suffering as it did in seeing virtuous suffering clearly rewarded. Nordisk was often more invested in the ethics and effects of performance than in establishing clear moral boundaries. Accentuating ambiguity and destabilizing identity—exploring the pleasures of a proto-modernist notion of self rather than the pleasure of disambiguation—align Nordisk *varieté* with the art cinema of art melodrama. We see this in *Jeanne d'Arc* as well; deciphering the ambiguities of the performing goodness overshadows any confirmation of goodness itself.

Denuding the *Varieté* Actress:
Falconetti's Body as Site of "Authentic" Melodrama

As he did with "Esther," Dreyer exploits the body of the *varieté* actress as a site of pathos and "authenticity" in *Jeanne d'Arc*. The rhetoric of eradicating melodrama becomes a drama that takes place diegetically and extra-diegetically on the body of the *varieté* actress Falconetti. As Neergaard puts it in his history of

Danish cinema, "Dreyer had chosen the *varieté* actress [*varietéskuespillerinden*] Marie Falconetti for the role of Jeanne d'Arc. When liberated from makeup, she became capable of displaying the naked, soulful face that Dreyer wanted."[37] Dreyer's strict prohibition of makeup on set attracted the attention of many contemporary critics and contributed to the project's "authenticity." And again, the stripping of embellishment actually reiterates and magnifies a dialectic of artifice and "authenticity" at the heart of melodrama: the perception of authenticity only pops in relation to the perception of artifice.

As if reenacting the scene between the baron and Esther, Dreyer's casting of Falconetti provides the cornerstone on which *Jeanne d'Arc's* extra-diegetic claims to "authenticity" are built. Dreyer first discovered the young actress of the *Comédie-Française* one evening while she was performing in the light comedy *Lorenzaccio* in Paris. From his seat in the audience, he recognized some aspect of Falconetti's humanity despite—or made possible by—her thick costuming and makeup. In a scene that uncannily rehearses the scenes of enthralled and reflective *varieté* spectators in "Esther" and "Lydia," Dreyer consumes and deciphers the embellishment of Falconetti's performing body. This marks the precondition for Dreyer, as a spectator, to recognize her "authentic" suffering. Jean and Dale Drum invest the encounter with a kind of mystical, wordless transmission between performer and spectator: "How Carl Dreyer was able to see beneath that surface to something deeper and more profound, was able to strip away the makeup, the urbanity, the sophistication and see the simple power and intensity of Joan, no one can say, not even Dreyer."[38] When Dreyer later invites Falconetti to his apartment for casting and asks her to wear no makeup, their greenroom encounter functions, in extra-filmic accounts, as a naturalistically coded performance between actress and spectator that structurally reinforces the film's "authentic" suffering. Offstage references to the actual suffering inscribed on Falconetti's face, the traces of some earlier drama in the actress's life, work to authenticate Jeanne's suffering on screen.

The film of *Jeanne d'Arc* reiterates the performance of disrobing a *varieté* star and also a saint. Falconetti plays the role of the true-hearted *varieté* performer, persecuted and redeemed through the making of the film. The *varieté* actress is seen elevated to tragic actress, but only by the kind of disclosure and recognition of suffering that is part of all melodrama. What makes this art melodrama is that Dreyer makes disclosure more extreme, taking it down to Falconetti's flesh. Nakedness becomes a guise equated with the ultimate "authentic" human experience; flesh becomes the most perfect exteriorization of interiority. Dreyer uses the body to represent the soul and express feeling. Returning to his 1950 introduction to the Danish Film Museum's screening of the film, Dreyer describes wanting "to strip [*afklæde*] Jeanne d'Arc of her halo and formal accoutrements of a saint and find a way into the actual little woman-child, who suffered death at the stake for her faith."[39] Dreyer cloaks the melodramatic desire for revelation and recognition within the rhetoric of austerity and nudity. The subdued, stylized costuming in *Jeanne d'Arc* and dialogue that evokes rather than shows beautification belie the fact that he retains melodrama's insistence on reading through disguise and deciphering bodies and bodily surfaces. The film introduces legibility as a central concern in opening intertitles where, interspersed with authenticating shots of the trial document, the spectator is tasked quite literally with reading a young woman's humanity obscured by a soldier's costuming: "Reading it, we discover the 'real Joan' not in armor, but simple and human." Dreyer's preoccupation with reading the body emerges again in sartorially focused dialogue from the trial that draws attention to clothing and hair while evoking the naked bodies underneath. A volley of questions about Jeanne's visions and her own ability to recognize a saint—essentially by differentiating between costuming and the bodies underneath—demonstrates the desire and inability of Jeanne's judges to read her. They demand to know how Saint Michael appeared to her. "Was he wearing a crown?" "Did he have wings?" "Was he dressed?" "How did you know if it was a man or a woman?" The ultimate question, "Was he naked?" and Jeanne's brilliant rejoinder, "Do you think God was unable to clothe him?" draw further attention to the film's hyperawareness of corporeality as demanding to be deciphered. Dreyer uses the question of how one recognizes the flesh of an angel or its equivalents—goodness, innocence, sainthood—to substitute for *variété*'s fascination with whether a performer is performing onstage or performing an identity coded as naturalistic. Each articulates melodrama's core humanist ambition to recognize suffering in another.

Being, Representing, the Haircut, and Tears

When one monk questions Jeanne's ability to recognize Saint Michael, asking "Did he have long hair?," and Jeanne responds, "Why would he have cut it?," her response foreshadows the film's climactic moment of "authenticity" accomplished by denuding her. The ultimate stripping of the *variété* actress in *Jeanne d'Arc* will be to cut her hair. The barber's insistent shears reveal strip after strip of her scalp—corporeal spectacle conveyed through the uncomfortable proximity of the close-up. Shreds of hair cling to Jeanne's tear-stained cheeks as she stares upward in exhausted submission. Dreyer's corporeal *coup de théâtre* is the most iconic sequence of the film. The tortured change of heart by which Jeanne retracts her confession, sending her to the stake, plays across her face in minute detail: quivering lips, the tears that dangle precipitously off her chin, the dry lips that bite nervously at trembling and despairing hands.

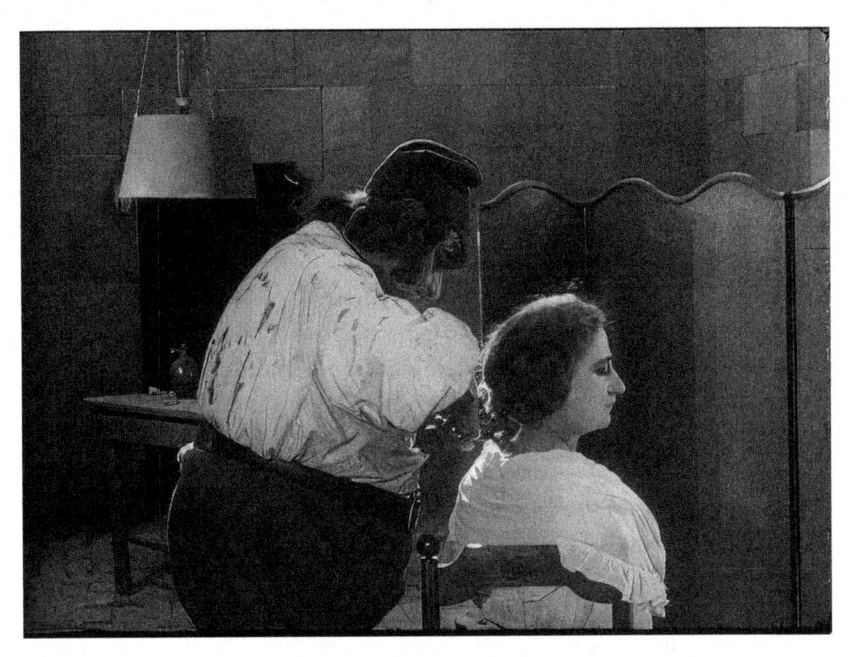

Figure 9. Marie Antoinette (Tenna Kraft) has her hair cut in preparation for her execution. Frame capture, *Leaves from Satan's Book*.

The haircut scene elicits pathos by exploiting the audience's awareness that Falconetti's hair was *actually* being cut. The pressure that the haircut puts on Falconetti and the material conditions of filming are reminiscent of avant-garde performance artists putting their bodies in harm's way.[40] The emotive impact of this sequence sets it apart from Dreyer's earlier experimentation with a similar spectacle in *Leaves from Satan's Book* (1921). There, a steadfast Marie Antoinette (Tenna Kraft) endures having her pigtail unceremoniously snipped in preparation for her execution, but the edit fails to fully suture the hair to the actress's body as not a wig. Marie Antoinette's haircut is also shot mostly from behind, underplaying any simultaneous reaction that might play across her face. In *Jeanne d'Arc*, Dreyer positions the camera in front of Jeanne, offering three extended shots of the barber cutting close to a scalp that can only be Falconetti's. *Leaves from Satan's Book* may represent a haircut, but in *Jeanne d'Arc*, the scene *is* a haircut.

Many critics viewed Falconetti's haircut as further proof of Dreyer's unrelenting commitment to a kind of "authenticity" through realism: "The ultimate act of reality for the film is of course the shaving of Joan's head."[41] This extreme engagement with realism and "authenticity" can also be understood as fully melodrama. The conflation of actress and role (representing and being) in the haircut sequence echoes traditions of extreme realism in spectacular stage melodrama where heroines and heroes could risk being cut in half by an actual log saw, trampled by real horses, or crushed by actual locomotives onstage. The pathos and thrill elicited by these scenes activated spectatorial concern for the actor's body that could rival identification with a fictional character. As Ben Singer writes, "They feared for the actor's flesh, not the protagonist's. This form of spectacular realism shifts the frame of attention from a believable diegetic realm, the frame one would expect realism to foster, to the material circumstances of the theater. Indeed, this is the precondition for the spectacle's effectiveness as a thrill."[42] That kind of corporeal spectacle, like Jeanne's haircut or the fire dance in *Lydia*, radically accentuates vacillations common to all mimetic performance—alternations between reading the phenomenological body of the actor and the semiotic body of the role she is playing.

Dreyer's art melodramatic "authenticity" enacts these vacillations spatially, as reflective distance and proximity to pathos. The haircut sequence thus intercuts intimate interior shots of Jeanne with exterior shots of sideshow spectacle, contrasting her agony with entertainment. Outside, the camera pans over circus sideshow performers entertaining the masses. A dancer prances in tights with a trained dog, contortionists wrap legs and arms behind their necks, and a sword-swallower plunges a sword down his throat. As these shots demonstrate, melodrama's *gøgl*, that is, the circus sideshow that Dreyer was supposed to have eradicated on leaving Nordisk, quite literally and vibrantly persists in his "mature" work. Sideshow performance here fully conflates representing and being: playing a contortionist means being one. Inside, Falconetti's luminous face, present in close-up and mid-shot, is both juxtaposed and elided with the spectacularly pliant bones and flesh of the sideshow performers, whose bodies are revealed at a greater remove, in long shot.

Here are dual, and interrelated, *cuts*: the hair*cut* and the inter*cut*.[43] The haircut is so striking because of its ontology. Falconetti's hair signals the material limits of the performing body onstage. Had something gone awry, Dreyer would have had to wait months to reshoot. As film spectators, the pathos of our response to Jeanne's experience is enmeshed in living Falconetti's sacrifice with her, in the real time of its performance. Also present is the quintessentially cinematic inter*cut*, which creates a simultaneity of experience by editing disparate experience (the circus sideshow and the jail) together. Again, the seemingly antithetical sensibilities of the cinematic and the theatrical coexist, feeding and informing one another in an intricate dialectic. The one begets and encompasses the other visually. The barber's scissors make graphic the cinematic cut even in the theater time of the cell, and the spectacle of sword

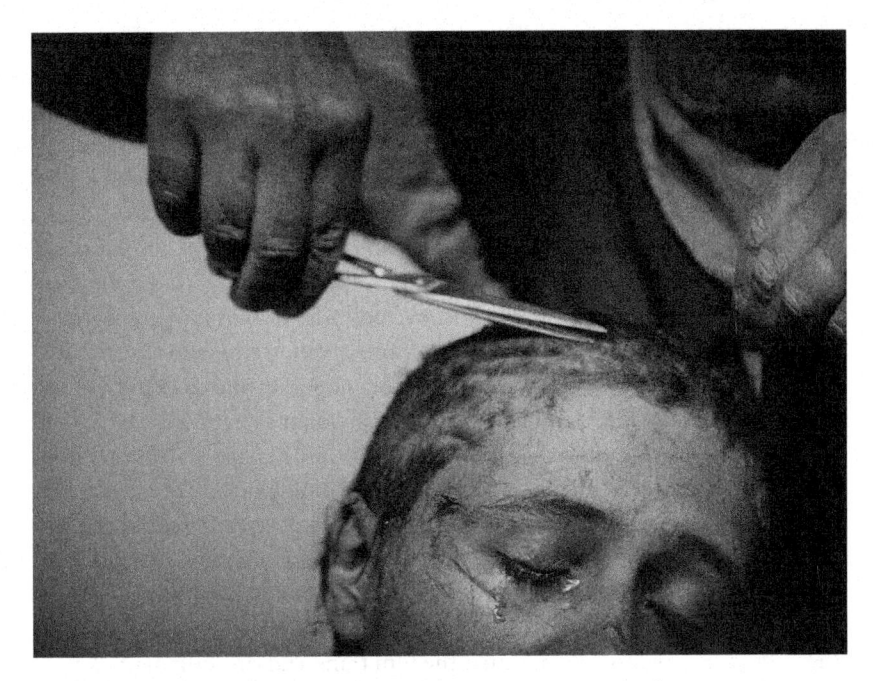

Figure 10. Dreyer captures Falconetti's haircut in gritty, extreme close-up. Frame capture, *La Passion de Jeanne d'Arc*.

Figure 11. Outside, contortionists, sword-swallowers, acrobats, and jugglers perform. Frame capture, *La Passion de Jeanne d'Arc*.

plunging deep into a performer's body communicates the cinematic within performance. Dreyer's mapping of proximity/distance, film/theater, being/ representing onto interior/exterior, intimate scale/long shot, naturalistic performance/circus spectacle makes vivid the dialectical underpinnings of art melodrama's performance in *varieté*. The rhetoric of "authenticity" allows Dreyer to turn the film and its production into a live experience, drawing out underlying connections between circus sideshow performance, avant-garde performance art, and religious ritual that transforms a young woman into a saint.[44] Exciting tensions in this way between seeming opposites and then performing a kind of reconciliation is emblematic of art melodrama's hybridity.

Falconetti's tears, captured in *Jeanne d'Arc*'s iconic barrage of extreme close-ups, perform a similar function, imbricating the ontologies of the cinema and of live performance. Historically, feminine tears are the quintessential mark of melodrama's profusions of pathos. *Jeanne d'Arc* is not a weepy; it is also not, not a weepy. On one hand, the extreme close-up that allows Jeanne's tears to be so prominent is understood as a framing impossible to replicate in the theater and often serves as evidence that the film transcends melodrama.[45] Yet the film's repetitive, emphatic, almost percussive use of that larger-than-life framing, particularly in conjunction with its lack of establishing shots, comes close to enacting the theater's quality of the "inauthentic." The stylization of so many close-up shots performs like Dreyer's "thick dollops of paint." On the other hand, while close-ups might be dismissed, rhetorically, as melodramatic insincerity when deployed in this manner, these larger-than-life tears also function as a metonym for Falconetti's experience of duress and emotion. By the logic of melodrama, tears provide a quintessential exteriorization of suffering—a kind of ontological proof of internal experience—proof also that pathos is communicable. As Steve Neale (1986) theorizes, when spectators cry at suffering, it signals that they are being moved by another's suffering. Tears in *Jeanne d'Arc* importantly communicate shared experience: the peasants witnessing Jeanne's immolation weep and her suffering moves at least one of her judges to tears. Put in terms of *varieté*, the tear affords important confirmation of affective interaction between performer and audience.

Accounts that document actual, on-set pathos often exceed the final cut of *Jeanne d'Arc*, further suggesting that Dreyer envisioned cinema as an interactive, immersive, and potentially transformative performance event. Eyewitness accounts of the filming, put into circulation by Dreyer and his cast and crew, constituted them as on-set reenactors and spectators. Costume designer Valentine Hugo's account of the scene in which Falconetti's head is shaved is particularly vivid in this regard: "In the silence of an operating room, in the pale light of the morning of the execution, Dreyer had Falconetti's head shaved. Although we had lost old prejudices [against short hair on women], we were as moved as if the infamous mark were being made there, in reality. The electricians and technicians held their breaths and their eyes filled with tears. Falconetti wept real tears. Then the director slowly approached her, gathered up some of her tears in his fingers, and carried them to his lips."[46] Dreyer's gesture—which replicates Massieu's wiping away of Jeanne's tears in the diegesis—performs a symbolic blessing of Falconetti's suffering performance. The tears of the assembled audience attest in turn to the affective, even transformative, potential of the film's production of performance. It is another embodied act, which, like the haircut, unsettles melodrama's purported artifice by drawing attention to the materiality of the suffering body—as well as to melodrama's potential affinities with performance art or the "quasi and queasy sensation of cross-temporal slippage" that Rebecca Schneider theorizes around historical reenactment.[47]

Jeanne d'Arc's affective transmission between bodies is also constituted as the film is projected. "Something is touched" also happens between the film spectator and the body of the screen. Luis Buñuel's description of tears in *Jeanne d'Arc* encapsulates this. He writes, "We have kept one of her tears, which rolled down to us, in a celluloid box. An odorless, tasteless, colorless tear, a drop from the purest spring."[48] A tear rolling down into the audience provides the most exquisite proof of cinema's capacity for pathetic communication. Buñuel's passage also evokes an embodied kind of archive; watching the film and collecting the tear become an act performatively preserving *varieté* for some future moment.

Tracing the body in this chapter has entailed looking at the ways that Dreyer returns to performing and spectating bodies in the enlivened filmic spaces of the *varieté*. The convention of the *varieté* offers another thread of art melodramatic continuity that loops through his archive, connecting Dreyer's script work at Nordisk to his later directorial pursuits. These are ties that Dreyer again purports rhetorically to sever, this time by purifying and stripping the literal *varieté* star of her melodramatic or inauthentic accoutrements and costuming—to elevate film and film performance as "authentic." In actuality, Dreyer doesn't eradicate Nordisk's art melodramatic impulses; he reimagines them as a more extreme form of art melodrama. He heightens the revelation of his true-hearted protagonist by cutting her hair to the scalp; he shatters the film's editing to emulate the minute experience of live, interactive theater space; and he turns the entire set of his film into a performance event. By reworking Nordisk *varieté* like this, *Jeanne d'Arc* reveals high and low, "authentic" and inauthentic, to be fully intertwined and negotiated in art melodrama. As we'll see in the next chapter, *Vampyr* similarly remakes another prominent figuration at Nordisk, the *Offer* film, but instead of tracing bodies and live performance, the ontology and media reflexivity of *Vampyr* revolve around bodies that are living but also dead.

Vampyr

Victims, Volition, and Melodrama of Consciousness

Dreyer's next film after *La Passion de Jeanne d'Arc* was *Vampyr* (1932), which he cowrote with Christen Jul, drawing loosely on "Carmilla" by Joseph Sheridan Le Fanu.[1] As Johannes Weber remarks in his essay on vampirism in the film, it will be "disappointing to viewers who approach it expecting a vampire film."[2] *Vampyr* doesn't adhere to the genre conventions as they have been established in the decades since it was made. The film pays scarce attention to the pursuit and elimination of the vampire, there's one measly vampire attack, the only blood spilled is a tiny puddle under a coach, and the film's main vampire, Marguerite Chopin (Henriette Gérard), "is neither alluring nor supernaturally gifted."[3] When the film does convey some of the familiar subject matter, it does so by means of lengthy, didactic intertitles containing passages from the monograph of vampire history, which figures prominently in the film's diegesis. Here we find, for instance, that "vampires are bodies and souls who are denied eternal rest because of the horrible deeds they have accomplished in life. In the light of the full moon, they rise from their graves to suck the blood of children and young adults and thus prolong their shadowy existence. The creatures haunt the abodes of the living where they sow death and decay."

Vampyr's experimentation with filmic style made its references to gothic or horror less immediately apparent to audiences. Typically read as a kind of early avant-garde vampire film and subgenre of the horror film, it premiered in Berlin in 1932 to fairly lackluster reviews, in part because neither spectators nor critics could reconcile the film's recognizable thematic appeal to the monstrous with its experimental and disorienting style, which some called avant-garde. *Vampyr* is one of the first vampire films alongside the expressionist ones (*Nosferatu*, etc.) to elevate the gothic, with its aesthetics of fear and haunting, in this way. The film disregards any attempt at continuity editing techniques, preferring instead to disorient the viewer in space and time, expressionistically. At times the camera seems to take on an embodied subject position of its own, moving without clearly expressing the point of view of any particular character in the diegesis. It's unclear whether it's day or night, dream or waking, and spectators have no clear sense of time elapsing other than the duration of the film. The film's formal aspects compound its narrative ambiguities. In many ways, *La Passion de Jeanne d'Arc* and *Vampyr* are Dreyer's most formally experimental films.

What *Vampyr* might withhold in terms of blood sucking or shedding it makes up for in its spooky ambiguation of embodiment; it features a profuse blurring of the line between physical flesh and immaterial kinds of experience (un-death, dreaming, shadows). Dreyer's film focalizes its action largely through the experience of the film's studious protagonist, Allan Gray (played by the Baron Nicolas de Gunzburg, under the pseudonym Julian West). Gunzburg, a journalist and fashion editor, financed the project on the condition that he be allowed to play the main character. Gray, as the film's opening text explains, has immersed himself so deeply in the study of the occult and ancient superstition that reality and unreality have become indistinguishable to him.[4] During one of his aimless treks about, he happens upon a desolate inn in the spooky French village of Courtempierre. That evening a stranger (Maurice Schutz) enters his room, issues him a mysterious warning, and leaves a small package with him on which is written, "To be opened upon my death." Later that evening, when he hears what must be a voice crying out for help, Gray follows it to a remote estate in the woods, where the peculiar man lives with his two daughters, Gisèle (Rena Mandel) and Léone (Sybille Schmitz), and the servants of the household. Léone is bedridden with a mysterious illness that has left two tiny marks on her neck. Shortly after Gray arrives, the father is shot and killed by shadowy creatures. Opening the package, Gray finds the book documenting the history of vampires, which references one vampire in particular, Marguerite Chopin, as having haunted the town for decades. After a few encounters with the stolid Chopin and her henchmen, including the devious doctor (Jan Hieronimko) who has been treating Léone, Gray and the devoted servant on the estate unearth Chopin's corpse and pierce her heart, freeing Léone from the spell. Gray also frees Gisèle, whom the doctor has kidnapped and bound, tying her wrists to a bed, and the film ends as the two flee across a river and through the forest to safety.

While *Vampyr* might depart from some conventions of vampirism, it excels in depicting its victims of vampirism in a variety of ways. The figure of the vampire gives Dreyer an excuse to focus instead on victimization. *Vampyr*'s fascination with the supernatural facilitates an extensive exercise in deciphering interiority that raises a slew of questions surrounding what it means to be a victim, including how to represent volition, desire, and consent. These states are manifested in characters ranging from victims of the vampire to her henchmen, who meet terrifying ends when she dies, and potentially Gray, too, as a victim of his own fantastical mind and memories. The vampire history book frequently relates information about vampires from the perspective of their victims: "A vampire's victim is doomed to perish without hope." And the book functions also as a guide to the ambiguities of vampire-related victimhood, for instance in this passage from the film: "Once the vampire senses that the victim is completely within its grasp, it does everything to drive the victim to the act of *suicide* and in this way *delivering that soul to the Evil One*." In the world of the film, vampires cannot simply seize their prey; they must control their victims and *drive* them to *choose*, leaving open what, precisely, the idea of control or choice or consent might mean.

This chapter explores Dreyer's art melodrama from an additional perspective: analyzing the influence of a melodramatic subgenre prevalent at Nordisk, what I call the *Offer* film, on his later film *Vampyr*. As *Jeanne d'Arc* reimagines *varieté*, *Vampyr* transmutes this subgenre of art melodrama. I consider how *Offer* films, which explore the body, desire, consent, and volition, partake of, and also question, what Peter Brooks calls melodrama of consciousness. Less about vampirism than about discerning the ambiguities of victimization and exploring embodied, mediated volition, *Vampyr* is art melodrama that comes about through Dreyer's fascinated transfusion and transmission of this Nordisk subgenre into a new form. The film performs Dreyer's Freudian screen memory—staging an encounter with his melodramatic past as simultaneously banal, alluring, and fundamentally threatening. And finally, I explore the queer subtexts in *Vampyr* in relation to horror and nonnormative bodies. But first, to examine the characteristics of the *Offer* subgenre.

The *Offer* Film

The virtuous suffering of innocent victims has often been held as an essential trait of melodrama. In this worldview, persecuted innocence becomes a focal point on which to anchor goodness. As Linda Williams writes of American melodrama, "If emotional and moral registers are sounded, if a work invites us to feel sympathy for the virtues of beset victims, if the narrative trajectory is ultimately more concerned with the retrieval and staging of innocence than with the psychological causes of motives and action, then the operative mode is melodrama."[5] Thomas Elsaesser makes the implications of human agency more explicit by arguing that Hollywood family melodrama of the 1950s represented worlds devoid of heroes and replete instead with constellations of passive victim-heroes inhabiting a world in which human agency is fundamentally constricted and characters are only acted upon. Victimization has also been critical to analyzing the melodramatic mode in other discursive spheres, for instance, in political discourse of national innocence, through which the rhetoric of injury and suffering to the body of the nation legitimates violent retribution in its defense.[6] Victims—and particularly innocently suffering ones—constitute a privileged site of pathos and morality in the melodramatic mode.

As I discussed in chapter 1, during the Golden Age of Danish melodrama at Nordisk (approximately 1910–20), the company didn't explicitly use the designation melodrama to market its films. Film production at that time is, however, full of victims, that is, *Offer* films; examining this archival subsection provides one way to trace the melodramatic mode at the studio in the absence of the specific genre designation "melodrama." Between 1909 and 1917, Nordisk produced about twenty-five films that explicitly included the word *Offer* either in the film's main title, a provisional script title, or in one of its several distribution titles.[7] *Offer* in Danish denotes victim and sacrifice simultaneously (often providing a layer of elegant interpretive ambiguity to the films), so this cross-section also includes Nordisk films with either "victim" or "sacrifice" in their English or German distribution titles. None of these *Offer* films were advertised explicitly as melodrama—a curious fact that I address in more detail below. Instead, their genre designations range from tragedy to film novel, reflecting the creative fluidity of genre categories at Nordisk. These films depict characters falling victim to all kinds of things—the stock market, the big city, the "white slave trade," for instance—and undertake many different kinds of sacrifices, from mothers sacrificing their own happiness for their children's to full-fledged spectacles of performative ritual sacrifice. *Offer* characters could be both male and female. The rhetoric and figuration of victim-sacrifice also pervaded many films not overtly billed as *Offer* films.

Offer films and scripts show that "victim" was very often neither a simple nor a straightforward category at Nordisk, despite the studio's general association with popular entertainment that drew upon schematic understandings of melodrama as striving for disambiguation of good and evil. Nordisk *Offer* films interspersed direct, clear-cut victims with more ambiguous ones, often in the same film. Victimization at Nordisk functioned less as a clear-cut tool for using pathos to establish moral clarity and more as a tool to explore the limits of human agency and will. Take, for instance, *Mormonens Offer* (*A Victim of the Mormons*, August Blom, 1911), starring Valdemar Psilander as Andrew, a charismatic Mormon preacher, and Clara Weith as Nina, who falls for his charms. At some points, the film blurs the line between willing and unwilling victims in intriguingly expressive ways, and at other points, it draws a clear distinction between the two. Most of the film exploits the more violent and spectacular thrills of clear violation, such as when Andrew abducts Nina by force from Denmark to Utah. There she plays the role of an immensely passive, innocent victim who swoons at every opportunity to free herself—the image of persecuted innocence in need of literal rescue rather than salvation. But the film also exploits the talents of two of the biggest stars of the era in an extraordinary scene of seduction that precedes the abduction. Sitting side by side on a couch in her drawing room, Andrew convinces Nina to follow him to Utah. Pictured in a medium close-up, Nina listens to Andrew whisper in her ear as her face registers a series of conflicting emotions roiling within her, one after the other in quick succession. Weith's magnificent facial expressions reveal her inner conflict as she must choose whether to follow her desire, and Andrew, or not. On one hand, she appears to choose on her own volition; it is only when she changes her mind, just before embarking, that Andrew forcibly kidnaps her. On the other hand, her consent is also potentially dubious in that we can read this scene as Nina falling victim to another kind of force, namely seduction. The film's printed program describes Nina's decision-making as potentially impaired by her altered consciousness. She is "half in ecstasy, half in hypnosis. . . . She is, in other words, completely spellbound by him."[8] Dreyer would later draw on Weith's prowess at conveying a similarly ecstatic dismay and agonizing choice—this time in a tighter close-up—for the Finnish episode of *Leaves from Satan's Book*, when her character must decide whether to commit suicide to save her country. These scenes with Weith convey Nordisk's imagination of internal conflict along a kind of spectrum of volition that includes clear-cut physical violation, dubious consent, self-sacrifice, and sacrifice under aspects of coercion. In contrast to other iterations of the melodramatic mode at the time, the Nordisk *Offer* film is more intent on using *vilje* (will, volition) to explore the limits of subjectivity, agency, and embodiment than it is in exploiting victims to establish clear moral categories. Exploring a character's volition creatively and spectacularly—abduction, hypnosis, life and death, violation—is more important than whether or not violations are punished and justice is restored, or whether or not good and evil are reinstated. Most important at Nordisk is the staging of these creative and exotic violations of will.

Put another way, Nordisk embodied victimization in ways that were overt, direct, physical, gestural, and what could be called *monopathetic*, a term Robert Heilman uses to describe the unified experience of melodrama, "a oneness of feeling—as competitor, crusader, aggressor; as defender, counterattacker, fighter for survival. He [*sic*] may be assertive or compelled, questing or

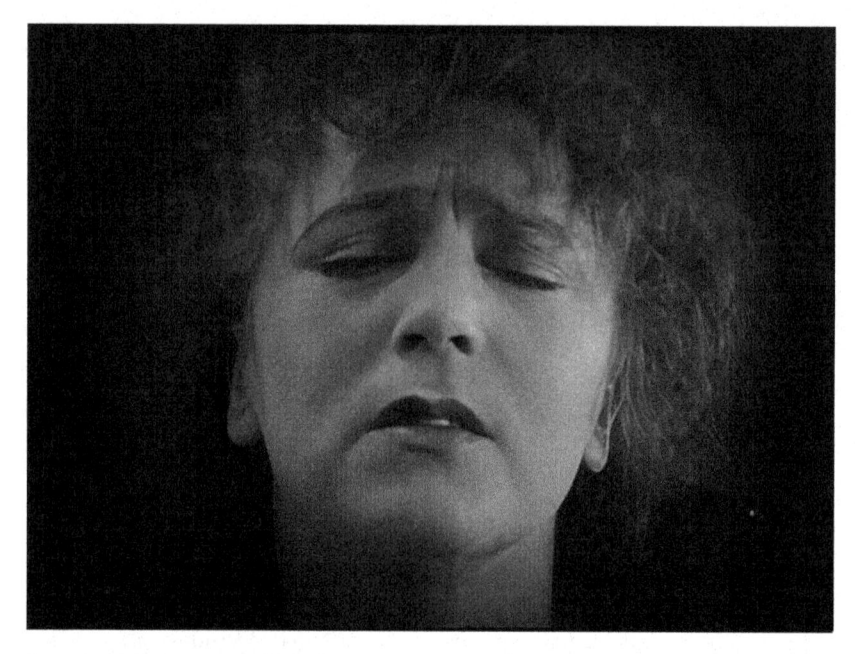

Figure 12. The incomparable Clara Pontoppidan (formerly Weith) performing Siri's tortured, ecstatic suicide in part 4 of *Leaves from Satan's Book*. Frame capture, *Leaves from Satan's Book*.

resistant, obsessed or desperate; he may triumph or lose, be victor or victim, exert pressure or be pressed. Always he is always undivided, unperplexed by alternatives, untorn by divergent impulses; all his strength or weakness faces one direction."[9] But Nordisk victims are also frequently torn by interior choices in ways that approach the cornerstone of tragic experience, which Heilman calls the *polypathetic*. This experience contends fundamentally with self-knowledge, or "the empathetically experienced conflict in a divided character struggling with counteroptions."[10] Heilman also describes "mixed feelings," for instance, when there are greater demands on a character than univocal monopathy, approaching but not achieving the divided interior conflict of tragedy. As an iteration of art melodrama, Nordisk *Offer* films throw these clear distinctions between unified and divided characters into disarray, in part by enlisting the spectator to grapple with pleasurable and torturous gradations.

Offer films provide another indication of effigy culture operating at Nordisk as introduced in chapter 2 and, consequently, heighten melodrama's pressures on physical, material bodies to express interiority, including emotion, thoughts, and other influential, invisible forces. This is quintessentially art melodrama: situations of extreme embodiment bring about the possibility for extreme kinds of reflection. Nordisk frequently juxtaposed and interrelated the spectacle of physical incapacitation with the spectacle of altered psychological states of consciousness related to the will, such as hypnosis, seduction, and shock. Dreyer's scripts, like many others at Nordisk, frequently employ stage directions for actors to respond *ufrivilligt* (involuntarily) or *uvilkaarligt* (literally, without complete intention or control of their volition) when reacting to a shocking sight or being overwhelmed with emotion. Dreyer also frequently employed the Nordisk stage direction *søvngangeriskt*—like a sleepwalker—indicating stiff, mechanical movements of the body as if possessed, overwhelmed, or hypnotized. Depicting characters in this way invites spectators to consider the limits of subjectivity and the claims to demonstrate mastery over one's mind or body. Melodrama of this era is not supposed to be psychological; psychological conflict and depth are some of the key terms that Dreyer employs to distance himself from Nordisk in order to make film art. Yet *Offer* films signal the pervasive fascination with psychological interiority and consciousness already operating in Nordisk's early iterations of art melodrama.

In addition to exploiting the unsettling ethical quandaries of such categories as a "willing victim," *Offer* figurations at Nordisk also took pleasure in heightening the ontological ambiguity of the embodied states. *Offer* films invite questioning, along the lines I discussed in the previous chapter on *variété*, of the ontological status of bodies depicted in extremis, and often in situations of performance. They explore the limits of the human through a deep investment in the pleasures and dangers of performing embodiment and victimization cinematically. Such ambiguous embodiments were a mainstay of effigy culture and afforded spectators an extraordinary display of spectacular bodies to consume (and desire) while reflecting on their ontological status.

Take for example, *The Vampire Dancer* (*Vampyrdanserinden*) directed by August Blom in 1912 at Nordisk—another *Offer* film that enlists the guise of the vampire, as *Vampyr* will, to probe questions of agency and control. The film's culminating sequence bears a striking resemblance to Dreyer's "Lydia" from the previous chapter, in that it also culminates with a dramatic suicide on stage. In *The Vampire Dancer*, Oscar Borch (Robert Dinesen), a young performer, has the misfortune to fall in love with Sylvia Lafont (Clara Weith), the diva with whom he performs and who does not return his love. Distraught, he ingests poison before the performance of their famous vampire dance, which culminates simultaneously in his performed death onstage and the actor's "actual" death. As I explore in more detail in the chapter on *Ordet*, male victims were also a mainstay at Nordisk. The description of the dance in the program accompanying the British distribution of *The Vampire Dancer* illustrates how the figuration of the vampire initiates larger, spectacular reflections on human agency, desire, seduction, and loss of control.

> Now comes a presentation of the Vampire Dance, mystic and thrilling, and laid in the underground haunt of the blood sucker, whose beauty, siren-like, holds her victims fascinated. The Vampire is roused out of her sleep by the noise of a human being approaching her lair. It is a young man who has stumbled unawares on the passage that leads from the outer world to her haunt. When he reaches the level he his [*sic*] surprised to see what appears to be the form of a beautiful woman but in whose eyes lurk [*sic*] the spirit of the devil. She dances backward and forward keeping her eyes upon him until, hypnotized, he has temporarily lost control of his will. Again and again he is enslaved by her charms. Thus the dance proceeds until the dénouement when the human heart ceases to beat and the Vampire, like some loathsome and nauseating beast, crouches over her prey.[11]

Deciphering these factors—of human volition, fascination, repeated enslavement, hypnosis, thrill, and innocently unwitting victims—goes hand in hand with coming to understand, along with the diegetic spectators (the unwitting Sylvia Lafont included among them), that Oscar Borch, and not just the character he plays in the vampire dance performance, has expired.

The Vampire Dancer illustrates how *Offer* films, as part of art melodrama's cerebral take on body genre, elicit unsettled feelings in spectators ranging from shock or surprise to curiosity and disorientation as well as reflection on the particular state of embodiment that they see represented. To decipher a fictional body's state of being is to reflect, pleasurably, at the same time that one feels. This lies at the core of art melodrama, which uses the body to heighten and dramatize the interrelationship of expressivity and reflexivity, feeling and thought, identification and estrangement. The following reading of *Vampyr* as an *Offer* film shows how the film reimagines and heightens schemes of victimization operating in the *Offer* subgenre, ultimately laying bare the underlying paradoxes of melodrama of consciousness.

Vampyr as Nordisk *Offer* Film

Although none of the Nordisk scripts that have been attributed to Dreyer, nor his feature films for that matter, include the word "*Offer*" explicitly in their titles, figurations of victimhood and volition nevertheless echo literally and figuratively throughout Dreyer's oeuvre. Victimhood and volition provide very concrete links between melodrama broadly conceived, Dreyer's work, and Nordisk art melodrama in particular. In *Glomdalsbruden* (*The Bride of Glom-*

dal, 1926), when the male protagonist, Tore, decides to save himself from the river rapids in which he finds himself, an intertitle describes that he doesn't want to become a "willing victim." Jeanne's heart-wrenching martyrdom in *Jeanne d'Arc*, the consequence of her victimization by patriarchal power structures, can be seen as an extreme test not only of faith but also of will. In *Day of Wrath*, Anne might exert her will over Martin and Absalon in the form of seductive influence, but she is also the victim of cruel betrayal by her beloved. Gertrud will suffer a similarly destructive betrayal by her lover, but her vicelike will enables her to survive and lead a life on her own hermetical terms—if a bit mummified—and the cinematic miracle in *Ordet* will provide a quintessential study of distinguishing cinematic life from cinematic death.

Vampyr is a prime example of an *Offer* film. Like *A Victim of the Mormons*, it also intertwines more straightforward melodramatic depictions of victims as innocents abducted, persecuted, and then rescued with more expressive, ambiguous explorations of victimization. Underlying the film's expressionistic form lies the quite common melodramatic trope by which heroic (masculine) figures rescue innocent (feminine) characters from the harm inflicted by evildoers. The film conveys a retrieval and staging of innocence to the extent that Gray—coded as masculine—undertakes to save feminine victims of the vampire and her henchmen. While still at the inn, in the beginning of the film, Gray hears the voice of a soul in mortal danger crying out for help.[12] Although film spectators aren't privy to this presumably agonized voice, it constitutes one of the most unambiguous moments in the otherwise quite narratively confusing film. The voice compels Gray to act; it leads him to the deserted manor house, where most of the film takes place. Dreyer overlays this melodramatic rescue with a valence of Christian salvation when a Christian cross flickers behind the intertitles as they scroll over the screen. When enquiring about Léone, the beautiful young woman lying upstairs in bed, weak, incapacitated, and ailing, Gray asks the attending doctor (who is secretly a henchman for the vampire), "Can't she be saved?" Gray then saves Léone's body by giving his own blood in transfusion; he also saves her soul by preventing her in the nick of time from ingesting poison to commit suicide, an act that would have condemned her soul to hell. The film's climactic ending also amounts to a rescue to the extent that Gray releases Léone from the vampire's spell and revives her when he assists the trusted manservant on the estate in driving a stake through Marguerite Chopin's heart. Gray also rescues Léone's sister, Gisèle, after she has been abducted by the nefarious doctor, who has locked her in a room and bound her to a bedframe by her wrists. After untying her, Gray and Gisèle escape as would-be lovers across a river, walk hand in hand through a glade of trees, and into the sunlight, as if toward some brighter

Figure 13. Gisèle forcibly tied to a bedframe, awaiting rescue. Frame capture, *Vampyr*.

future together. Melodrama is not always defined by such narrative resolution, but this narrative twist allows *Vampyr* to culminate with a quick-fix, happy ending that tempts the spectator to take it at face value.

Vampyr makes extensive use of fairly unambiguous, monopathetic characterization. Gisèle, and to a certain degree Léone, each emote one unified emotion at a time. Facial expression and bodily gesture align to exteriorize that single emotion. When she sees her father die, Gisèle's body stiffens and she walks haltingly, or mechanically, according to the English translation of the screenplay.[13] With a fixed expression of shock and wide-eyed disbelief on her face, she stares straight ahead as a kind of dazed, hypnotized sleepwalker. Overwrought, she leans heavily on one of the female servants who helps her across the room to sit. With a much more naturalistic expression, the tenderly emotive servant (N. Babanini) weeps as she supports the weight of the young girl. Gisèle's stylized gestures broadcast her mental state of shock and dismay. Later, her abduction is represented in a similarly unambiguous fashion. The spectacle of a young woman with her wrists tied to a bedframe, constricted, and needing to be rescued, elicits pathos for a victim whose will has clearly been violated.

Vampyr also presents Léone as an innocently suffering victim by drawing on the semiotics of the hypnotized female body. As Gray reaches the mysterious estate, the doctor arrives to treat to the bedridden Léone. In close-up, she covers her face with her hands in pain and dismay. She is teary and distraught. Not long thereafter, instigating a key sequence in the film, Léone flees her sickbed—the camera pans away from her and then back to reveal her empty bed—and we see her walking, barefoot, outside in the hazy moonlight. The rest of the household heads out in anxious pursuit. In a long shot, the search party sees her from afar in mid-rendezvous with Marguerite Chopin, the vampire who leans over Léone, with a kiss on the neck, presumably having sucked more of her blood, before fleeing. Léone, here, assumes a quintessential pose of incapacitated victimhood. She lies on a forest bench in statuesque, languid repose, her head tilted upward, her eyes closed, and her arm grazing the ground, as if having fainted. The incapacitation of her body is sensual, heavy. The two servants who carry her body back to the house and up the stairs struggle under the weight.

Stage directions explicitly evoking these hypnotic states of heightened affect in *Vampyr*'s script and program demonstrate its continuity with Nordisk *Offer* scripts; the fascination with manipulated consciousness is palpable throughout. As mentioned above, Gisèle walks "mechanically"—much like the sleepwalker that frequents Nordisk scripts. When Nikolas recoils in his chair, and later, when the manservant grabs Nikolas's arm, their actions are both described as happening "involuntarily."[14] At several moments in *Vampyr*, Gray also comes close to fainting and losing consciousness. And after the head of the estate is murdered, the manservant makes a series of "unconscious movements" with his hands, as if wanting to keep someone quiet. In many ways, *Vampyr* perpetuates conventional links between hysteria and melodrama, suggesting that Dreyer's attraction to Nordisk remained on melodramatic terms.

As with *A Victim of the Mormons*, *Vampyr* also interweaves more ambiguous and conflicted kinds of victimization. As the screenplay describes Léone lying in bed: "She looks like a medium under hypnosis. She is visibly no longer a master of her own will, or she is under the influence of a power stronger than herself."[15] In a key scene between the two sisters, *Vampyr* stages different styles of victimization as potentially in conflict. Back inside the house again after her escapade in the woods, Gisèle wraps Léone up to her neck in a blanket, framing her face, highlighting the series of intense emotions that play across her face in quick succession: her eyes roll upward to the ceiling as if she is possessed, then her face snarls demonically, and then it softens, and she weeps.

Figure 14. Léone lies in bed, displaying a fleeting expression of manic possession. Frame capture, *Vampyr*.

Gisèle stares back in horror with her fixed, stylized expression of fear and disbelief. Her sister has become unrecognizable to her. The alternating point-of-view shots that convey this sisterly stare-down completely disregard eyeline matches, further emphasizing the juxtaposing styles of victimization that each sister embodies in the scene. Gisèle's vacant stare of horror appears even more stylized when intercut with the more naturalistic and varied expressivity of Léone's countenances. The variation of Léone's expressions—and the way she emotes multiple, distinct feelings in quick succession—make apparent that her mind and will are in conflict rather than unified. Léone's varied facial expressions also suggest that she suffers not simply from an incapacitated will but also from a conflicted one. A battle rages inside her; some part of her is attracted to the vampire's seduction, while other parts are clearly repulsed by it. Consequently, her range of facial expressions encompasses pain, perhaps remorse for acts undertaken with very dubious consent, but also, crucially, ecstasy. Léone performs psychological complexity, like a serial monopathy, that makes her status as victim more open to (critical) discernment about her agency, will, and desires.

Léone's dramatic scene of possession reminds us of Dreyer's extensive melodramatic practice of employing mixed feelings or serial monopathy to convey psychological depth and complex interiority. He continues to draw on this technique in his later films such as *Day of Wrath*, when Absalon visits Herlofs-Marthe immediately before she is about to be burned as a witch and she emotes multiple violent, contrasting emotions in quick succession. She weeps, pleading for her life, then immediately becomes defiant, then reflective, and, ultimately, irate when naming Absalon's brazen hypocrisy and pathological use of his power for the satisfaction of his own desires. The close-up shots of Léone's bedridden suffering in *Vampyr* will similarly foreshadow key close-ups of aestheticized feminine suffering and resurrection in *Ordet*. Both Léone and Inger are depicted (either dead or ailing) with the sheets pulled up to their necks, leaving only their faces visible. Léone, like Inger, also experiences a resurrection of sorts, albeit on a much more modest scale. At the moment that a stake is driven through the vampire's corpse, she sits up in bed, her soul suddenly restored, and returns to life. In each case, Dreyer's images of feminine suffering and the dramatic prowess by which they are accomplished inspires a perverse beauty, attraction as well as repulsion.

Offer Film as Melodrama of Consciousness

Continuities between Nordisk art melodrama and Dreyer's art melodrama—such as the figure of the *Offer*—draw attention to interesting, undertheorized paradoxes implicit in Peter Brooks's argument in *The Melodramatic Imagination*. Brooks's work on Henry James, in particular, pertains to my reading of *Vampyr* and this study as another model for grappling with depictions of interiority and corporeality within the melodramatic mode. Although collections like *Melodrama Unbound* have sought to decenter Brooks's work by incorporating other approaches, this canonical work remains a key text in melodrama studies for defining excess and putting melodrama on the radar of literary and film scholars. *The Melodramatic Imagination* is less frequently read as making a claim about how melodrama develops within a single authorship. Reading Dreyer's early and late careers together with James's early and late careers shows that Brooks contends with the expressive tensions of art melodrama without explicitly labeling it as such.

At the macro level, *The Melodramatic Imagination* traces a genealogy from René-Charles Guilbert de Pixérécourt to Balzac to James, documenting a course of artistic influence by which one melodramatic artist inspires the deferential appropriation and imitation of the next. Shame doesn't enter into the equation; each author openly appreciates the melodrama that has come before. Neither do they perform anything like Harold Bloom's anxiety of influence, in which offspring must symbolically kill their patriarchal predecessor to assert their place.[16] Brooks's reading of Henry James's career also resonates with Dreyer's in interesting ways. His analysis of James's career is, on one hand, teleological and implicitly hierarchical. Artistic nuance effectively distinguishes James's early work, or "primary melodrama," from his late work, "secondary melodrama," the latter characterized primarily by "the melodrama of consciousness."[17] On the other hand, both still function as melodrama, existing, in Brooks's formulation of the mode, "to permit the isolation and dramatization of integral ethical forces, to impose their evidence and a recognition of the force of the right" and clarify good and evil.[18] They function differently: primary melodrama is outward, explicit, and manifest, while secondary melodrama is inward and latent. Primary melodrama explicitly "facilitates the 'circuit' of desire, permits its break through repression, [and] brings its satisfaction in full expression," while secondary melodrama is reflexive, constrained, and remains implicit.[19] Secondary melodrama draws on less overt expressions of victimhood by emphasizing psychological rather than physical distress, puts increased pressure on the plane of representation to yield meaning, and incorporates a potential for irony, all of which contribute to James's highly stylized later work. Brooks also complicates the teleology by arguing that James *transmutes* primary melodrama into secondary, melodrama of "external action—the suspenseful menace, pursuit, and the combat" becomes a melodrama of ethical choice.[20] Transmutation remains a curiously ambiguous and fluid term that resonates with Dreyer's art melodrama. Sometimes the charge of James's early work persists in the late work. Sometimes consciousness itself becomes explicitly dramatic and thrilling. Moments of direct, bold, dramatic, or violent action—the domain of primary melodrama—continue to be vitally present in James's later work. Brooks justifies the presence of dramatic and violent endings in James's "mature" work, saying that "such action best correlates to and delivers, over the footlights as it were, the intensity of his melodrama of consciousness."[21] Being just barely contained by the veneer of social propriety in James, primary melodrama charges secondary melodrama in ways that "both indicate and mask its hidden presence."[22] Brooks can also read James's work through the kind of attraction-repulsion of Dreyer's art melodrama—figured as renunciation. I return to explore the (archival) traces of melodrama refused in chapter 6 on *Gertrud*, but important for our discussion of *Vampyr*, the renunciation of primary melodrama prompts melodramatic clashes to veer into *horror*. Referring to a passage in *The Golden Bowl*, Brooks writes,

Nowhere more effectively than in this renunciation of melodrama did James image the melodramatic tenor of his imagination, the attraction of melodrama, the continuing need for it as a mode of consciousness and rhetorical stance, as well as the need to conquer it. The true horror is that of the thing hideously *behind*, the latent lurking horror, concealed by manners, yet just visible through them; unconscious horror, welling, as the nearly surrealistic imagery of the passage suggests, from the deepest recesses, the abysses of the soul. The metaphor stands for James's constant fictional technique: the pressure to reach through to the "behind," and then the pressure to keep it behind.[23]

This account of horror, imagining the unconscious and the deepest recesses of the soul, reads like a description of *Vampyr*, which also transmutes the repulsion of melodramatic energy to charge art melodramatic expressivities. As we will see in the next chapter on *Day of Wrath*, the surfaces of art melodrama in Dreyer's late work, like James's, will mostly contain the surges of illicit desire and emotion pulsing beneath them. In *Vampyr*, however, Dreyer experiments with giving them freer rein, unleashing and embodying all the latent, lurking horrors "behind."

We can think of *Vampyr* through another psychoanalytic framework as a cinematic version of a Freudian screen memory. Screen memories, as Freud outlines in his 1899 essay, are a kind of defense mechanism combining aspects of repression and transference that result in a creative reconstruction of the past—often memories of childhood—that combine memory and fantasy.[24] The analysand reconstructs elements of traumatic, dangerous, seductive, or perilous events creatively, by transmuting them into memory that is part fantasy. Often, some early unremarkable memory is used as a screen for a later event. Similar to dreams and parapraxes, screen memories manifest what has come before but don't articulate past events directly. At the same time, they help explain why we often remember insignificant details from childhood rather than traumatic ones or remember the two alongside one another. Interestingly, screen memories frequently incorporate out-of-body scenes in which the analysand watches themselves watching themselves, a scenario that *Vampyr* encapsulates in the most iconic sequences of Gray peering down at his own corpse.

As a screen memory, *Vampyr* figures Dreyer's creatively grappling with—here traumatic—aspects of his melodramatic past. Effectively a cautionary tale about the risks of immersing oneself in the past, *Vampyr* carefully explains from its opening sequence that Gray is a dreamer obsessively preoccupied with past beliefs and superstitions. His inability to distinguish between reality and unreality stems from this preoccupation. Screen memory helps situate some of the more banal, less supernatural or horrific details in *Vampyr* as Dreyer's distancing himself from Nordisk. The first person whom Gray encounters at the inn, which initially seems abandoned (his knocks on the door and window go unanswered), is a child, a young girl who shouts down to him through a rooftop window, "Who's there?" and then, "Go around." She wears round glasses and a nightdress and, holding a candle, leads him through to his room. She regards Gray warily, keeping an eye on him as she backs out of the room, closing the door as she goes, wishing Gray goodnight. The film then continues to make this child present, if not visible, as audible corollary to this child, namely, when Gray watches the doctor's hand along the railing and then the doctor, descending the stairs, passing him, turns to Gray and asks, "Did you hear that?" To which Gray responds, "Yes. The child." The doctor turns back toward him, suspiciously alarmed or as if trying to hide something. "The child?" he asks. "Yes, the child," is Gray's response. "There's no child here," the doctor shoots back accusingly, his brow furrowed. Their peculiar argument over the status of what has been or might be subject to hearing continues. Gray responds, "But the dogs!" And the doctor angrily says, "There are no children or dogs here!" "No?" "No! Good night." The curious exchange casts Dreyer's melodramatic past as also potentially banal in its contested presence or absence, visibility or invisibility. The child reads as Dreyer's displacing and reworking the raw material of Danish cinema's childhood in banal ways as well, creating film memory that combines fantasy and reality.

Throughout *Vampyr* Dreyer heightens the interiority of the *Offer* film—and particularly Allan Gray's subjectivity—by making it an explicit externalization of the character's psyche that confronts him from without. Although Nordisk was already creating characters with complex inner experience and conflicted psyches, Dreyer sought to elevate *Vampyr* by making its psychological stakes explicit and by emphasizing Allan Gray as an individual ego under investigation. This psychologization wasn't conceived as an extension of art melodramatic practices already operating at Nordisk but rather as a move away from the studio and toward elevating film as an art. As Brooks has argued, melodrama is already intimately intertwined with psychology, psychoanalysis, and hysteria. "Psychoanalysis can be read as a systematic realization of the melodramatic aesthetic, applied to the structure and dynamics of the mind. Psychoanalysis is a version of melodrama first of all in its conception of the nature of conflict, which is stark and unremitting, possibly disabling, menacing to the ego, which must find ways to reduce or discharge it. The dynamics of repression and the return of the repressed figure the plot of melodrama."[25] That said, as a particularly embodied kind of melodrama of consciousness, *Offer* films like *Vampyr* also continued to juxtapose and combine elements of primary and secondary melodrama to simultaneously elicit pathos and unsettling kinds of reflection and ambiguity. They also exemplify Dreyer's art melodrama as continuously hybrid, dynamic, and nonteleological.

The Ambiguous Victimization of Gray's Psyche

Dreyer's interest in the psychological *Offer* film is made palpable in the many explicit references to categories like consciousness, unconsciousness, and the subconscious in *Vampyr*'s script. The script frequently references psychological categories such as hypnotic suggestion, being fully conscious and yet far away, and being in a semiconscious state.[26] One prime example that would be conveyed in the film using superimposition reads, "A FIELD Nikolas is lying on the spot where he fell. Suddenly his body divides in two. One part remains lying unconscious, while the other (Nikolas's ego) gets up with obvious difficulty. He slowly comes to and looks round in amazement."[27] Gray's body splits, one half remaining slumped on a bench, whether because he is weary after his blood transfusion or dreaming, while the other part of him leaves to walk around, a ghostly presence.

Figure 15. Gray's ego departs from his own body. Frame capture, *Vampyr*.

As the reference to Gray's ego indicates, Dreyer's most prominent move to psychologize the *Offer* film is to explore the boundaries of a single psyche and body, Gray's. The haze of ambiguity that pervades the film emanates from its central premise that neither Gray, the characters in the film, nor spectators watching it all can easily decipher what actually exists in reality and what exists as a projection of Gray's mind, consciousness, dream, possession, or fantasy. Gray's status as a victim is compounded by his inability to distinguish between reality and unreality, which links the film aesthetically to Dreyer's larger archive of exploring how to convey unreal bodies on film (and also on stage).[28] The character's subjectivity fractures and splits most iconically in the sequence culminating in the translucent Gray's face-to-face encounter with his own corpse as he is being buried alive. The film's peculiar tracking shots, which are often not associated with any observable character's POV, also contribute to the feeling that the camera is one of Gray's mental projections. In one of the film's opening sequences, Gray knocks on the door to the seemingly abandoned bar of the inn. From inside, the camera tracks toward him. Sometimes it predicts his movements, sometimes it tracks reactively behind him. Sometimes it is as if Gray were observing himself from within and sometimes observing himself from without—inside and outside the room, in and out of his mind. While entirely fragmented and unsteady, Gray's psyche is the entity that comes closest to providing coherence to *Vampyr*'s narrative.

Vampyr's heightened investment in a kind of overtly psychological consciousness remains at the same time invested in the hypermateriality of effigy culture as discussed in chapter 1. It alternates persistently between ephemeral and solid bodies. The film serves up an unparalleled array of effigy culture's ontological mediation of the body in, and as, opaqueness, transparency, reality, projection, contamination, possession, shadow, dancing, disability, alertness, incapacitation, deadness, and aliveness. Characters are depicted in the script as dead but appearing to sleep (as the coachman or the unearthed vampire), or are referred to as being "truly dead," or being dead but appearing peaceful, or as if sleeping normally; but it also references being hypnotized or of a "normal" state of mind.[29] The film's camerawork mystifies and accentuates the contours of Gray's body and character. The film's spectral shades and shadows are curiously ephemeral and physical at once—in one scene they even fire rifles. With the death of the doctor, the vampire's henchman, *Vampyr* culminates with peculiarly gruesome attention to the physicality and corporeality of the actor's body, and the projected body. The script is quite clear about the underlying, grotesque corporeality that subtends the film's projections, conveying the doctor's (Marc's) gory demise in a bog.

The water is up to his face; he closes his mouth and presses his lips together; it reaches his mouth; he lowers his head and moans. At the moment his head disappears into the mud, his face is red and flushed as if it were about to burst. His last expression is a malevolent grimace. He raises his hand above his head, and this hand resembling a claw, with fingers tight together, covered in mud and bulging veins, is soon the only witness to Marc's death. Then it too disappears.[30]

In the film we see the nefarious doctor suffocate in the silo of a mill as flour sifts down to cover him—another scene of corporeal spectacle that, like the haircut in *Jeanne d'Arc*, inspires concern for the body of the actor rather than its character and reminds us that Dreyer never abandons corporeal spectacle for psychological interiority. *Vampyr* combines melodrama's privileging of the expressive potential of the suffering human body, emotion, and spectacle, on the one hand, with art cinema's claims to ambiguity, aesthetic distance, media consciousness, reflexivity, authorial subjectivity, and formal experimentation on the other.

As an *Offer* film with a heightened sensibility for horror, *Vampyr* adds an interesting twist to what Carol Clover calls "body genres," that is, film genres that privilege sensational bodies, like horror and pornography, to produce bodily sensation in spectators that mimics what they see on screen, whether horripilation (horror) or ejaculation (pornography).[31] In her 1991 essay, "Film Bodies: Gender, Genre, and Excess," Linda Williams added melodrama to the list of body genres, citing its depictions of profusely weeping bodies and the "spectacle of a body caught in the grip of intense sensation or emotion," including ecstasy; but in a subsequent piece revising her stance, she deemphasized that categorization, preferring to analyze melodrama expansively as a mode rather than more narrowly, as a genre.[32] The notion of body genre is useful in discussing what art melodrama does in terms of spectatorship, especially in the case of Dreyer's films. Clover's formulation brings the embodied experience of spectatorship into the matter of defining genre in a way that ultimately reaffirms the link between the body and popular culture genres. Art cinema, which is implicitly understood as more cerebral than embodied, doesn't figure into Clover's equation.[33] But as a cerebral body genre, art melodrama expands what we think of as body genre by taking the exploration of spectatorship a step further and representing diegetic spectators on screen. As we saw in the previous chapter on *Jeanne d'Arc*, the performance situation of the *variété*, in which fictional bodies of characters watch, consume, and react to the suffering of other characters in the fictional world of the film, multiplies questions of spectating bodies and contributes a layer of media reflexivity.

Contemplating the act of watching suffering sparks a cerebral body awareness of one's own status as a spectator of a fiction and raises ethical questions about the aestheticized or realistic representations of pathos that one is consuming.

Part of what makes *Vampyr* interesting as art melodrama are the ethical questions it raises about bodies, vision, and spectatorship. Amid *Vampyr*'s relatively nuanced and more ephemeral, cinematic explorations of the psychological potentials of effigy culture, Dreyer also continues to employ very overt corporeality and corporeal spectacle in heavy-handed ways that align with regimes of ablism. The characters and actors in the film who experience forms of disability function as external threats to Gray's coherence as an embodied subject. As Gray is led into his room at the inn toward the beginning of the film, Dreyer intercuts shots of an old man with no eyes, holding onto a large scythe, about to be shuttled across the river. Then once in his room, a sound leads Gray to the hallway, where he peers up the stairs to where a second blind man walks haltingly toward him. Later in the film, one of the shadow vampires is shown as having lost the lower part of his leg and walking with a prosthesis. The film's main vampire, Marguerite Chopin, embodies multiple threats, as simultaneously androgenous, aged, and walking with a cane. The vampire and disability each perform the threat of difference and in so doing constitute Gray's subjectivity from without. The older, masculine figures that Gray encounters, with their distinctive physiognomies, are at once intriguing but also meant to be unsettling. Corporeality, and particularly in the depiction of older male figures in *Vampyr*, dramatizes the inherent threat of emasculation. Deploying victimization in these problematically ageist and ableist schemes consolidates Gray as a figure of perceived coherence and mastery. No matter what befalls him, he remains impeccably spry in his tailored suit, with hair that is perfectly parted, trimmed, and shiny. To a certain degree, *Vampyr* echoes Dreyer's physiognomic casting in *Jeanne d'Arc*, which juxtaposes the skin of Falconetti's smooth, unadorned face with the wrinkles, hairs, and warts on the faces of her church interrogators. But whereas the corporeal contrast in *Jeanne d'Arc* has the effect of confirming Jeanne's persecution and innocence, in *Vampyr*, Gray is a more ambiguous character, who can sometimes seem to participate in the monstrous himself. His gaze is that of a scientist, if an amateur one. He stares. No matter what befalls him, the dark pools of his brown eyes remain wide, vapid, and doe-like. In this context, Gray's stare takes on a valence beyond that of a fascinated and obsessed protagonist struggling with the integrity of his own perceptual apparatus, or the default fixity of an amateur actor tasked with expressing more than he is able. The way that Gray stares—particularly at disability—offers an important reminder of the political stakes of being offered unadulterated access to consume corporeal spectacle as body genre on film. As Sharon Snyder and David Mitchell write in their work on body genre and disability sensations, "Film spectators arrive at the screen prepared to glimpse the extraordinary body displayed for moments of uninterrupted visual access—a practice shared by clinical assessment rituals associated with the medical gaze."[34] For Snyder and Mitchell, the construction of disability remains as integral to the functioning of body genre as gender does: "Because body genres rely on extreme sensation, we argue that disability is as crucial as gender in the primal structuring fantasies of these formulas. Body genres are so dependent on disability as a representational device (a process we have referred to as 'narrative prosthesis') that each formula can be recognized by its reliance on particular kinds of disabled bodies to produce the desired sensational extremes."[35] *Vampyr* is a fitting example of this narrative use of disability as representational device, and we can be critical of the seemingly uninterrupted visual access with which Gray stares at the bodies moving around him as well as the way they are exoticized.

At the same time, *Vampyr* intertwines spectacles of disability with a perhaps more subtle spectacle of gender queer victimhood. Gray's dapper style and exquisitely coiffed body allows him to be read as a beautifully feminized victim; a queer subtext helps ensure that the normativity of his male body remains productively in question. The *Offer* film, as art melodrama, participates in body genre by exploiting a heightened media awareness that challenges distinctions between reflection, emotion, and physical suffering. *Vampyr*'s unique innovation of this, as a revamped *Offer* film, is to present Gray as threatened by—potentially a victim of—his own interior vampire. He becomes the spectator of his own corporeal spectacle as his inner visions seduce and confront him from without as exteriorized projections of himself. At the same time that the vampire, Marguerite Chopin, motivates his heroic acts in ways that align with traditional notions of masculine agency, such as saving imperiled female characters, the androgenous woman also emasculates him. Like the beautifully unwitting Oscar Borch in *The Vampire Dancer*, Gray is also an *Offer* figure who undergoes the same ecstatic victimization that Léone does—both pleasurable and painful. In a scene of corporeal spectacle that visually echoes the bloodletting in *Jeanne d'Arc* and foreshadows the torturous medical procedure to which Inger will be subjected in *Ordet*, Gray rolls up his crisply pressed sleeve to provide a blood transfusion for Léone and the camera cuts to an array of medical instruments spread out on the table beside him. The transfusion incapacitates him—he rests limply back in a chair, in a languid posture reminiscent of Léone after she encounters the vampire on the moonlit grounds of the estate. The film leaves the spectator to decipher whether he has lost consciousness, fainted, or collapsed into a dream state within an entire film that might be a dream. In typical *Offer* film fashion, Dreyer's script makes clear that Gray's interior experience constitutes a sensuous battle of volition and describes him as "in the throes of paroxysm, as if some stranger's will is trying to gain control over him."[36] The luminous, hallucinatory passages that follow in the script depict a gauzy, shadowy creature emerging in his mind, a seductively riveting force that at one point takes on the appearance of a skull that brushes its mouth against the sensitive skin of his throat. Gray closes his eyes, in ecstasy, agony, and horror; he comes close to being possessed by the same luminous, shadow creature vying for Léone's soul.[37] Had Gunzburg possessed Schmitz's talent as an actor, perhaps Dreyer would have asked him to convey a similar series of facial expressions in quick succession, from ecstasy and placidity to terror, depression, anxiety, and despondency, that Léone's character performs.[38] Lacking that option, Dreyer exteriorizes Gray's internal conflict through a series of special effect shots and flashes. We see Gray with his eyes closed in the chair. A beam of light shines down on his face through the door, open just a crack, and a voice (from the other room? from his mind?) calls to him, "Come . . . follow me. We shall become one soul, one blood. Follow me. Death is waiting," as he nods his heavy head back and forth. The spectator bears witness to Gray's battered psyche as he struggles to maintain coherence. The queer potential of Allan Gray's shattered masculine subjectivity in *Vampyr* becomes emblematic of the complexities of attraction-repulsion in Dreyer's art melodrama writ large. The hope is that art melodrama, to the extent that it partakes of body genre, might also be capable of employing corporeal spectacle in ways that ultimately repulse its entanglement with ageist, ableist, gendered logics.

An immense body of scholarship has interrogated the associations between, as Harry M. Benshoff puts it, "the monster and the homosexual," contending with the reality that representations of the former in popular culture significantly outnumber representations of the latter. "For the better part of the twentieth century, homosexuals, like vampires, have rarely cast a reflection in the social looking glass of popular culture."[39] *Vampyr* is interesting to read in this context, as incorporating something of the visual resonance with a decadent or dandy, but then positioning Gray as less vampire than exquisite victim or Marguerite Chopin as a butch, lesbian vampire. The interaction between the two evokes something of Sue-Ellen Case's personal narrative of cross-gender identification, coming to queer theory as a lesbian consuming the poetry of Arthur Rimbaud, and ultimately, her identification with the unnaturalness of the vampire. Queer desire, she writes, "is constituted as a transgression

Figure 16. Gray, another exquisitely incapacitated victim. Frame capture, *Vampyr*.

of these boundaries and of the organicism which defines the living as the good."[40] *Vampyr* shines particularly queerly in light of Case's construction of queer theory from the site of ontology, blurring the boundaries between life and death.

This chapter has explored how *Vampyr* employs, exploits, and transforms the category of victim in the *Offer* film at Nordisk by drawing explicitly on its fascination with volition, extending established configurations of melodrama of consciousness operating at Nordisk. As Dreyer's attempt to imbue the subgenre more explicitly with psychological terminology and set it apart from popular culture, *Vampyr* helps articulate the mechanisms by which the stigma of Nordisk melodrama as an external threat consolidates Dreyer's artistic persona. At the same time, the film reverberates with the attraction-repulsion that Robert Heilman notes when he writes, "Melodrama is alluring; as a tonic or tranquilizer, it unifies. It may be that our tendency to use the generic term disparagingly reflects an unarticulated resistance against an unacknowledged seductiveness."[41] And this gesture finds a corollary in a passage from the book of vampire history in the film that reads, "Like a plague, the vampire's lust infects the victim who is torn between a lust for blood and a desperate repulsion toward this craving." As we will see in the chapter on *Day of Wrath* to follow, life will again be reinvested with lust, blood, and a desperate revulsion. This time-contested seduction will invade the domestic sphere and initiate not from the vampire but from the witch.

Day of Wrath and "Kniplinger"

Melodramatic Inheritance and the Domestic Sphere

In one of the most iconic scenes from *Day of Wrath* (1943), Dreyer's tale of incestuous, intergenerational love triangles and psychic murder set against the backdrop of the seventeenth-century witch persecutions in Denmark, the main protagonist, Anne (Lisbeth Movin), sits down behind a gauzy needlework scrim to stitch. She peers slightly upward toward the camera, through the rectangular frame over which her needlework is stretched. It is a meta-cinematic moment, when the frame of her needlework nearly coincides with the frame of the film itself, a frame within a frame. A following reverse shot reveals the object of her desire, Martin (Preben Lerdorff Rye), her new lover, a young man who is also her husband's son from an earlier marriage. He smiles back, through the same scrim, and we see him through her eyes, in a softened, dreamy haze—a focus made soft by the materiality of the scrim. The textile sensibility of the scene extends also to the crisp white collars and cuffs edged with decorative lace that frame Anne's face, neck, and hands. This lace pops against the modest cut of her black dress as an intriguing, if understated, flourish within the film's otherwise austere Puritan aesthetic. A few curls of her blond hair have escaped her tight bonnet; its lace edging inspires titillating thoughts about the flowing hair that remains hidden in much the same way as her severe clothing conceals her desirous body. Lace and needlework draw the spectator toward this young woman's eyes and face, which are alternately seductive, playful, and delighted as she laughs. The lace of her cuffs accentuate the elegant movements of her body, her hand as she stitches, or the palm she holds against the scrim to steady it. The needlework scrim and the lace are integral to revealing and concealing Anne's illicit, carnal desires in the scene.

As Andrew Webber writes in his reading of Luis Buñuel's *Un Chien Andalou*, lace can be considered a kind of "viewing material" that occupies "a special sort of space between: innocence and guile, sacred and profane, the

Figure 17. Anne peering playfully, longingly, through her needlework. Frame capture, *Day of Wrath*.

infantile and the adult only, inside and out. Whether on bodies or buildings, it is a cover for intimacy. It is designed to be seen as well as to hide, and in many cases, be hidden, or at least partially so."[1] In Dreyer's scene as well, textiles provide surfaces on which and through which to express Anne's unspoken thoughts and dreams. We find out that the figure yet to be stitched into the idyll of the needlework is the young child that Anne longs for but which her much older husband is incapable of giving her. Also, in keeping with the ambiguous constitution of lace itself, which is made of holes but also catches, inhibits, and restricts, lace conveys the taboo that will keep these two characters apart. Layers of lace separate the two lovers visually. The mesh accentuates and articulates Anne's desire for Martin, but it also bears something ominous. It makes manifest barriers to the life that she imagines the two might have together. Both the medium close-up framing and the layers of clothing constrict her body in ways that foreshadow the violent stifling of her desires that will befall her by the end of the film.

The visual material of lace, along with its adjacent textile arts—spinning, weaving, and stitching—runs like a proverbial red thread of art melodrama throughout Dreyer's *oeuvre*. Dreyer employs this motif and a similar framing of shots between potential lovers much earlier in films like *The Parson's Widow*, in which the loom facilitates a comical scene of mistaken identity. Its iterations will be felt later in his career as well, for instance, in the *Medea* script that Lars von Trier would later adapt for the screen, in which sheets flapping in the wind serve a similar scrim-like function on which to imagine a woman's fundamental betrayal, or in *Ordet*, when Inger playfully traps Morten into a conversation he doesn't want to have by asking him to hold yarn between his arms so that she can wind it into a ball. Lace signals Dreyer's larger interest in employing the domestic sphere and domestic labor to address questions of interpersonal relationships, power, traditional gender roles, and female desire.

One of the most intriguing examples of Dreyer's exploration of lace as a trope for illuminating the contingencies of female desire and the domestic sphere is his Nordisk script "Kniplinger" (Lace).[2] Dreyer wrote "Kniplinger" around 1919, adapting it from a novel of the same name by Paul Lindau. August Blom would direct the script as *Grevindens ære* (*The Countess's Honour*), and it was distributed in the UK under the title *Lace*. In an interesting example of how fluid authorship practices at Nordisk could be, the film's accompanying Danish program contains no mention of Blom at all, crediting Dreyer with the adaptation instead. Text in block letters beneath the title on the front cover reads, "A play in five acts based on Paul Lindau's novel 'Lace,'" followed by, "Adapted for film by Carl Th. Dreyer," with Dreyer's name in even bolder type.[3] The recent release of *The President* had perhaps made Dreyer's name a more prominent draw than Blom's.

Grevindens ære no longer exists as a projectable film, but the "Kniplinger" script includes a strikingly graphic, early moment of the body in extremis, when Juliane, the film's protagonist, experiences a feverish dream in which lace takes on the suffocating manifestation of heartbreak, crushed desires, betrayal, and guilt. The material forms a noose around her neck and presses down on her chest and body with the weight of a death cloak. Dreyer's graphic passage reads,

> Miserable, Juliane thrashes back and forth on her bed. [*sic*] with a terrible raging fever. Reality and dream, and even more awful images of what *might* happen, blend in and out of one another becoming some insufferable, compact thing that in her excited mind takes on the form of the Lamoral lace. It soon binds her mouth like a muzzle, soon winds itself like a noose around her neck, soon coils her chest together like an awful compress, and finally spreads out like a shroud over her stiff limbs. And she groans and incessantly repeats the old verse: Dentelle Lamoral / Ecrase la moral, / Puis donne la mort a l' / Adultere fatale. She repeats it incessantly throughout the long, endlessly long night.[4]

Looking at the "Kniplinger" script and program raises the evocative possibility that in some sense, *Day of Wrath* will eventually figure the return of this cursed piece of handiwork as the manifestation of "what might happen." Dreyer attended a performance of the play from which *Day of Wrath* was adapted, *Anne Pedersdotter* by Norwegian playwright Hans Wiers-Jenssen, around the same time that he was writing "Kniplinger," but this only partially accounts for ties that bind the two pieces together. More than two decades would elapse between that performance and his production of *Day of Wrath* in 1943, another example of Dreyer's ongoing film practice of returning to and repurposing material from Nordisk, of restitching the old with the new.

This chapter reads "Kniplinger" and *Day of Wrath* together within a larger mesh of what might be called art melodrama of the domestic sphere. Domestic life figures prominently in Dreyer's work, and lace functions as a multifaceted metaphor signaling the nuanced conflicts of the home. Lace stands in for the negotiation of female desire—its expression and constriction—within traditional gender roles and patriarchy. Lace also tells the story of Dreyer's ambitions to make cinema artistic, by constricting the overt expressivity of "Kniplinger" to bring about a stunningly repressive piece of art melodrama. Dreyer attempts to distance himself from Nordisk melodrama by untangling the knots of "Kniplinger" and making a more elegant film about the pressures and contradictions of Anne's lived experience. To accomplish this, he paradoxically employs techniques of displacement in which desire that cannot be outwardly expressed in dialogue is made manifest through various displacements into the soundtrack, the mise-en-scène, and onto the bodies of other characters besides Anne. All of these resonate with melodrama as it has been theorized in the films of Douglas Sirk, which have been read as sophisticated, highly stylized, ironic, and subversive melodrama—a theorization that resonates with art melodrama as I'm defining it.[5] Despite the parallels explored in detail below, we shall also see that the preconditions for Dreyer's art melodrama differ from Sirk's by juxtaposing reflective aspects of melodrama of consciousness with powerfully empathetic corporeal spectacle in *Day of Wrath*. The ambiguous presence of witchcraft allows Dreyer to imbue a melodramatic worldview with the kind of epistemological uncertainty and ambiguous causality associated with art cinema. Finally, in another meta-cinematic performance, *Day of Wrath* stages Dreyer's attraction-repulsion to his melodramatic past. In this film, Nordisk figures as an ambiguous, seductive, powerful femininity that is also a potentially cursed, demonic inheritance that Dreyer must exorcise. The temptations of melodrama must be denied for Dreyer to be taken seriously as an artistic film director. *Day of Wrath*'s ambivalent ending—

in which Anne is condemned to the flames, her desires fully repressed and punished, shedding luminous, fully melodramatic tears—reflects Dreyer's ambivalent inscription of his own body into the film.

The Pleasurable Pain of Renewing Danish Cinema, Again

Day of Wrath holds an important position in Dreyer's oeuvre as the first in his suite of late, "mature" films (to be followed by *Ordet* and *Gertrud*). Its status was evident even in advertising materials at the time, which reflected pressures put on Dreyer to develop Danish cinema by cleaning up its messy associations with immature popular culture and bringing Danish cinema as a whole to a new artistic level. That Dreyer was making a feature film in Denmark, after an eleven-year hiatus, was cause for celebration.[6] In production materials accompanying *Day of Wrath*, Christen Jul (who had collaborated with Dreyer on the *Vampyr* script) writes in language echoing the antimelodramatic rhetoric discussed in chapter 2: "Carl Th. Dreyer returns to Danish film! What could be better? We need him! For the reason that this Danish man is known the world over is simply that he was one of the very first to teach the world that film is something to be taken seriously. He was a part of raising it from tomfoolery [*Gøgl*] to art, showing what depths of the mind and what great arenas of the imagination film is capable of depicting."[7] The extra attention paid to the project can be traced partly from the historical moment, given that Denmark was occupied by German forces in World War II, and making a Danish film production constituted an important act of national resistance. Film scholars from Ebbe Neergaard onward have read *Day of Wrath* as a broad cautionary tale against religious intolerance, often in relation to World War II. On the other hand, raising the status of Danish film by innovation was something Dreyer would be tasked with again and again throughout his career. It's part of the function that he served as an internationally recognized Danish director, to bolster a small national cinema.

As usual, Dreyer's innovation and push to make film of the future involves dipping backward into his archive, and to the past. *Anne Pedersdotter*, the play on which *Day of Wrath* is based, was written in 1908. Its action is set three centuries earlier. Dreyer and others draw attention to earlier forms in order to position themselves, rhetorically, as doing something new. With *Day of Wrath*, Dreyer brings in the director's artistic personality as a crucial factor in redeeming film from the factory-like production environment of early Danish cinema discussed in chapter 1 and advancing it as a medium. As Dreyer wrote in his article "A Little on Film Style" (1943), a detailed account of his ambitions with the *Day of Wrath* project, "We directors [have] a great responsibility. It is in *our* hands to raise film from industry to art. If film as an art form is not to stand still, we must seek to create films that are marked with style and personality. Only from them can we await renewal."[8] Imbuing film with one's personality and artistic vision, Dreyer writes, entails confronting the influence of two residual forces from the past: the silent cinema and the theater. Film, he contends, must extricate itself from each. Too much sound film, he laments, still bears traces of silent era rhythm in which editing exceeded narrative purposes by being too fast, resulting in numerous flourishes of empty action such as actors flying across the screen. Much like Dreyer's aspersion of the theater that I detailed in chapter 2, Dreyer describes the problem as "actually a legacy [*arv*] from the silent era—a legacy, that sound film has yet to shake off."[9] Dreyer's attraction-repulsion to melodrama in *Day of Wrath* takes the form of repeatedly rejecting the past, but only after resurrecting it in spectacular, and spectacularly ambiguous, ways.

With *Day of Wrath, shaking off* actually takes the form of *tying oneself up.* The systematic constriction, repression, and punishment that Anne experiences in the diegesis for acting on her desires have an on-set corollary. Dreyer's account of his collaboration with cast and crew for *Day of Wrath* is rich with the language of emotional restraint, resisted temptations, and intentional deprivations—the widescale, collective denial of the expressive, gestural tools available to the theater (and implicitly, melodrama) in order to achieve film art. He writes, "The actors and I [have], in a good, unified effort, worked to 'de-theatricalize' the film's intrinsically very tense and concentrated scenes."[10] Constriction produces a more focused, "truthful" affective appeal—reminiscent of the rhetoric surrounding *Jeanne d'Arc* as a stripping down to achieve authenticity. He writes, "There is no shortage of conflicts of the soul [*sjælelige*] in 'Day of Wrath.' On the other hand, one would have to search for a long time to find material that tempts one to external drama to the same degree. I—and I dare say my actors with me—have chosen not to fall for this temptation. We have been equally zealous in our hunt for false exaggeration and established clichés. We forced ourselves to the truth."[11] Rhetorically speaking, Dreyer proposes to hunt melodramatic excess with the same zeal that characters in the film espouse in their persecution of witches. The paradox, of course, is that achieving this subdued, nuanced art involves deliberately choosing to present oneself with spectacular, highly dramatic subject material such as witch trials and incestuous love triangles in order then to deprive oneself of its temptations. In order not to fall for the temptation, the temptation must first be brought into play. At the center of the performative "shaking off" of melodrama in *Day of Wrath* that I explore in this chapter is the need for the effusive presentation of sensational subject matter and corporeal spectacle that can then be restrained in various ways, whether bound, constricted, or compressed. The attraction-repulsion to melodrama in *Day of Wrath* results in an art melodrama that is performatively self-teasing, self-tempting, and potentially self-denying.

This attraction-repulsion in the narrative finds interesting parallels in production on set and also in the film's reception, which has often struggled to contend with the film's overtly melodramatic aspects. One dramatic example is Raymond Carney's monograph on Dreyer, *Speaking the Language of Desire*, which I return to in more detail in chapter 6. The book's title is a direct citation from Peter Brooks's *The Melodramatic Imagination*, yet the word "melodrama" remains conspicuously absent from the book's argumentation, signaling the persistent curse of melodrama's stigma in scholarship on Dreyer.[12] Bordwell's reading of *Day of Wrath* similarly presents the film's proximity to popular culture as troubling to its status as an art film, which Bordwell sees as inherently a problem to be solved. He writes, "*Day of Wrath* is probably Dreyer's most popular film, which already indicates something of the problems it poses. . . . A tale of witchcraft, passion, and murder, it has more melodramatic appeal than *Ordet* and *Gertrud*."[13] The spectacular subject matter in *Day of Wrath* poses problems for Bordwell's formalist reading, which is interested largely in narrative ambiguity. Melodrama simply doesn't align with the images of Dreyer as an artist and formalist, and Bordwell must work hard to argue that despite its popularity, *Day of Wrath* is in fact not popular film. For Bordwell, narrative ambiguity is a constitutive feature of art cinema that distinguishes it from the normative interaction of cause and effect that dominates "Classical" Hollywood editing.[14] In the standard reception of *Day of Wrath*, narrative ambiguity and its epistemological uncertainties trump the film's "melodramatic" subject matter. Bordwell and Thompson write, "In films like *Day of Wrath*, the questions we ask often do not get definite answers; endings don't tie everything up; film technique is not always functioning to 'invisibly' advance the narrative. . . . As a narrative film, *Day of Wrath* depends on cause-and-effect relations, but what strikes us immediately is its unusual number of parallels."[15] Reading *Day of Wrath* and "Kniplinger" together allows us to reimagine what it means to "tie everything up" in a more expansive way and to imagine the energy of Nordisk art melodrama as continuing to inhabit and animate *Day of Wrath* in ways that are sometimes visible, sometimes invisible. In *Day of Wrath*, instead of expunging the legacy of the silent era—a legacy that functions as a slot-substitution for the legacy of Nordisk melodrama in art cinema—Dreyer makes it lacy, both manifest and occluded (and ambiguously embodied as the occult). Performatively "shaking it off," then, entails various mechanisms of silencing, repressing, and constricting in ways that both deny and suggestively affirm a melodramatic past.

Interwoven Plots of Domestic Art Melodrama

Despite Dreyer's expressive claims to break with his past, the plots of "Kniplinger" and *Day of Wrath* remain interwoven; Nordisk allowed Dreyer enough creative freedom to work through ideas that would continue to motivate—or perhaps haunt—him later in his career. For one thing, the two works remain clearly and provocatively bound together by domestic melodrama. *Day of Wrath* and "Kniplinger" each figure a desiring female body maneuvering within the constraints of a domestic sphere dominated by the patriarchal institution of marriage. In each case, female desire threatens these institutions, prompting the institutions to bolster defenses in order to perpetuate themselves. This threat can be figured as external and as emerging from within the protagonist's body. Threat is also causally ambiguous and mysterious, taking the form of inheritance or ambiguous powers that raise questions about how institutions are perpetuated from one generation to the next. "Kniplinger" and *Day of Wrath* each examine core conflicts having to do with marital ties, oppressive family secrets, and desires through the experience of a strong-willed, decisive female lead who falls in love in a way that leads her to perform a gesture of self-denial that signals the end of a lineage. These female protagonists each end up heartbroken yet are redeemed by keeping their honor and self-awareness intact. The beauty of their suffering and self-sacrifice also makes ambiguous the pessimistic ends for these protagonists.

Set in 1623 in the era of pious Lutheran Denmark, where witchcraft was understood to be an everyday reality, *Day of Wrath* tells the story of Anne, a young woman who is married to pastor Absalon (Thorkild Roose), a man much her senior. They live together in the parsonage under the ever-watchful eye of Absalon's domineering and austere mother, Merete (Sigrid Neiiendam), who wields all the power in the household, a fact symbolized by the heavy ring of keys she wears at her waist. Merete remains suspicious of her son's young wife, whose very presence threatens the hierarchy of the parsonage that she dominates. The status quo of domestic life becomes unsettled when forces descend on it from without. First, an older woman named Herlofs-Marthe (Anna Svierkier), a local healer who, among other things, gleans the powerful herbs growing beneath the executioner's scaffold, is accused of witchcraft and seeks refuge in the parsonage from the vicious mob pursuing her. Herlofs-Marthe is also an unsettling force because she brings knowledge of Anne's past. She knew Anne's mother before she passed and bears the secret that Absalon spared Anne's mother, who had also been accused of witchcraft, from perishing at the stake under the condition that Anna be given to him in marriage. Anna's mother, as Herlofs-Marthe tells it, had the power to call people to her, such that it was impossible to resist. Anna allows Herlofs-Marthe to hide in the parsonage, but the drops of blood she sheds on the stairs betray her hiding place and she is captured by the mob. In his capacity as head of the church, Absalon will eventually torture a confession out of Herlofs-Marthe and condemn her to be burned alive as a witch. Herlofs-Marthe's secret will not come to light to save her from perishing in the flames, but before she dies, she plants the seed in Anne that she might have inherited occult powers from her mother, a common trope in folklore of witches in the Nordic region and elsewhere. It is a seductive but ambiguous gift. Absalon, too, suffers pangs of guilt, knowing that in indulging his own desire for Anne, he has stolen her youth, dashed her dreams of being a mother herself, and potentially also betrayed his religious calling. He struggles as well with his hypocrisy; he saved Anne's mother but consigned Herlofs-Marthe to the flames. The other force of upheaval to unsettle the parsonage from without will be Absalon's beautiful son, Martin, who returns home from his university studies to visit his family and meet his new stepmother, Anne. In part because they are of the same generation, Martin ignites passions and desires in Anna that she had never before realized had been denied her. Anne and Martin have an affair and fall in love. In a moment of political awareness, Anne realizes that she never actually *chose* to be with Absalon. The open floodgates of Anne's desires lead her to explore the occult potential of the powers that she might have inherited. When she wishes Absalon dead, he dies. This act, with all its ambiguous causality, allows the tables to turn. Martin, whether because he is confused and grieving, or simply feckless, falls under the sway of Merete, who has never approved of Anne, and turns against Anne. The film ends at Absalon's funeral, when Anne, betrayed and alone, confesses to being a witch and consigns herself to share Herlofs-Marthe's fate at the stake.

Similarly, "Kniplinger" also revolves around an intergenerational marriage and conflict, resulting in another adulterous affair that will have disastrous consequences. Juliane, a vivacious, eighteen-year-old countess, marries Grev Albert v. Iseneck, an ambitious politician many years her senior. In contrast to men her own age, the count possesses an honor and forthrightness that she admires. But the marriage doesn't work out as Juliane has planned. As the film's program describes it, "The marriage was a bitter disappointment for her. He was too old to understand her natural need to enjoy the joys of life, and the demands of his work left little time for companionship with his wife. The unavoidable dissolution arrived. He was forced to acknowledge that their marriage had been a terrible mistake and granted her the freedom to live her life, as she wished, within the boundaries that morality and honor required."[16] The scene in *Day of Wrath*, in which Anne confronts Absalon about his inability to fulfill her desires could almost have been taken verbatim from this Nordisk script. Juliane's expression reads, "You don't even touch me. You have nothing to do with me. I haven't given you my youth and my love of life merely for you to feed and clothe me. I have grand ambitions, and you know that. I'll tell you this much: I will not have my life destroyed!"[17] Juliane's tale is told through a series of flashbacks when, as an older woman, she writes entries in her diary. While both Anne and Juliane have affairs out of wedlock, Juliane's evokes the affair in *Gertrud*, in that she is a married and mature woman who initiates a relationship with a younger man, Prince Ulrich Engernheim-Kypstein. Juliane will be compelled to abandon her own desires when Ulrich falls in love with Juliane's young niece, the Princess Alix. Juliane's misery is further compounded by the fact that, not only must she stifle her feelings for a lover she has lamentably (but honorably) forsaken to ensure the happiness of her niece, but their mutual lover suffers the terrible fate of dying in a dual. As the script reads, he dies with a clear conscience, "a calm, peaceful, smiling expression on his face."[18] In a moment that foreshadows Dreyer's epilogue for *Gertrud*, to which I return in chapter 6, "Kniplinger" ends by showing spectators that Juliane's hair has turned white overnight. She survives the incestuous, intergenerational love triangle to live out the rest of her life alone, in a perpetual state of mourning, and with a neurotic compulsion to make lace.

Both films indulge in quite lascivious material—multigenerational, multiply incestuous love triangles—but in one sense, Dreyer did succeed in resisting the temptation to clutter *Day of Wrath* with the thrilling-if-confusing tangles of minor characters, subplots, intrigues, and dramatic pursuit of the titular needlework at the center of the film that make "Kniplinger" such a wild ride. Servants conspire to steal from their aristocratic employers and get caught in the act, lovers get caught in clandestine meetings, a devious newspaper editor eager to sully the reputation of the noble house instigates a public trial for perjury, and a prince dies in a spectacular duel. Masterfully, a fatal bullet pierces not only his heart but also a revelatory, exculpatory letter concealed in his breast pocket. Tying everything together is the Lamoral lace that changes hands legally and illegally, is duplicated, disguised, lost, and then found again. This laden object ties the narrative together tenuously; the sheer variety and number of plot twists means that it is difficult to follow. Originally a royal wedding gift, the beautiful, and beautifully overdetermined, piece of handiwork brings with it a curse of adultery on all married couples who own it. In the beginning of the script, Juliane, who has long been interested in lace making, and her fiancé the count attend an industry exhibition, where she sees a replica of the famous Lamoral lace displayed and for sale. Seeing her enthusiasm for the piece, he buys the imitation lace for Juliane as a wedding gift. The original Lamoral lace, however, is part of the famed Kypsteiners collection. The original version is owned by her future lover, Prince Ulrich, who lends it to Juliane to enjoy as they commence their love affair. While the real Lamoral lace is in her possession, he takes her imitation piece to include in his collection. The prince will inadvertently also be accused of stealing the lace when at Juliane's, where he meets her for a tryst. Juliane's servants, who know of her secret affair, scheme to steal the lace, but before they are caught, they stitch it into a shawl. The extended conceit of the film as written revolves around who has the real lace and who, the fake lace, or whether someone has it but doesn't realize they do. As a narrative device, the lace drives the script's wildly circuitous plot, and it takes serious effort to keep track of its various travails and transformations.

More than simply motivating the main action of the film, however, lace in "Kniplinger" functions as an overdetermined object imbued with symbolic meaning as the physical manifestation of past sins—adultery and greed—in the present. It is the material instantiation of the violation of marital vows and the institution of marriage. The curse of actions in the past are brought to bear on actors in the present moment, another example of the temporality of effigy culture as I discussed it in chapter 2, by which the sins of past generations return to exact their revenge and what is repressed returns.

Many of Dreyer's early scenarios from Nordisk also feature protagonists who must test their will in "shaking off" their unsavory pasts when family secrets come to light that threaten future generations. Dreyer's script *Ned med Vaabnene!* (*Lay Down Your Arms!*, Holger-Madsen, 1915), adapted from Bertha von Suttner's 1889 pacifist novel, *Die Waffen nieder! Eine Lebensgeschichte*, exploits the mechanism to consider whether women, as wives and daughters, will ever interrupt men, husbands, fathers, and brothers who perpetuate generations of destructive war-making when society continues to deem such acts as honorable. Dreyer's directorial debut, *The President* (1919), which came into being around the same time as he wrote "Kniplinger," also revolves around the fundamental question of whether the protagonist, Carl Victor, will be able to break with his patrilineal inheritance of behavior that involves romancing young women of lower classes, only to then abandon them and their offspring or bring them into legitimate but unhappy marriages. For both *Day of Wrath* and "Kniplinger," lace allows Dreyer to explore representing the pleasures and pitfalls of the archive—past behavior, values, traditions, and proscriptions— and to play with different mechanisms for representing its perpetuation from one generation to the next. Further, the plot of each film is clearly a variation on domestic melodrama, which displaces the large-scale conflict of the public sphere, including war or class or patriarchal oppression, onto relationships within the domestic sphere.

Latent Tensions: Emotion and Art Melodrama of the Domestic

The veneer of domesticity in the parsonage will be stretched to its utter limits by the mortal conflicts between its inhabitants raging just beneath it. Dreyer describes the crux of tensions in *Day of Wrath* in the following way: "And isn't it true that the great dramas are played out in silence? People hide their feelings and avoid showing on their faces the storms that are raging inside them. Tension lies under the surface only to be released the day that catastrophe strikes. It is this latent tension, this smoldering unease behind the daily life of the family at the parsonage, that I have been compelled to bring forth."[19] The rhetoric of repression that Dreyer employs, describing latent tension and conflict barely contained by (bodily) surfaces, resonates with foundational scholarship in melodrama studies about how the mode operates in film. The move toward the psychological is another moment when Dreyer purports to move film away from melodrama and toward art. But in doing so, he actually renews domestic melodrama in ways that resonate with discussions of melodramatic narrative and style in American film in the 1930s–1950s, predominantly revolving around work by Vicente Minnelli, Nicholas Ray, and Douglas Sirk. Take, for instance, Sirk's comments regarding his use of color and deep-focus lenses in *Written on the Wind*, which echo Dreyer's in an uncanny way: "I wanted this to bring out the inner violence, the energy of the characters which is all inside them and can't break through."[20]

Sirk offers an interesting point of comparison for Dreyer as another director of what I would call art melodrama. Although both directors were consummate stylists, Dreyer never articulated any overt aspiration to ideological or political critique the way that Sirk's 1950s melodrama at Universal has been read as central to scholarship on film melodrama. The elevation of Sirk's melodrama to a legitimate object of study happened through Marxist scholars undertaking the ideological critique of postwar American capitalism. Dreyer also never recuperated his earlier work as ironic or claimed to employ cliché subversively as Sirk, and film scholars working on Sirk, claimed he was doing.[21] Dreyer was much more sincere in his use of expressivity and emotion. And although Dreyer possessed as acute an awareness of his public persona as the critically savvy Sirk did, Dreyer never performed a public, retrospectively melodramatic recuperation of his own earlier work. Sirk's look back at his early work, however, does resonate in an interesting way with the look back to Nordisk that I see happening through Dreyer's oeuvre. Scholarship on Sirk's melodrama is important to my discussion of Dreyer because with Sirk, melo-drama ceases to be the unsophisticated or unaesthetic antithesis to artistic film and becomes a privileged form of high melodrama, as artistic and sophisti-cated. Sirk elevates melodrama within and as melodrama rather than making it not-melodrama. At the same time, this elevation as ideologically sophisti-cated work undertakes its own problematic disparagement of other kinds of melodrama that supposedly only elicit spectator identification absent of reflec-tive distance.

There are connections to be drawn between Dreyer's stylized treatment of the domestic sphere and Sirk's treatment of conventional subject matter with an elaborate, excessive, cinematic style. Sirkian style is distinguished by its use of elaborately composed, sometimes claustrophobic mise-en-scène, in which each detail or object is laden with symbolic meaning: the expressive or sym-bolic use of lighting and color, music that expresses mood in contradiction to narrative situations, and the frequent use of long- and midrange shots to pro-duce a stage-like impression. Dreyer's approach to mise-en-scène is as laden with meaning but is excessively austere rather than excessively sensual. From the 1970s onward, melodrama scholarship could have accommodated Dreyer's aesthetic sensibility, including his willingness to spend endless hours research-ing his stage-like mise-en-scène, composing shots and lighting schemes in order to compress action into visual metaphor rather than dialogue. We can think of both Sirk and Dreyer developing this mastery of imbuing surfaces with meaning during the silent era when directors, as Elsaesser puts it, devel-oped "an extremely subtle and yet precise formal language (of lighting, stag-ing, décor, acting, close-up, montage, and camera movement), because they were deliberately looking to compensate for the expressiveness, range of in-flection and tonality, rhythmic emphasis and tension normally present in the spoken word."[22] With sound, too, voice and dialogue simply became addi-tional scenic elements (additional plasticity) to manipulate.

To the extent that *Day of Wrath* and "Kniplinger" contend with the con-striction and punishment of female desire, particularly its violation within the institution of marriage, and set their circuits of passion and repression in the domestic sphere, they are examples of domestic melodrama or the family melodrama. Again, melodrama's low-culture stigma and Dreyer's reputation for art cinema have caused the film's obvious connections to domestic melo-drama to be repressed in their own right. Domestic melodrama again puts Dreyer's work in conversation with a prominent vein of scholarship on film melodrama. The staging of Dreyer's films, like Sirk's or Max Ophuls's, place universal, humanist concerns in the domestic sphere. This is typical of melo-drama's origins in post-Enlightenment liberalism, by which large-scale social uncertainty found its expression in personalized, emotional terms and inter-generational conflict. As Elsaesser conceives it, the family melodrama, too, invests normal life with "an intensified symbolisation of everyday actions, the heightening of the ordinary gesture and a use of setting and décor so as to reflect the characters' fetishist fixations."[23] Elsaesser calls this "displacement-by-substitution" and attributes a certain potential for false (or apolitical) con-sciousness to it. Dreyer, meanwhile, invests the everyday with heightened drama but with a less clearly politically subversive intent than Sirk. Dreyer's characters often suffer from the constriction of their agency and the inability to realize their desires. Dreyer, like Vincente Minnelli, puts "a pervasive psy-chological pressure on the characters," whose desires remain unvoiced or un-realized, present and almost palpable, contained, but just barely.[24] The im-maculately detailed surfaces in Dreyer's films produce, like Minnelli's, "an acute sense of claustrophobia and decor and locale [that] translates itself into a restless and yet suppressed energy surfacing sporadically in the actions and the behavior of the protagonists, . . . with hysteria bubbling all the time just below the surface."[25]

In a sense, Dreyer was operating under the false assumption that melodrama couldn't be psychological. Scholarship on Minnelli or Sirk demonstrates that as a mode, melodrama can incapsulate protagonists that demonstrate psychologi-cal development, a seeming violation of conceptions of melodrama as enlisting only monopathic characterization. Elsaesser's work on Sirk, for instance, ex-pands melodramatic characterization to include the more complex and "psy-chological" kinds of characterization that are consistent with Dreyer's films and resonate with art melodrama as I theorize it. Aligning with the family melo-drama as Elsaesser defines it, many of Dreyer's films show the failure of pro-tagonists "to act in a way that could shape the events and influence the emo-tional environment, let alone change the stifling social milieu. The world is closed, and the characters are acted upon."[26] They also include the intricate al-ternation between constellations of dramatis personae and identification with a single, central protagonist that Elsaesser sees in Sirk (but that arguably exists in all melodrama). In other words, the family melodrama tends to "place a victim hero/ine at the centre of the narrative and afford them privileged audience identification and knowledge" but also distributes victimhood onto a whole constellation of characters.[27] Elsaesser writes: "One of the characteristic features of melodramas in general is that they concentrate on the point of view of the victim: what makes the films mentioned above exceptional is the way that they manage to present *all* of the characters convincingly as victims. The critique—the questions of 'evil,' of responsibility—is firmly placed on a social and exis-tential level, away from the arbitrary and finally obtuse logic of private motives

and individualised psychology."[28] Such juxtaposition between individual protagonists and constellations of characters—taking action to an abstract level—
occurs throughout Dreyer's oeuvre both early and late. As I discussed in relation to *Vampyr* and return to presently, in *Day of Wrath*, Dreyer's art melodrama
juxtaposes protagonists who demonstrate psychological interiority with characters who do not.

Anecdotally, the fact that Dreyer sought work in Hollywood at several
points during his career and that he admired Nicholas Ray's *East of Eden* (1955)
and chose to screen such psychologically engaging, quality Hollywood films in
his years running the Dagmar theater in Copenhagen (where 1960s art-house
fare was scarce) further establishes links toward this Hollywood melodrama
and away from Dreyer's exclusive identification as an art cinema auteur. Although we might trace certain affinities between Dreyer's late work and Sirkian melodrama to currents of influence in the 1940s or 1950s—and putting
Sirkian melodrama in conversation with Dreyer's oeuvre would be an interesting project in its own right—more interesting to my mind is the possibility
that Dreyer and Sirk draw upon a shared, European tradition of art melodrama, with its own mechanisms of identification, media reflexivity, and estrangement. Better understanding of Dreyer's relationship with his early roots
in early Danish film melodrama might allow us to see Sirk's work as part of a
larger European tradition as well.

The Curse of the Lace Returns:
Repression of Desire in the Ending of *Day of Wrath*

Nordisk art melodrama, like the cursed Lamoral lace, is woven through *Day
of Wrath* in ways that are visible and invisible. Another look at the scrim scene
above reveals it to be stitched into a broader swath of references to textiles that
tie together Anne's passions, her desire for an imagined future, and a past that
will seal her fate. We first see Anne wear lace in a scene in which the household
has gathered around the table to pray and read from scripture. To Anne's right
sits her husband, across from her, Martin, her new lover. As Absalon finishes
guiding them in prayer, Anne asks if she might read another passage from the
Bible and chooses the description of Charon's rose and apple tree from the
Song of Songs, with its blossoming imagery and scarcely disguised sensuality.
As we know from the sequence immediately preceding this prayer, Anne and
Martin have lain down together in the tall grass of a lush meadow, consummating their adulterous and incestuous love. The lace she wears on her body
thus signals the shift that has taken place within her. As Dreyer writes in pre-
production materials, Anne has awakened from a dream. A quick glance up at
Martin hints at her desire for him. Her ignited passions will embolden her to

challenge power dynamics in the parsonage, including Merete, the stolid matriarch and upholder of propriety in the household, who senses the exchange of inappropriate looks at the other end of the table and demands that Anne cease reading. This scene around the table brings Anne's newly enflamed desires inside the parsonage, charging the quotidian. Anne's newfound irreverence continues to reverberate through the motif of textiles, yarn, and needlework. After her reading from the Song of Songs is cut short, Anne gets up from the table and sets about winding the yarn she has spun, humming audaciously all the while. Again, Merete commands her to stop, but Anne persists, even going so far as to give her spinning wheel a dismissive final spin right in the face of Merete's vicelike authority. Merete responds to the affront uttering, "Bitch," under her breath, a condemnation that Martin overhears. What follows is the scene of needlework referenced at the opening of this chapter, when the two new lovers find themselves suddenly alone together in the main room of the parsonage. Merete's warning still resonating in his mind, Martin asks, "Anne, what will become of us?" When Anne says, "Kiss me," he hesitates, and she expresses her agency, saying, "Then I'll kiss *you*." But at the sound of footsteps, the lovers scurry apart; Martin picks up a book and Anne sits down behind a panel of her needlework. Dreyer's modulation of Anne's wardrobe mirrors his fascination with the blossoming and constriction of her desire. Anne will wear this lace until the climactic scene in which she confronts Absalon about Martin and wishes him dead. In this climactic moment, her bonnet has disappeared, leaving her wild, flowing hair to frame her face. We see more of Anne's body, and her face conveys full expression of her desire, something that also reads as her possible bedevilment. Her body will be constrained once again in the final funeral scenes of the film—to which I return below—when Anne dons a satiny white, hooded cape that envelops her body. The image of Anne in this garb evokes the curse of the Lamoral lace itself—her body and hair are tamed once again. This parallels Dreyer's performative self-denial of theatrical expression, which, ambiguously, also enables the exquisite reading of pathos on her face, in her eyes, and through a single, poignant tear Anne sheds. The denial of melodramatic expression distills and transforms it.

References to spinning and lace in *Day of Wrath* imbue quotidian activities of the mise-en-scène with layers of symbolic meaning that point to the dangers of femininity to patriarchal order. In addition to winding Anne into the incestuous love triangle with father and son and articulating the power dynamic between Anne and Merete, spinning also gestures toward the ambiguous, and dangerous, connection between Anne, her mother, and Herlofs-Marthe. The first scene in *Day of Wrath* to show the bodies of actors—after the opening Deus Irae scroll and image of the document declaring Herlofs-

Figure 18. An emboldened and radiant Anne smirks defiantly at her judgmental mother-in-law. Frame capture, *Day of Wrath*.

Marthe's death sentence—is the darkened space of Herlofs-Marthe's hovel. Included among the silhouetted objects in the foreground of the film's opening tracking shot in Herlofs-Marthe's home is a spinning wheel. The strategic placement of this prop gestures toward the dark matriarchal ties that bind Herlofs-Marthe, Anne, and Anne's dead mother, who is never physically or visually represented in the film but who we know, thanks to Herlofs-Marthe, also possessed occult powers. In a sense, the spinning wheel foreshadows the fate that Herlofs-Marthe and Anne will share: perishing in flames as a witch.

As we saw in *Vampyr*, different forms of art melodramatic expression that map onto categories of older and newer, past and present, coexist and compete in *Day of Wrath*. Given that she elicits an extraordinary pathos in the film, Herlofs-Marthe's character troubles the linear chronology in which secondary melodrama supersedes primary melodrama, to put it in Brooks's terminology. Dreyer enlists rhetoric that the past must be laid to rest, yet he continues to engage with it. Characters representing the previous generation remain a substantial source of emotion in the film. Herlofs-Marthe's character elicits an undeniably direct appeal to pathos in a way that Anne's seemingly more psychological characterization does not. *Day of Wrath* also makes little effort to understand Herlofs-Marthe's interiority; her character shows no real evidence of development, and her suffering is overwhelmingly corporeal and visceral. From her initial arrival at the parsonage where she appeals to Anne to grant her refuge from the mob pursuing her, her disheveled hair signals her distress, eliciting sympathy for her plight. Although not made visible to the cinema spectator, drops of her blood on the stairs, the bodily traces of her suffering, lead the townsmen to her hiding place in the attic above. In the scene in which Absalon attempts to extract a confession, he commands Herlofs-Marthe to fall to her knees and be silent. As with the conflation of Falconetti's phenomenological body with her character in *Jeanne d'Arc*, Dreyer exploits the fact that the actor Anna Svierkier falters unsteadily when attempting to rise to her feet again. Cinematically as well, Dreyer creates a direct appeal to identify with Herlofs-Marthe's suffering, for when Absalon commands Herlofs-Marthe to kneel, he stares straight down at her—in a frontal shot straight into the camera—bringing the spectator to her knees as well, to peer up at him and plead for her life. It is the only such overtly subjective moment in *Day of Wrath*. Narratively we can understand Herlofs-Marthe's corporeality as exteriorizing the quandary roiling within Anne as well as the boldness of her choice to pursue Martin despite knowing the risks. But the force of pathos that is Herlofs-Marthe transcends her function as a secondary character in the narrative; she shines.

Although Dreyer extracted a range of tortured confessions at different moments in his oeuvre, from *Leaves from Satan's Book* to *Jeanne d'Arc*, the immense pathetic charge that Dreyer derives from Herlofs-Marthe's "beautiful confession," as one churchman refers to it, is unprecedented. It is, as François Truffaut puts it, "the most beautiful image of female nudity in the history of cinema—the least erotic and most carnal nakedness—the white body of Marthe Herloff [*sic*], the old woman burned as a witch."[29] The presence of this explicit sequence in a film that purports to privilege psychological interiority speaks to the continued power of the persecuted female body to seduce art cinema directors. A slow, tracking pan shot across the hyper-clothed, hyper-concealed bodies of the male persecuting judges eventually reaches Herlofs-Marthe's naked torso from behind as she lies on her side. Verbal cues issuing from within the room further indicate the brutality of her experience. We understand that she has momentarily been taken down after being suspended by her hands, her limbs stretched by the executioner. The extreme close-up of Herlofs-Marthe's face immediately following, in which the camera tilts up as she rises, haltingly, to a seated position, is one of the film's most affective moments. Tears glisten on the older woman's cheek, physical evidence of her an-

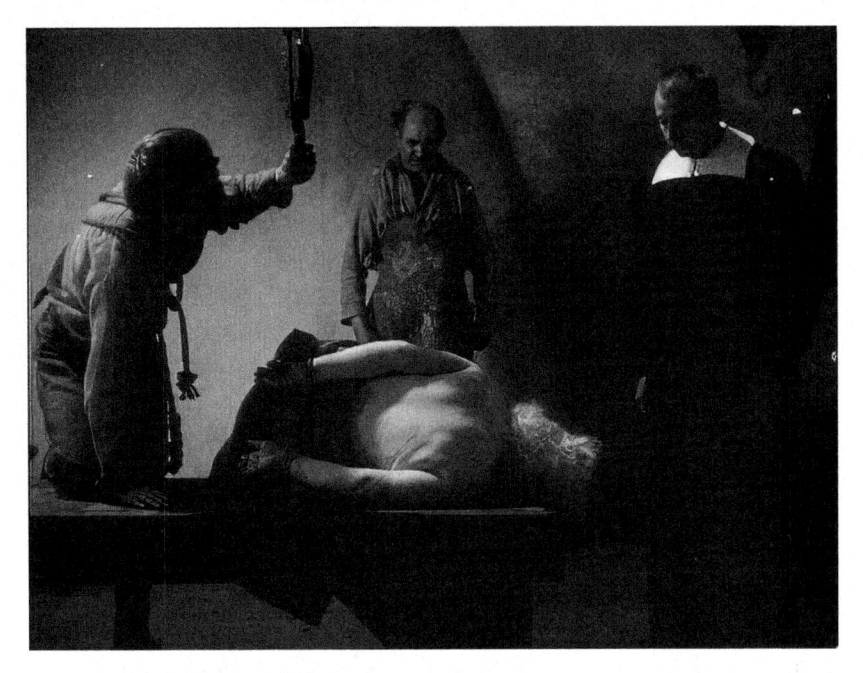

Figure 19. Herlofs-Marthe's tortured confession, one of the most powerful moments of corporeality and pathos in the film. Frame capture, *Day of Wrath*.

guish. Her disheveled hair creates an aura glowing around her head as she gazes imploringly up at Mæster Laurentius. In the following shots, in which Laurentius exacts her "voluntary" confession, she sobs softly as he looms over her in the upper right half of the screen. Absalon will also loom over her in a similar framing. In a sense, the literal binding of Herlofs-Marthe's body in the torture chamber and again when tied to the ladder on which she will be immolated make manifest the overtly corporeal and graphic moments of binding that Dreyer imagines in "Kniplinger."

Dreyer's use of sound in *Day of Wrath* heightens the impact of corporeal spectacle further. *Day of Wrath* is Dreyer's first feature film to incorporate sound technology in a comprehensive way, *Vampyr* having been an initial, partial experiment. And in a way we can think of this technology as legitimizing the melodramatic subject matter by appealing to artistic innovation via sound technology. But Dreyer's use of sound ultimately attests to his interest in corporeal spectacle, in that he uses it not to make expression subtler but rather to amplify the impact of physical suffering in the film. This is perhaps unexpected, considering the way in which, in "A Little on Film Style," Dreyer emphasizes sound film's innovative capacity for both authenticity and subdued gesture and cites its ability to capture actors' natural voices and subtle gestures. As he writes, "This is the great advantage of the film over the theater—that the actor can let his voice rest in natural position; yes, he can whisper if the role demands it."[30] Although much of *Day of Wrath* does rest in a decidedly muted register, Dreyer exploits Herlofs-Marthe's blood-curdling screams to punctuate this same register, exemplifying melodrama's use of non-verbal sound to express pure suffering not able to be articulated in language. As Linda Williams puts it in an early discussion of body genre, "Aurally, excess is marked by recourse not to the coded articulations of language but to inar-ticulate cries of pleasure in porn, screams of fear in horror, sobs of anguish in melodrama."[31] Herlofs-Marthe's screams and suffering are narratively justified to make very clear to Anne, and the spectator, the mortal risk involved in consummating her desires. But as the only character in the film to perform in this heightened, nonverbal register, Herlofs-Marthe stands apart as a remark-ably forceful and empathetic embodiment of primary melodrama.

Herlofs-Marthe's immolation is, of course, another version of corporeal spectacle and *varieté*, another iteration of the art melodramatic immolation that we see at the end of *Jeanne d'Arc*. Dreyer presents Herlofs-Marthe's death at the stake largely for Anne to witness as a spectator. The immolation se-quence opens with Anne climbing the stairs in an adjacent building, after which a series of her POV shots through a window convey what she sees: the fire raging, Herlofs-Marthe being led in by Absalon, Mæster Lauretius at-tempting to support her when she falters while the old woman pushes him away defiantly, men lifting her onto the ladder to be tied down, another pan-ning shot of church fathers gathered to watch the spectacle (Martin among them initially), a procession of choirboys singing. At the terrible sight, Anne must step away from the window and cover her face with her hands. As a *va-rieté* space of performance and spectatorship, the scene opens up various view-ing perspectives: Absalon who watches and refuses again to pardon Herlofs-Marthe; the various church fathers who stare in staid contemplation; and Martin, who seemingly shows compassion by joining Anne. Each character reacts to the burning in a way that illuminates his or her character and opens up points for the cinema audience to identify with or judge those responsible for this gruesome death. Meta-cinematically, the sequence questions and cri-tiques watching torture and church-sanctioned murder. Perversely, when Herlofs-Marthe, in the last moments of her life, pleads for Absalom to spare her, he ignores her by praying for God to open her eyes. The sequence culminates with graphically corporeal shots that echo Jeanne's immolation—this time the horrific figure of a woman, terrified and bound to a ladder, plunging face-first into the fire. The art melodrama of this scene emerges from its extreme pathos, which instigates reflection, both on the ethical question of whether or not to watch, or perhaps whether or not to take pleasure in watching such scenes, and also speculation of how the film might have been shot, what kind of effigy was burned.

We can imagine that making Herlofs-Marthe's suffering very physical and graphic in order to emphasize Anne's vicarious experience of it without also torturing or stripping Anne might read as an instance in which Dreyer resists the temptation of melodramatic expressivity. While *Day of Wrath* might spare Anne the same overt, physical tortures, the film ensures that her fate will be equally grave by employing a discordant, unsettling soundtrack. Through the immolation sequence we hear the sounds that we could only sense in *Jeanne d'Arc*, the crackle of the fire, emphatic church bells, the ominous chanting of the mob of spectators (out of frame), the wicked sweetness of singing choir-boys, and crucially, Herlofs-Marthe's shouts that Absalon has lied accompanied by her screams of terror. The first screams that Anne will hear Herlofs-Marthe emit happen earlier in the film as she is captured in the parsonage attic. But these screams will echo within Anne throughout the film. "I keep hearing her screams," she remarks to Martin in one of their meetings outside the sacristy. Anne's utterance hangs in the air a moment as the boys choir practices the song it will later sing at the burning. A sound bridge then takes us to the screams that initiate the sequence of Herlofs-Marthe's immolation. Sound allows Dreyer to enhance the corporeality of Herlofs-Marthe's suffering in the film, even in shots that withhold her body from view, out of frame. Spectators, as with Anne, still imagine her body in pain. These screams reverberate not only through Anne's interior but also through the mind of the cinema spectator. Dreyer reproduces this subjective aurality again in the final scene of *Två människor* (*Two People*, 1945), when the sounds of sirens and bells meld together in the minds of both the protagonists and the audience. In *Day of Wrath*, voice in particular offers proof of interiority and presence much like the tear does in *Jeanne d'Arc*. We can read sound and the tear as each contributing to the discourse of "authenticity" in which Dreyer is enmeshed. This voiced appeal to authentic interiority and presence will become most acute in *Ordet* when Dreyer includes the actual recording of actor Birgitte Federspiel giving birth to her child. In sum, while Dreyer's innovation of cinematic technique purports to move film beyond the theater or beyond film's melodramatic past, his innovations with sound produce new expressions of art melodrama.

Performing Melodrama's Fate: Dreyer as Anne

Day of Wrath ends pessimistically, or at the very least with an ambivalent flourish of attraction-repulsion to melodrama. When Anne confronts Absalon,

Figure 20. The tear-filled pathos of Anne's climactic scene of confession. Frame capture, *Day of Wrath*.

revealing her affair with Martin, and then wishing that he were dead, he collapses and dies. Initially Martin is filled with shame and confusion but believes in his love for Anne. Ultimately, he abandons her. The ambivalence of the film's culminating sequence depicting Absalon's funeral makes it apparent that Dreyer struggled to abandon melodrama as well. After a slow, circular tracking shot follows the same procession of young boys around the room, ringing bells foreshadowing that Anne will share the fate of Herlofs Marthe, the camera settles on Martin. Beside him sits Anne, who is enveloped in a gauzy, white satin cape. His speech, delivered in a wavering voice over his father's dead body, asserts Anne's innocence. Merete, however, draped entirely in a black satin cape on the other side of the casket, stands, points an accusatory finger at Anne, and proclaims her to be a witch. In a whiplash *coup-de-théâtre*, Martin takes his grandmother's side. In the face of the accusation, a church father in attendance approaches Anne and asks her to swear on the body of her husband—pulling back the covering to reveal Absalon's corpse from the head up. Anne approaches the casket, starts to address Absalon, but can't complete her sentences, "I have . . . ," "I swear that . . . ," until, with increasing weariness, she sits on the edge of the casket saying, "Absalon, you got your revenge at last." What follows is Anne's version of a beautiful confession, that she murdered Absalon and brought Martin under her power, each with the devil's help.

On one hand, the extended medium shot of Anne's face, luminous amid the soft white gathering of her cape and set against a diaphanous wall behind her, reads pessimistically. Anne will be condemned to the flames—her desires fully expressed but, ultimately, constrained again. The ending stands as another instance when the expression of feminine desire, particularly in violation of the institution of marriage, is narratively punishable by death. A powerful maternal line will end and the patriarchal status quo will be restored. The ending of *Day of Wrath* in one sense participates in melodrama's fundamental conservatism, its yearning for a nostalgic return to a prelapsarian past and a return to the status quo. Alternatively, as Christine Gledhill theorizes it, a "third way," between realism and modernism, by which melodrama adapts to conventions of realistic representation in ways that pressure realism but without going so far as modernism does in seeking to reveal all representation as constructed. Melodrama's peculiar power lies in simultaneously depicting what is and what is not; it employs emotion to trigger awareness of felt contradiction within institutions, but without sparking revolution and overturning them. Though possessing the power to imagine and refigure the world, melodrama doesn't ultimately strive to upend the status quo. As Brooks writes, "Melodrama cannot figure the birth of a new society—the role of comedy— but only the old society reformed."[32] Dreyer's reimagination of melodrama as art melodrama in *Day of Wrath* problematizes human, and particularly feminine, agency within a worldview bounded by constraint—whether the institution of marriage or church patriarchy, but seemingly without razing these structures. At the end of the film, they persist. Repetitions of the past in Dreyer's *oeuvre* similarly suggest that artistic renewal and casting off the past are never accomplished in one go (if ever), but again and again.

Case in point: *Day of Wrath* reenacts aspects of "Kniplinger" even when that version seemed to offer psychological resolution. The script, at least, gestures toward the end of the curse of Lamoral lace. As a correlate for, or symptom of, Juliane's psychological state or well-being, Dreyer provided an opening for past trauma to be worked out in a Freudian sense. He describes Julianne's perturbed state as in a terrible headache, "a compact mass, that presses down on her brain in the form of a heap of lace," but also the possibility of relieving her symptoms in what amounts to the visual corollary to Freud's talking cure.[33] "She has made it her mission to untangle the heap and smooth it out. After she has successfully accomplished this, the unbearable pressure will also disappear."[34] "Kniplinger" untangles, while *Day of Wrath*, in some sense embodying the return of this cursed lace, provides neither expressive freedom nor cure, only further repression, further tightening, binding, and constricting.

And yet, melodrama, and art melodrama in particular, also operates according to its own logic of emotional privilege and its related economy of tears, and by this logic, the pathos of Anne's final scene exceeds the pessimism of her impending death. Narratively, Anne holds the privileged position of the last character to be depicted in the film. She, rather than the film's hypocrites, Martin, Merete, Absalom, or any of the church fathers, gets the last word. The fact that Anne is awash in a whiteness coded—albeit problematically—as innocent tells the true story, the one contrary to the purported "guilt" conveyed verbally in her confession. By enveloping Anne's body in the cape and framing her face, Dreyer channels all of Lisbeth Movin's expressive prowess as an actor into her facial expression. Reminiscent of Jeanne d'Arc, Anne expresses persecuted innocence by means of the tears streaming down her cheeks, the truth of which trumps any accusation her persecutors might utter. Also echoing Jeanne, Anne peers upward, saintlike, as a radiantly beautiful Madonna figure, with the trace of a smile on her face. Her remark "I see you through my tears, but no one will come to dry them" is a reference to Martin's betrayal; earlier in the film, at the height of their love, he was there to wipe away her tears. Throughout *Day of Wrath*, Anne's eyes have provided a key site through which to interpret her interiority as a character—some look into her eyes and see purity, others the bedevilment of her mother. Here, I read Anne's tear-filled eyes—which hold the powerful flame of melodrama inherited from her mother and also the gust of air that makes it flicker—as also Dreyer's.

Alongside the rhetoric of collective self-constriction surrounding the *Day of Wrath* production, Dreyer also describes the function of an art cinema director in language that borders on mystical, even occult. The powers that Anne inherits from her mother in *Day of Wrath* bear an intriguing resemblance to the powers that Dreyer will ascribe to the director of artistic film. The film becomes a body into which the director must breathe life and to which he grants his own face: "It is through style that he breathes the soul into the work, that makes it art. It is he who is responsible for giving the film a face—namely his own."[35] And the director possesses the power to "get others to see the material through his eyes." Anne's final close-up, then, might stand in metonymically for the film as a whole. Dreyer couches the task of the director in language that evokes possession and embodiment. A director vivifies his film with a style that mystically permeates and saturates it, all the while remaining invisible and indemonstrable.[36] Dreyer's ideal director possesses telepathic powers of transmission reminiscent of Anne's power to call people to her, casting his aim of eliciting affect in the spectator through a kind of telepathy, another kind of direct, but invisible, transmission or seduction: "It should be his feelings and moods that color the film and arouse corresponding feelings and moods in the mind of the spectator."[37] Similar connections will secure the correspondence between external expression, via legible signs on the body, and internal experience; gesture has the bewitching power to communicate emotions directly into others. Dreyer writes, "Gesture has a direct effect on us and calls forth our feelings without any thought at all as an intermediary. It is gesture that imbues the face with a soul."[38] While shaking off his Nordisk inheritance to assert his agency as a director involves a repulsion to past forms of expressivity and content, for Dreyer, the *Day of Wrath* project also frames his attraction to this past as equally bewitching. Anne's passions will live on.

The ability to conjure up and reimagine his archive in film after film—controlling and adjusting variables and outcomes each time—illuminates Dreyer's creative agency as a director of art melodrama. As Mark Sandberg describes his creative agency directing *The Parson's Widow*, another film about generational conflict in the parsonage, "Art can be trusted to keep the dead at bay, to keep tradition in its proper place, and to allow for a meaningful performance of inhabitation."[39] But Dreyer clearly delights not only in putting the dead to rest but in bringing them to life again and again. Melodrama's miraculous resurrection takes its fullest form in Dreyer's next film, *Ordet*, with which we contend in the following chapter.

Ordet

Art Melodrama and the Miracle

Dreyer's penultimate feature film, *Ordet* (*The Word*, 1955), is probably his greatest critical and popular success, winning multiple awards on the newly emerging film festival circuit in Europe: a Golden Lion at the 1955 Venice Film Festival as well as similar awards at the Edinburgh and Finnish film festivals, a Golden Globe, and a Bodil Award (the Danish equivalent of an Oscar) for best film.[1] Two of the actors won Bodils for their performances. The film secured Dreyer's position internationally as Denmark's most distinguished auteur film director and established his reputation for being a paragon of serious European art cinema. Even today, *Ordet* regularly gets voted onto "best film" lists by cinephile journals such as the British Film Institute's *Sight and Sound*. The fact that *Ordet* is one of the three feature films that regularly appear on this list, along with *La Passion de Jeanne d'Arc* (1929) and *Day of Wrath* (1943), offers a sense of Dreyer's central status in the canon of European art cinema.

Ordet is a miraculous project that allowed Dreyer to continue reworking melodramatic popular culture as art melodrama. The film's overtly melodramatic mechanisms have either escaped attention or been repressed in its critical reception. Much as the melodramatic impulses in *Day of Wrath* could pose a problem to reading its art, *Ordet* is, as Bordwell puts it, "the most obvious film Dreyer ever made."[2] This chapter explores *Ordet* as Dreyer's most obviously melodramatic film by reading its representation of hysterical male bodies, the carnality with which it depicts female bodies experiencing desire and pain, its idealized representation of maternal plenitude, and the masterful paroxysm of pathos and action with which it culminates. More than any other film in Dreyer's oeuvre, *Ordet* stages a reconciliation of the tensions between the melodramatic mode and art cinema—becoming a fantasy of art melodrama. With *Ordet*, Dreyer reconciles his attraction-repulsion to melodrama, and as such, the film is something of an anomaly in his art melodrama archive. The magnificent resolution with which *Ordet* culminates stands in stark contrast to the films that come before and after it, *Day of Wrath* and *Gertrud*, each of which leaves the spectator feeling something between dismay and ambivalence. In contrast to so many of Dreyer's other films that grapple with the tensions of past and present, *Ordet* relieves these contradictory energies to gesture, lovingly, toward a beautiful future. With *Ordet*, Dreyer miraculously resurrects Nordisk melodrama as an exceedingly reconciliatory iteration of art melodrama, in terms of both temporality and gender.

Based on a 1925 play by the same name written by Kaj Munk, *Ordet* tells the story of a prosperous farming family led by the curmudgeonly widower Morten Borgen (Henrik Malberg). Borgen professes a joyful faith in a Christian God—a life-affirming form of Christianity embraced by N. F. S Gruntvig—and a profound love for his three sons: Mikkel (Emil Hass Christensen), the eldest, married to Inger (Birgitte Federspiel), who is pregnant with the couple's third child; Johannes (Preben Lerdorff Rye), the middle son, a theology student who after some undisclosed trauma at school—perhaps related to having read too much of Søren Kierkegaard's work—believes he is Jesus Christ resurrected and acts the part; and Anders (Cay Kristiansen), the youngest. Anders falls in love with Anne (Gerda Nielsen), the daughter of Peder the tailor (Ejner Federspiel), who believes in a more fundamentalist Christianity—a faction of the Danish Lutheran Church called IndreMission—and forbids the marriage. As the two stubborn patriarchs, Morten and Peder, quarrel over the prospective marriage of their offspring, Inger undergoes an agonizing labor. Although she loses her child, she appears initially to have pulled through, resting peacefully as the men of the household gather at her bedside—the first of the film's two key deathbed scenes. This peace will be short lived, however, when Inger dies. Ultimately, though, Inger is miraculously and tearfully brought back to life by the faith of Johannes and her daughter, Karin, who hold hands and pray to God for a miracle. The film's second, climactic deathbed scene in which Inger is reunited with her husband and family lasts an agonizingly pleasurable seventeen minutes. Inger's resurrection and reunification with her husband, Mikkel, is one of the most extended explorations of pathos and embodiment in Dreyer's archive.

Ordet reads as art cinema in multiple ways, whether through its treatment of "serious" religious themes or the existential conflict between science and faith. The film's formal innovation—its use of long takes; its flowing, ethereal dolly shots; its stylized acting, dialogue, and slow, deliberate pacing—has also captivated critics and scholars as art cinema. *Ordet*, as Paul Schrader writes in his 1971 *Transcendental Style in Film: Ozu, Bresson, Dreyer*, is the film with which Dreyer most self-consciously employs "transcendental style," which Schrader theorizes as cinema's approximation of a religious system designed to elicit a spiritual commitment or induce belief in a viewer.[3] The style entails detachment, stasis, and examination of the details of cold, everyday reality in order to achieve the expression of the transcendent in motion picture form.[4] *Transcendental Style* was reissued in 2018 with a new introduction by Schrader in which he further bolsters Dreyer's position in the genealogy of art cinema by situating transcendental style as a precursor to another form of art cinema, slow cinema. Schrader's book continues to play an important role in establishing Dreyer as a transcendental "artist with spiritual intentions" as well as an art cinema director par excellence, despite the fact that Schrader in fact juxtaposes Dreyer's work with both Ozu's and Bresson's to argue that Dreyer only ever partially approached transcendental style with his work, remaining, instead, fundamentally dualistic—as invested in the body as the spirit.[5] According to Schrader, "Dreyer uses the decisive action to reaffirm humanity; it does not disembody the passion, it reembodies it."[6] In 1981 film scholar and theologian Martin Drouzy positioned his psychobiographical reading of Dreyer's work as overtly interceding against the persistent—and by his account, inaccurate—characterization of Dreyer as a director interested most intently in spirituality. Drouzy writes against Dreyer's reputation as "a more or less uncorporeal, angel-like artist, with a direct connection to the divine—an artist, who concerns himself above all with spiritual problems, as if that sort of thing could be perceived as entirely independent of the body and society."[7] Aspects of Schrader and Drouzy's work unsettle Dreyer's reputation for disembodied formalism or spiritualism. Schrader's work picks up on the tensions I also see in Dreyer's work, which he casts in terms of Dreyer's pervasive tendency to combine antithetical styles and contents in his films. Schrader, of course, doesn't use the word "melodrama," but he does refer to *Ordet* as embracing a tenacious dualism that evokes the emphasis on the quotidian often foregrounded in domestic melodrama, for instance. Dreyer, he argues, refuses to abandon the immanent completely in *Ordet* and, instead, continues to engage with psychology and societal context. Schrader's reading of *Ordet* as imbuing *Kammerspiel* situations with elements of transcendental style resonates with art melodrama's hybridity. Scholarship on Dreyer by Claire Thomson, who reads his fascination not only with slowness but with speed as well, also complicates Dreyer's received reputation.[8] Ultimately, however, the high-low binary undergirding Dreyer's rise to prominence remains strong. To a great degree, the picture of Dreyer as a genius, an austere director of art cinema pursuing otherworldly ambitions and formal experimentation as an end in and of itself, persists. Dreyer's work is still implicitly understood as antithetical to melodrama and all that the term encompasses: Nordisk, popular culture, worldly identifications, and corporeality.

This chapter first reads *Ordet* as engaging with gender in the form of key nodes of melodrama genre studies that have developed in recent decades: the maternal melodrama, the woman's film, and the male weepie.[9] The film's fantasy of maternal plentitude reproduces a rather normative, if idealized, white femininity. At the same time, the aestheticization of pain in the scene of Inger's traumatic labor also inscribes the pregnant female body with carnality and the status as a sexual being that opens up the possibility of queer identification with her character. Alternatives to the heteronormative identifications that Dreyer engages are possible. Similarly, the male figures and patriarchs in *Ordet* perform an exceedingly concrete embodiment of masculinity while also gently questioning it. Dreyer tempers the film's traditional representations of patriarchy, including characters who espouse scientific or medical discourse, by including highly emotive male characters who are hysterical or weep profusely. The film's depiction of masculinity puts it into conversation with what Thomas Schatz calls a male weepie, and what Tom Lutz, in his study of the emasculated father figures and collapsed Oedipal triangles in postwar American cinema like Nicholas Ray's *Rebel without a Cause* (1955), has theorized as male melodrama. Interestingly, *Rebel without a Cause* came out the same year as *Ordet* (1955). I also read these representations of masculinity in relation to figurations of male victimhood at Nordisk, as aestheticized, sleepwalking, or hypnotized male hysterics. Given that Dreyer made *Ordet* in part so that he could experiment with cinematic miracles as well as represent the historical Jesus for his unrealized "Jesus of Nazareth" script, we should consider the masculine bodies in *Ordet* alongside those in the Jesus script, which are aligned explicitly with hysteria. Together, these two texts constitute a religiously infused iteration of effigy culture; Dreyer's art melodrama explored bodies in extremis—not only dead-but-not-dead and resurrected but also bodies experiencing ecstatic, aesthetic pain of labor as well as hypnosis and hysteria. As previous chapters have demonstrated, key scenes of Dreyer's late career often allow him to rework a scene or figure from his earlier archive. Here, we shall see that *Ordet*'s extended final sequence reimagines a past moment in Dreyer's archive, namely, the deathbed pathos in "Chatollets Hemelighed" (*The Secret of the Bureau*, 1913), one of Dreyer's earliest Nordisk scripts. Reading these two texts together further establishes *Ordet* as engaging particularly with temporality, transforming the pathos and action engendered by the experience of arriving "too late" into the experience of arriving "just in time." This becomes most apparent in *Ordet*'s miraculous, and miraculously extended, climax, as what Linda Williams has identified as melodrama's alternation between paroxysm of pathos and action. The ultimately ephemeral art melodramatic resurrection that Dreyer stages with *Ordet* reaffirms corporeality and unites competing temporalities of past and present and, implicitly also, of melodrama and art cinema.

Ordet and Maternal Melodrama

Ordet is special in Dreyer's archive. There's something remarkably forthright, earnest, and even naive about the film's iteration of art melodrama that sets it apart from Dreyer's other late, "mature" films. Religious themes and the trappings of transcendental style provide the guise that allow him, in effect, to engage with a particularly straightforward iteration of maternal melodrama, incorporating elements of the woman's film and paternal, or male, melodrama as it has been theorized in Hollywood film of the 1940s and 1950s. The heart of the film is the character of Inger, who is luminously sacrificial, kind to the point of self-effacement, domestic, and very pregnant. She is a vision of hyperwhite, maternal femininity. In contrast to the complex, divided personalities of almost all of Dreyer's other female protagonists, Inger neither changes nor develops through the course of the film. She is a force of nurturing, maternal plentitude who experiences no internal conflict; we also learn little about her own desires. Aligning *Ordet* with the woman's film, Inger reads as an angel-in-the-home character who represents an idealized version of "good mothering." Those she cares for come first, whether this means filling Morten Borgen's pipe, providing visitors with endless cups of coffee, making cookies, reminding slightly soured old men of the inherent goodness of their sons and urging them to be patient, making sure everyone dresses warmly, meeting children as they return from school, reminding Mikkel to show compassion for Johannes, or pleading the cause of young lovers. At the same time, as an exceedingly pure presence of unadulterated maternal plentitude in the film, Inger functions abstractly, activating notions of maternal presence that have more to do with motherhood as wish fulfillment than actual lived experience. Offering no insight into her interiority, *Ordet* presents Inger as an abstract type. She is an innocent, luminous, and sacrificial mother and caregiver, whose suffering functions to heal the rifts between male characters in conflict.

Ordet stages the juxtaposition between earthly and ethereal mothering as a kind of competition in a conversation between Johannes, acting like Jesus, and his niece Maren (Ann Elisabeth Groth Hansen). The scene between these two characters occurs just past the film's midpoint as Inger lies in an adjacent room, agonizing in childbirth—we hear her sighs of pain each time the door opens. Johannes has promised Maren that if Inger dies, he will raise her from the dead. Johannes and Maren then calmly discuss whether it is better to have

Figure 21. Inger, illuminated as an angelic figure of maternal plenitude.

a mother in heaven or on earth. Maren wishes her mother to die so that she can be resurrected; Johannes explains that the others (the unbelieving adults on the farm) won't let him resurrect her, but he reassures Maren that her mother will go to heaven, which is better. Johannes says, "Little girl, you don't know what it's like to have one's mother in heaven," to which Maren answers, "Is it better than having her on earth?" Johannes, whose own mother has passed, then describes the protective presence of a mother in heaven, felt everywhere, near, constantly at your side. Maren, in turn, prefers to have her mother living and also always nearby. In contrast to Johannes's disembodied maternal presence, Maren's mother is material. She cares for you when you get hurt, washes the floors, does the dishes, and milks the cows. The dead, as Maren points out, can't do housework. Dreyer conveys these two competing ideals of mothering in two extended takes. An initial long shot with a fixed camera shows Maren's ideal as she initiates the conversation by coming up to kneel behind Johannes on the chair where he is sitting, staring at the ground. For the subsequent shot, which traces the bulk of the exchange, the camera has been moved to the other side of Johannes, and a slow, smooth tracking shot traces a half-circle around the two as they exchange views. The camera movement of this second take enacts a slow, delicate voyeurism, as if granting the spectator the POV of Martin's dead, heavenly mother as she watches over him, perceptible yet invisible, immaterial.

The scenes preceding Inger's death during childbirth provide ample evidence of her fulfilling the role of Maren's "mother on earth." Inger's domestic prowess and seemingly endless caregiving energies show her to be a strong maternal presence gently dominating the home. In this her position resonates with maternal melodrama as theorized by early melodrama scholarship that initially framed discussions of melodrama in terms of "the woman's film." For instance, E. Ann Kaplan's work on the woman's film of the 1930s and 1940s traces representations of motherhood and mothering from nineteenth-century France to the US, through popular literature and psychoanalysis, to inform categories of both maternal melodrama and the woman's film in Hollywood. The woman's film depicts positions of domestic feminism, including values of domestic work and strong mothering, as morally superior to "a male public order that is either corrupt or inadequate."[10] Inger embodies the domestic reconciliation and domesticity that Kaplan argues are synonymous with a moral high ground in the woman's film. *Ordet* clearly privileges the goodness of Inger's work in the home—she is an untiring force of diplomacy—in contrast to the squabbling pettiness of the film's many patriarchs, including the doctor and the pastor. This domestic version of the woman's film that Kaplan outlines as operating in Hollywood in the 1920s exacts a subtly transgressive potential by making explicit a cognitive dissatisfaction with patriarchal structures. This raises interesting questions about whether it is possible to discern anything approximating a cognitive dissatisfaction with patriarchy in Dreyer's film. The beauty of *Ordet*'s domestic sphere seems to cast a soft haze over any claim that the film offers a criticism of patriarchy per se, especially if we need this critique somehow to be reflected by Inger's character. In contrast to Dreyer's *Master of the House* (1925), the story of a tyranical husband served a taste of his own medicine by his no-nonsense mother-in-law, which is more in keeping with this model of the woman's film, given its explicit treatment of gender roles in the domestic sphere—nothing in Inger's disposition betrays the least frustration with or desire to change the patriarchal status quo. Further, *Ordet* even confirms the caretaking mother as a role decidedly subject to slot substitution, further dispelling any suggestion of critique. As will become apparent later in the film, despite the immense loss that Inger's death wreaks upon Borgensgaard, she will also be replaced almost immediately after she dies. Distraught at the prospect of losing his wife, Mikkel declares to Borgen that he cannot go on without Inger, but in the next breath, he implores his father to do everything in his power to arrange the marriage between Anders and Anne so that Anne might be brought to Borgensgaard to mother his children. Inger's domestic benevolence in *Ordet* is not conspicuously critical.

Inger's self-sacrificing motherhood in *Ordet* glows pure against the numerous self-sacrificing mothers in Hollywood melodrama of the 1950s. We can read the film in conversation with films central to the construction of melodrama studies, like Douglas Sirk's *All That Heaven Allows* and King Vidor's *Stella Dallas,* in which motherhood becomes such an immense project of self-sacrifice that it takes on an ominous hue, particularly to second-wave feminist critics. In these films, sacrificial mothering has the potential to stifle a child's development into their own individual self. One contributing difference is the fact that Inger's offspring are small children rather than young adults, and their still-developing psychosexual identities give them less impetus to react to their mothers. Still, it is as if, with *Ordet,* Dreyer sought an antidote to Anne's pessimistic fate in *Day of Wrath* by allowing a gorgeously nostalgic indulgence in a kind of "pure" fantasy of maternal plentitude. And if we think of Dreyer's attraction to melodrama as figured in part through such immaterial maternal force, then *Ordet* figures another fantasy of reviving melodrama as one might revive a departed mother—albeit as a domestic goddess this time rather than as the occult seductress in *Day of Wrath*. *Ordet*'s idealized depiction of motherhood stands as an intriguing moment in Dreyer's ongoing conflict with the melodramatic mode.

Ordet is striking also because motherhood is more complicated in almost all of Dreyer's other films, many of which actually critique self-sacrificing motherhood. In his public service film, *The Fight against Cancer,* a young mother discovers a lump in her breast, and a doctor—a calm and nurturing patriarchal authority—recommends that she be treated immediately. She disregards his orders, sacrificing her own well-being so that the family can go on vacation to celebrate her husband's birthday. Maternal sacrifice here entails her own demise, conveyed with a shot of the young woman's headstone. Importantly, maternal sacrifice for family is represented here as distinctly the wrong choice, in terms of both public health and, implicitly, for her family. Nor is there anything in the film that aestheticizes or idealizes this mother's self-sacrifice. *Master of the House* is another narrative that calls into question the idealization of motherhood, in part by chiding its patriarch for not appreciating domestic labor as such. Inger also personifies motherhood in a way that appears more innocent and uncomplicated than Nordisk early melodrama. Looking at the cross section of Nordisk melodrama that includes *Offer* scripts, Dreyer's extant Nordisk scripts, and still-extant films, as described in chapter 2, indicate that mothers served a variety of narrative functions in melodrama's ideational complex at the studio. Mother characters could elicit pathos in fairly traditional roles as virtuous victim heroes who "achieve recognition of their virtue through the more passive 'deeds' of suffering and sacrifice."[11] August Blom's 1911 film *Ekspeditricen* (*The Girl behind the Counter*), for instance, features a young woman of a lower social class impregnated by an upper-class lover who later abandons her. Like Inger, the main character also dies in childbirth, illustrating that deathbed scenes were a reliable source of pathos for Nordisk to exploit. Mother figures could also elicit pathos by sacrificing their desires, ambitions, or lives—reminiscent of maternal sacrifice in "classical" melodrama of Hollywood in the 1940s and 1950s. Sometimes this suffering is revealed as virtuous, but sometimes it is shown to be utterly in vain, in a seeming challenge to traditional norms of maternal femininity. In *Moderen* (Robert Dinesen, Denmark, 1914, distributed in the UK as *A Mother's Sacrifice*), for instance, a widowed mother sacrifices her own chance of happiness and love for her ungrateful teenage daughter who has fallen for the same man. *A Mother's Sacrifice* ends ambiguously when the young engineer, the object of desire for both mother and daughter, plummets to his death during a mountain expedition. By the time the heartbroken mother delivers the news to her daughter, she is already engaged to another man, effectively ridiculing her mother's sacrifice.[12] And although, as we'll see, *Ordet's* final scene is spectacular in its own right, "maternal" could also be spectacularly unconventional at Nordisk. Mothers could be forceful agents of reconciliation at Nordisk in nonnormative ways, for instance, pursuing their callow, wayward sons into the nefarious city to retrieve them from the grips of seedy *varieté demimondes*. In *Massøssens Offer* (*The Masseuse's Victim/Sacrifice*, Alfred Lind, 1910), Henry Vinge, another naive son recently relocated to big-city Copenhagen, falls in with women of dubious moral repute and is so comprehensively seduced that he no longer recognizes his own mother's face when she arrives to help him. Affecting a spectacular Oedipal whirlwind, his mother disguises herself as a "woman of the world" and seduces him back to propriety. Compared with these mothers, Inger represents an exceedingly pure and conventional maternal presence.

Being narratively positioned as an angelic force of maternal goodness in the film accentuates the graphic depiction and pathos of Inger's suffering in childbirth. The strikingly extended labor sequence, the first of two corporeal spectacles that Dreyer incorporates in *Ordet* (the second being Inger's resurrection), overlays Inger's idealization as mother with the pathos elicited by the materiality of bodies suffering in extremis. Dreyer conveys both the childbirth sequence and the resurrection sequence with more complicated editing than the rest of the film's long takes, which ties the two scenes together as privileged, interrelated moments of pathos. As Drum and Drum write,

Figure 22. Another scene of ecstatic suffering, Inger in labor. Frame capture, *Ordet*.

The birth scene had aroused a good deal of comment, but Dreyer defended it. "People have complained that the long birth scene had nothing to do with the miracle, but it does. All the women in the audience must identify with Inger and the men with Mikkel. If they do that they will also experience the same passion as Inger and Mikkel and they will hope that the miracle will occur, and so the miracle will come as a liberation for both those on the screen and those in the audience."[13]

From my perspective, as a white, feminist, female-identified spectator reading the birth scene, it poses the same problems and pleasures—the same attraction-repulsion—that H.D. does in her response to *Jeanne d'Arc*. Inger's agonized countenance is unavoidably beautiful, her torture by the stolid and arrogant doctor is also somehow inexcusable. The patriarchal authority of the medical discourse in the scene avails itself of the same implements we saw the doctor use in *Vampyr* and the torturers use in *Jeanne d'Arc*. Much like Anne's tears in the final sequence of *Day of Wrath*, the close-up of Inger's face in this scene, along with the soundtrack of her moaning in pain, signal at once incredible discomfort and also, perversely, pleasure—an ecstatic moment that verges on orgasmic. Inger's suffering is breathtakingly aestheticized. It's another scene of possession, not unlike those we saw in *Vampyr*, that connects instruments of torture with the image of ecstatic possession. The female spectator also is invited to consume Inger's visage through Mikkel's POV, queering the schematically gendered identification that Dreyer proposes. Reading the childbirth sequence in relation to *Ordet*'s climactic miracle scene, which I return to presently, affirms Dreyer's elevation and love of flesh, and Inger's flesh in particular, as a critical counterpoint to disembodied motherhood. But first, we must consider male bodies and tears in *Ordet*.

Male Melodrama and Jesus of Nazareth

The resistance in scholarship on Dreyer to using the term "melodrama" to talk about his work might be strongest in relation to the masculine bodies he depicts as overcome with emotion or hysterical. But these, too, constitute a very significant instantiation of melodrama. Men feel, and weep, and are overcome by affect in *Ordet*. Johannes conveys a strong somatic presence in the film. Although dialogue and family discussion in *Ordet* will clarify for the spectator that Johannes is not in his right mind, Dreyer also makes Johannes's mental state immediately apparent through his bodily posture and gesture. He walks with a slow gait, does not focus his gaze on those with whom he is conversing, speaks in a curiously drawn-out and high-pitched voice, and reports having visions of a man with a scythe that neither the other characters nor the film spectator can discern. This depiction of male hysteria is commensurate with melodrama's aesthetics of embodiment, the full, symptomatic exteriorization of internal experience that cannot be expressed verbally. Laying out the parallels between melodrama and hysteria, Brooks writes:

> Melodrama constantly reminds us of the psychoanalytic concept of "acting out": the use of the body itself, its actions, gestures, its sites of irritation and excitation, to represent meanings that might otherwise be unavailable to representation because they are somehow under the bar of repression. Melodrama refuses repression or, rather, repeatedly strives towards moments where repression is broken through, to the physical and verbal staging of the essential: moments where repressed content returns as recognition, of the deepest relations of life, as in the celebrated *voix du sang* ("You! my father!"), and of moral identities ("So you are the author of all my wrongs!").[14]

Johannes's condition is the result of some undisclosed experience while away studying—in Kai Munk's play text, his hysteria has a more explicit, traumatic cause: the death of his fiancée. Unable to express this trauma in words, it is displaced to be read on his body, in the Freudian sense. Dreyer's version keeps the underlying cause of Johannes's hysteria ambiguous but accentuates the moment when melodrama breaks through repression and repressed content returns as recognition: Johannes glimpses what he understands to be Inger's corpse, after she has died in childbirth, and swoons. Dreyer here depicts the masculine body in extremis, heightening its materiality with a graphic thud. Johannes's floundering, off-kilter swoon registers with a resounding thwack as he stumbles and hits the end board of her bed that knocks him unconscious. His limp body must be carried out of the room, but typical of a hysteria cure scenario, the strong shock restores Johannes to sanity.

Dreyer's empathetic depiction of the relatively rare sight of a male body gone limp with emotion is in some sense indicative of *Ordet*'s interesting take on masculine melodrama. As I have argued elsewhere, *Ordet* reimagines elements of male melodrama, as Thomas Schatz and Tom Lutz have theorized it, in part by rewriting gendered scripts about how male bodies are permitted to show emotion and convey hysteria. In contrast to the fully emasculated father figures in postwar American cinema like Nicholas Ray's *Rebel without a Cause* (1955), the stolid Borgen men are subtly feminized—their chins quiver as they cry and mourn, and they openly care for one another—in ways that nuance the film's depiction of conventional masculinity.

Perhaps as important as expanding traditional notions of what it means to be a man, Dreyer embraced *Ordet* as a project because it allowed him the opportunity to practice depicting both Jesus and the graphically corporeal miracles for what was to be his magnum opus, titled *Jesus of Nazareth*. Dreyer worked on his script about the historical life of Jesus intermittently for more than thirty years until his death; it was also to be his Hollywood breakthrough that never materialized.[15] The script was written in English during his stay in Independence, Missouri, in 1949–50, and in 1951 he completed a draft of *Ordet*'s filmization.[16] Only in 1968 would the Jesus script be published in Danish as *Jesus fra Nazaret*. In his book about his experience with Dreyer on the set of *Ordet*, Jan Wahl recounts Dreyer saying that *Ordet* "will be an 'in-between' experience for me. I want to see how people will react to a miracle, since the Christ film will be full of them."[17] Dreyer worked on the *Jesus of Nazareth* script so intently, for so long, that it grants an invaluable insight into Dreyer's thoughts and long-standing aesthetic interests. Accounts of Dreyer's work on the Jesus script tend to cite it as an example of his tenacious genius or his interest in historical accuracy, particularly given that he traveled to Palestine and learned to read Hebrew as part of his research. But the Jesus script is also a surprisingly graphic and exhilarating account of what are effectively art melodramatic embodiments.

In a sense, Johannes's character pales in comparison with the fascinating examples of hysterical male embodiment that Dreyer planned to employ in *Jesus of Nazareth*. Scenes of spiritual and corporeal fascination allow Dreyer further opportunity to exteriorize interiority as mental illness. I cite the scene in which Jesus first performs a miracle in some length as an indication of Dreyer's enduring fascination with—as well as his attraction-repulsion to—psychologizing corporeal spectacle as hysteria.

> In the darkness of a side-aisle is a man known to all the town. He is thought to be possessed of an evil spirit and his frequent fits of rage lend credence to that opinion. In fact, he suffers from a mental disease which shows itself in periodic bursts of hysteria. The following scene depicts the ambivalent mind which characterizes those afflicted. On the one hand, he is *attracted* by Jesus and wishes to be healed; on the other he is *repelled* and wants nothing to do with him. The religious excitement is only the incidental cause of his rage.[18]

The man, though captivated by Jesus's preaching, nevertheless grows restless but cannot move because he cannot make his way to the door, for he is trapped by the large audience surrounding him. As his anxiety overwhelms him, he leaps to his feet. Dreyer describes his eyes, much like Anne's in *Day of Wrath*, as "aflame with excitement." Just as Johannes's possessed ranting will have a truth-telling quality to it, the man shouts foreboding words to Jesus about the fear that will lead to his crucifixion as his body succumbs to a fit of hysteria:

> *Let us alone. What have we to do with you—you Jesus of Nazareth? Are you come to destroy us? I know who you are.* His outburst instigates a full hysterical fit. He beats the air violently. Those sitting nearby draw away from him as he repeats again and again / *I know who you are* / He becomes incoherent and starts to scream. Seized with a cramp, he falls to the floor. His lips covered with foam and his face distorted, he screams out time and again. Involuntarily, his arms are thrust back. His hands look stunted and his fingers are crooked like claws.[19]

Dreyer's use of the word "involuntarily" corresponds to the word *uvilkaarligt*, another common term at Nordisk in the silent era that sutured gesture with authentic emotive response. As we saw with *Vampyr*, it served the same function in Nordisk scripts that *søvngængerisk* (as if sleepwalking) often did, namely, providing direct indication of interiority through bodily response to situations of duress or strong emotion. In *Vampyr*, the supernatural or the monstrous allows Dreyer the possibility of experimenting with the body and volition. Similarly, *Ordet* and the Jesus script enlist religious experience to reaffirm the imminent experience of the body rather than its transcendence.

The Jesus script is full of miracles that provide ample opportunity for Dreyer to continue exploring art melodrama's media reflexivity. Miracles, with their ambiguous materiality and bodies in extremis, allow Dreyer to remake corporeal spectacle. The process of instilling in spectators the capacity to believe onscreen miracles could be downright gruesome, as evidenced in another early scene in the Jesus script. Having heard rumors that a man named Jesus has been performing miracles, four men carry another man on a pallet to meet him. The script reads, "One of the sons tells of his father's illness. *This is my father. . . . He is taken with palsy. . . . Look, both his legs are lame.* Another son uncovers the legs of the father and demonstrates that the muscles are loose and flabby. He says / *Look.* / He takes a long needle and drives it into the calf of his father's leg. Philip addresses the lame man. PHILLIP: *You feel no pain?* / LAME MAN: *None at all.*"[20] As Dreyer writes it, the needle in this scene helps elicit the film spectator's identification with the lame man who suffers the inability to walk and who anxiously awaits a cure, and perhaps also with the relatives who are concerned for his well-being.[21] The graphic, deliberate fact of a needle entering flesh also elicits the kind of empathetic wince that we experience in the birth scene in *Ordet* when the doctor chooses a gruesome set of scissors from among his medical instruments and the soundtrack gives us the brutal crunching of bones. These scenes of corporeal spectacle function much like those in *Jeanne d'Arc*, namely, eliciting identification and reflection at the same time. They draw the spectator out of the fictional world by prompting her also to reflect on the material experience that the actor's body underwent while creating the scene. Did the actor actually experience pain or was it a fake needle? Such questioning ultimately also signals reflection about the ethical limits of creating and consuming such visceral images of suffering, harm, and pain. This reflection is integral to the complex identificatory thrill of the scene.

We can only speculate about how Dreyer would have filmed the Jesus script, whether he might have emphasized God's immaterial presence as spirit or whether it might perhaps have resonated with the Jesus section of *Leaves from Satan's Book*, in which Jesus walks around the Garden of Gethsemane and to the last supper as if in soft focus, beautifully entranced and entrancing, the actor's beauty and white robes subtly illuminated. Dreyer's Jesus script does, however, culminate with what looks on the page to be an overtly unidealized image of the historical Jesus's body suffering and dying on the cross. Roman soldiers pierce his body to ensure that he is dead and then sit down around him, matter-of-factly, to eat their lunch. "The centurion and a soldier approach the cross. It was the duty of the centurion to make sure that those crucified were really dead and he motions to the soldier to pierce the side of Jesus with his spear. The soldier does so and 'forthwith came there out blood and water.'"[22] As written, Jesus's resurrection is only accomplished through the voiceover narrator's accounting of his deeds and not made visual. The script reads, "NARRATOR: Jesus dies, but in death he accomplished what he had begun in life. His body was killed, but his spirit lived. His immortal sayings brought to humanity all over the world the good tidings of love and charity foretold by the Jewish prophets of old."[23] The graphic corporeality of Jesus's death further suggests that *Ordet*, with its luminous resurrection sequence and, well, its happy ending, is an unusually effusive moment in Dreyer's art melodrama archive. *Ordet*, which we turn to now, culminates with an unironic fantasy of reunification: *Ordet* offers spectators the resurrection of flesh.

Ordet's Luminous Corporeality

Ordet's climactic resurrection is often read for its figuration of spiritual and cinematic transcendence. Narratively, this is the moment that affirms the existence of a loving God, whom Mikkel comes to embrace along with Inger. Stylistically, this is the moment when the film transcends its materiality as film to approximate religious experience. But film spectators have grown accustomed to the everyday miracle of cinema, which effectively resurrects humans who have died or who are otherwise absent. By its very nature, cinema reanimates dead bodies to appear lifelike again. *Ordet*'s miracle, then, is as much about making the spectator believe in the material corporeality of the characters represented, or making the spectator believe that intense emotional response is synonymous with media reflexivity, as it is about transcendence. Media reflexivity grounded on the body in extremis will be acutely tied to pathos derived from grief, loss, and mourning rather than shock or other more violent forms of corporeal spectacle. *Ordet* encapsulates effigy culture at its most moving, most artful.

Before Dreyer can depict Inger's miraculous resurrection from corpse to living woman again, he must first convince spectators of the utterly beautiful corporeality of these filmic bodies. To do this, he incorporates ambiguous scenes of suffering, sleep, and near death that foreshadow the film's resolution. Each draws attention to the task of deciphering a body's ontological status—a hallmark of effigy culture—and, importantly, marks this as agonizing. Spectators are granted firsthand access to witness Inger's suffering in the childbirth scene, but in the subsequent deathbed scene, when Inger appears to have survived that trauma but, ultimately, passes away, it happens behind closed doors.

Mikkel comes out of the sickroom, stunned, conveying the news that Inger has died in her sleep. When Morten and Anders express their shock at the news, he impels them to see for themselves, typical of the way that *Ordet* overtly draws attention to the body. Cutting to the room in which Inger lies in her sickbed (a mid-length shot) covered up to her neck with a sheet, completely still, the film spectator only has visual access to Inger's face, so Dreyer conveys and heightens the deadness of Inger's body through Mikkel's account of holding her as she passed: "I felt her grow stiff in my arms, her lips turned blue." As he speaks, his younger brother crouches toward Inger's body in hyperbolic disbelief. Morten, incredulous too, hunches over, staring intently at his daughter-in-law's unmoving face, close enough to feel her breath. Here Dreyer cuts to a close-up of Inger's face against the bed—a shot that again evokes the ethereal agony of the childbirth scene—and provides film spectators the opportunity to confirm for themselves that her body is become flesh. A clock ticks. Back out in the living room, Mikkel turns to still the pendulum of the clock. Johannes, still performing as Jesus, utters another line of dialogue drawing attention to deciphering bodies, saying, "She's not dead. She's just sleeping." Mikkel then leads Johannes back into the room, as the spectator just

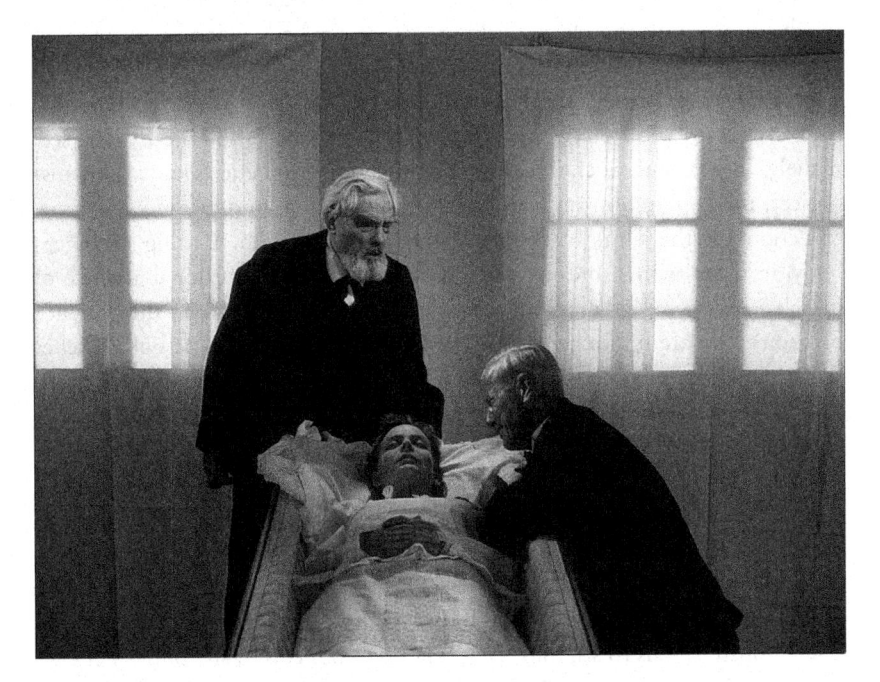

Figure 23. After much agonizing dismay, Mikkel finally breaks down in tears. Frame capture, *Ordet*.

was, to judge for himself. This is the scene of psychic shock and hysterical cure mentioned above.

The climactic sequence of Inger's funeral, where we see her lying peacefully in an open casket, continues the task of establishing the luminous corporeality of Inger's body. At one moment Mikkel leans over her coffin, weeping, and Morten attempts to comfort him by appealing to the bare materiality of her dead body, saying, "Mikkel, her soul is with God. It's not here any longer, surely you see that?" But Mikkel weeps in reply, "But her body. I loved her body too." As dialogue draws attention to the scene's corporeality, the duration of this media-reflexive moment refigures the corporeal spectacle of the haircutting scene in *Jeanne d'Arc*. Here the spectator is drawn to consider the actor's body during production, not because she might be experiencing pain per se but rather an extended period of having to hold her breath and remain still. Watching the climactic, eight-minute-long miracle sequence grants ample time to gaze on the stilled body of Birgitte Federspiel, performing the role of the dead-but-about-to-be-resurrected Inger. Her corpse is extraordinarily beautiful. And while the spectator admires it, she also wonders how long the actress had to lie still during the shooting or how long she could hold her breath. The question effectively demands that Mikkel, in this moment very much aligned with the film's spectator, situate the body along an ontological spectrum of representation of consciousness (dead? faking? manikin? unconscious? sleeping? acting? alive? real? sedated?). The scene draws attention to Inger's flesh to prompt the spectator to think about what she cannot see, namely, Inger's soul. Such imaginings contribute at once to *Ordet's* humanist project, the exploration of love, death, and suffering, and at the same time, reflection on the film's status as media, play, and film. Gazing at Inger's body, in other words, means contending with the constitutional absence of film as a photographic medium that asks spectators to believe in the presence of bodies that are no longer material; the presence of cinematic bodies belies their ontological absence. When Morten Borgen asks everyone to *look* carefully at Inger's body and confirm that it is actually dead, this is Dreyer carefully encouraging the spectator to believe what she sees *on film*. Dreyer needs the spectator, with all his diegetic characters, to think epistemologically about Inger's dead body so that he can believe the cinematic miracle of her resurrection. Mikkel's response to his father, "But I loved her body too," spoken so earnestly and sweetly, initiates the viewer into the physical longing he feels for the lover he is now grieving. The beauty of flesh is confirmed also as Inger miraculously begins to stir. Slowly sitting up in her coffin, she blinks her eyes incredulously and embraces Mikkel with an extraordinary, ravenous desire. As if trying to consume him, she opens her mouth wide, biting his cheek and

Figure 24. Inger voraciously embraces Mikkel upon being restored to life. Frame capture, *Ordet*.

chin. The strand of saliva that clings to Mikkel's cheek offers its own miraculous proof of desire embodied. *Ordet*'s climactic miracle may serve to reconcile obstinate patriarchs and unite a community in faith, but any purported spiritual or familial resolution pales in comparison to the film's intimate spectacle of carnality: one of the most impassioned reunions ever to be captured on film.

Reversing and Resurrecting Nordisk Art Melodrama

Ordet's luminous corporeality is also fully art melodramatic, in the sense of resurrecting scenes from earlier in Dreyer's archive. Not surprisingly, the trope of a mother on her deathbed was a tried-and-true source of pathos and reflection as well as narrative tension, which Dreyer had begun exploring at Nordisk. There, a deathbed often facilitated the dramatic revelation of identities and exploited the suspense of potentially not getting there "in time" for some daring rescue, or alternatively, the agony of arriving "too late." We'll see Dreyer's experimentation with bodies, death, mothers, pathos, coffins, and just-in-time narratives later, in films like *The Fight against Cancer*, which shows that treating pathology in time can save you. Another of Dreyer's public service shorts, *They Caught the Ferry*, created to discourage driving over the speed limit, is another kind of just-in-time narrative in which a young couple race against the clock and against the anthropomorphized figure of death driving alongside them, in order to reach the ferry in time. They do make the ferry, but only as corpses in two coffins. Deathbed scenes are a key topos of effigy culture, affording opportunities for spectators to reflect on the ontological status and materiality or media of the bodies performing death or false death on film.

Dreyer's Nordisk script "Chatollets Hemmelighed," which would later be realized by Hjalmar Davidsen as *The Secret of the Bureau* in 1913, offers an interesting counterpoint to *Ordet* in this sense. Rather than culminating in a death scene, this film opens with a wealthy countess lying on her deathbed, gesturing feverishly toward her bureau in the corner but unable to speak. Her efforts are in vain for she dies before the meaning behind her frantic gestures can come to light. The full import of this scene will become apparent only later, after the bureau has been auctioned off to a young soldier by the last name Høfft, who discovers a document hidden in a secret compartment revealing—in an extraordinary coincidence—that he is the countess's illegitimate son and rightful heir who had been adopted away at birth. In "Chatollets Hemmelighed," the countess yearns to clear her conscience and reconcile with her lost son before she dies, but she is too late. As written in the script, her death at the outset of the film instigates effusive action. The countess's nephew, who happens to be in love with the same woman as Høfft and who would inherit everything if the document were to disappear—steals it in the hopes of securing his own inheritance. After the deathbed scene, the rest of the film consists of an elaborate, death-defying, adventurous chase; the document is nearly destroyed numerous times in the process. Eventually, the good-hearted protagonist, Høfft, prevails and the film resolves happily, providing a counterbalance to the narrative "too lateness" with which it opens.[24]

As will be the case with *Ordet*, "Chatollets Hemelighed" figures another moment in which Dreyer contends with his personal and professional past at once, this time through the fantasy of a dying mother character. In an extraordinary moment from Dreyer's early archive, we find out that not only were both Dreyer and his true-hearted protagonist Høfft adopted away at birth, but they also shared the same birthday, February 3.[25] In Dreyer's script, the hidden document the countess struggles to disclose reads, "If I die before I have mustered the courage to confess the error I made in my youth, this document shall verify that I have a son, who was born on February 3, 1884, but who was given up for adoption to the Fang Family and given the name Arthur. This family has since disappeared completely, but, if my son is found, then he is, in other words, my only sole rightful heir.—Countess de la Garde."[26] This passage provides suggestive evidence that Nordisk scriptwork allowed Dreyer the space to reimagine elements of his own past creatively. This maternal reckoning also aligns with Drouzy's psychobiographical reading of Dreyer's oeuvre mentioned above, which contends that his career-long interest in suffering maternal figures emerges from his attempts to grapple with the trauma of being born out of wedlock, given up at birth for adoption to new parents who were strict and unloving, and then later learning that his biological mother died, sadly, after consuming the tops of matchsticks in a desperate attempt to abort another child. Some scholars have criticized Drouzy's work as providing neither a great biography nor a satisfying analysis of Dreyer's films, but the document and deathbed scene in "Chatollet's Hemelighed" certainly resonate with Drouzy's contention that Dreyer's work reflects the impact of this early childhood trauma.[27] In only a couple of short passages, Dreyer's script dispenses with the adoptive family, reveals the lost son to have a heart of gold, makes a biological mother lament her adoption as a mistake she wholeheartedly regrets, and punishes her—narratively speaking—by killing her character off. *Ordet* also connects a child lost at birth and a mother suffering on her deathbed, albeit with a significantly different resolution.

Seen from the perspective of my argument, Drouzy makes an important intervention in pointing out that Dreyer's creative process is not exclusively forward-looking. I also see the need to account for persisting, idealized depictions of female suffering and longing in Dreyer's films. Drouzy's work also raises broader questions about the possible integration between individual artistic agency and melodrama's broader narratives of loss, longing, and the desire for narrative resolution. We can situate Dreyer's impulse to depict private trauma or maternal suffering as enmeshed in much broader cultural understandings of traditional gender roles. As I discuss in chapter 1, this maps onto the intersection of Dreyer's art melodrama with queer pessimism and queer historiography. Staging his traumatic backstory allows Dreyer to imbue melodrama's yearning back to a moment of prelapsarian plentitude or happy, unknowing innocence, with something like the negative affect. We can think of theorists like Heather Love embracing figures in queer history who are melancholy or who perform a more complicated position than simply being out and proud. In a similar vein, Dreyer's look back to a mother figure in his own past who suffers, is unhappy, and self-destructs after becoming pregnant with a child out of wedlock tempers melodrama's impossible fantasy of reunification—that is, until he, somewhat incredulously, makes it all possible again in *Ordet*'s miracle.

Inger's Resurrection

In a reversal of the too-late narrative in "Chatollets Hemelighed," *Ordet*'s narrative trajectory produces a slow build of emotional charge surrounding the threat of being too late and eventually provides an immensely gratifying just-in-time resolution. Characters casually discuss time, whether how to reconcile miracles with medical science or with the laws of nature and chat nonchalantly about whether or not the time of Old Testament miracles has in fact passed. Rather than trying to catch something in time, the miracle in *Ordet* allows Inger not only to defeat death but also to start the clock over, with resurrection to a new life.

The resurrection sequence with which *Ordet* culminates is an art melodrama miracle par excellence; art cinema's ambiguity and accentuated duration and the pathos of melodramatic time coincide. Fundamentally a nostalgic, conservative mode, melodrama often elicits pathos by exploiting a desire to return to an earlier moment of lost innocence. Symbolically, the miracle of Inger's resurrection achieves the gloriously impossible return to an undifferentiated maternal state. The funeral sequence itself operates according to the temporal logic of what Linda Williams, in her theorization of how American melodrama employs a dialectic of pathos and action for emotional effect, calls a "paroxysm of pathos."[28] Melodrama produces climactic, tearful release by prolonging resolution (for instance by cutting to action sequences) and temporarily denying the spectator the satisfaction of either a happy, just-in-time rescue, producing tears of joy, or the release that comes with a too-late rescue, when tears flow in a surrender to time's inevitable forward progression. The death-turned-resurrection sequence in *Ordet* constitutes an extraordinary paroxysm of pathos—a key tool of the melodramatic mode referring to a sequence constructed to achieve a sustained escalation of dramatic anticipation and emotion punctuated by moments of expressive, minor release—such as Mikkel's tears—that allows the moral goodness of the victim-hero, for whom sympathy has been generated throughout the film, to be revealed to great effect. The exceedingly long takes and lugubrious pace that Dreyer employs in *Ordet* have been read as a key aspect of its transcendental style—which I equate with art cinema estrangement—film announcing its mediality as film. As David Bordwell writes, "The primary function of these long takes, I suggest, is to foreground *the shot itself* as a component of cinematic perception."[29] Melodramatically, however, *Ordet*'s slow pace contributes to its overall strategy for delaying climactic resolution in order to elicit and release the most potent expression of emotion possible. Linda Williams writes, "[The] teasing delay of the forward march of time has not been sufficiently appreciated as key to the melodramatic effect."[30] On one hand, *Ordet* exemplifies Franco Moretti's theorization of hopeless tears in his essay "Kindergarten," in which he explores crying in situations in which something is experienced as lost and impossible to be regained. "This is what the protagonist's death is for: to show that time is *irreversible*. And this irreversibility is perceived that much more clearly if there are no doubts about the different direction one would like to impose on the course of events."[31] *Ordet's* temporality has put this "different direction"— Inger's resurrection—quite palpably on the table, along with the characters' repeated deferral of the knowledge that it is already too late. Dreyer signals the importance of "too late" quite overtly, by positioning the clock (stopped at Inger's death) directly opposite her coffin. Funerals, much like deathbeds, provide a quintessential topos for the release of tears. Moretti notes that people cry, at funerals in particular, because it is then that one "knows," finally and forever, that it is too late. Mikkel's final, effusive burst of tears illustrates Moretti's assertion that "tears are always the product of *powerlessness*. They presume two mutually opposed facts: that it is clear how the present state of things should be changed—and that this change is impossible."[32] For Moretti, tears mark the release of tension between two mutually opposed points of view (*agnition*). Finally letting go of desire and conceding reality produces sadness but also a sense of release. But Mikkel's tears of "hopelessness" are not the film's final melodramatic climax; instead, they serve to delay the paroxysm of pathos with which the film actually ends. Lasting about seventeen minutes, Dreyer's resurrection sequence in the film is an exquisite paroxysm of pathos. On the other hand, the miracle of Inger's resurrection will, of course, occur just in time. In contrast to Moretti, Steve Neale theorizes that melodrama's tears result not only from sadness and loss but from happily melodramatic, just-in-time endings as well. The coincidence or chance recognitions that bring lovers together just before they lose one another forever produce tears of joy. Dreyer's decision to raise a woman from the dead—reuniting her with her lover—affords a magnificent example of producing tears not only in the spectator but also in the embracing couple. In returning Inger to life, Dreyer pushes melodramatic temporality to the limits of realistic conventions. Time begins again as Anders restarts the clock. This glorious moment of melodramatic temporality registers in Bordwell's formalist reading as a moment in which art cinema and Hollywood norms of continuity editing merge and cause and effect normality is restored. In my reading, the resurrection marks Dreyer's resolution of art cinema estrangement with melodramatic pathos: an art melodrama miracle. Cheating death's supposedly inevitable temporality,

Ordet culminates in a reunification fantasy, as the dream of reuniting with maternal plentitude—one that makes manifest Dreyer's faith in film's potential to overcome absence.

Ordet's miraculous ending might also be considered as another example of melodrama's problematic love of resolution, reunification, and "happy ending" at all cost, with little care for logical structures of cause and effect or narrative plausibility. For this, melodrama has been dismissed as unrealistic or as promoting false consciousness. *Ordet*'s extraordinary resurrection miracle violates logical cause and effect conventions, making it legible as an act of faith, melodrama's stunning, if notorious, excess, and the unification of art cinema and melodrama. In the chapter to follow on *Gertrud*—a film in which the tensions between melodrama and art cinema, the past and the present, return in a magnificent way—we will see *Ordet*'s effusive fantasy of resolution repressed—such that it emerges, again, full force, in the archive.

Gertrud

Melodramatic Refusal and the
Art Melodrama Archive

In many respects, Dreyer's last feature film, *Gertrud* (1964), appears to be his most confounding. Considering that European art cinema in the mid-1960s was pulsing with vibrant experimentation and innovation such as the French New Wave or films like *The Silence* (1963) or *Persona* (1966) by Ingmar Bergman, Dreyer's choice to adapt a play of Hjalmar Söderberg's by the same name from 1906 was a curiously uncontemporary choice. *Gertrud*'s opening credits designate it as an image emanating very intentionally from the past, a "tidsbillede fra århundredets begyndelse," literally, a time picture or snapshot from the beginning of the century. In addition to evoking the cross-temporal sensibilities I discuss in chapter 2, Dreyer had explicitly used this formulation earlier in his career to gesture toward an earlier historical time.[1] Shot in black and white and consisting almost entirely of interior shots, *Gertrud* feels strangely out of sync with its mid-1960s production moment. The film's exceedingly long takes, glacial pacing, sparce interiors, and hyperstylized acting further contributed to critics deriding it as stagy and uncinematic—of the past. *Gertrud* was not particularly well received by critics in Paris, where it premiered, and only ran in theaters for one week. *Gertrud* would be the last feature film that Dreyer directed before his death in 1968, but as a text overtly anchored in the early twentieth century, it gestures evocatively toward the very beginning of his career.

Set at the intersection of bourgeois and bohemian social circles in fin-de-siècle Stockholm, *Gertrud*'s daisy chain of love affairs, heartbreaks, betrayal, and misunderstandings, combined with its questioning of institutions of marriage and class, tie it to plot structures of domestic melodrama or the woman's film. The film's formal estrangements and glassy surfaces barely contain the repressed passions of its female protagonist, Gertrud (Nina Pens Rode), an elegant, reserved opera singer with uncompromising convictions about love between equals. She leaves her ambitious politician husband, Gustav (Bendt Rothe), for a talented young composer, Erland (Baard Owe), a dashing genius who proves too foolhardy to understand the immensity of her love let alone return it, and after they make love, he brags about his conquest. Gertrud's former lover, Gabriel (Ebbe Rode), a famous poet who had returned to Stockholm to be honored on his fiftieth birthday, witnesses this bragging and recounts what he has heard to Gertrud, whom he still laments having lost so many years earlier. He too had failed to appreciate her capacity for love, rashly neglecting her in favor of his career, and begs her to take him back. On the face of it, the passions that undergird *Gertrud*'s depictions of love and loss endure endless challenge to their full expression and culminate in an ambivalence that appears particularly chilly when compared to the miraculously happy ending of *Ordet*, Dreyer's film immediately preceding it. In *Gertrud*'s extended epilogue, spectators meet Gertrud in her old age leading the quiet life of a hermit, proud, unflinchingly independent, and resolute in her ideal of love but alone nevertheless. But there is more than meets the eye in the epilogue of this art melodrama masterpiece.

While each of Dreyer's films bears the trace of its coming into being via Dreyer's complex engagement with his art melodrama archive, *Gertrud* is Dreyer's most metareflexive experiment. *Gertrud* stages art melodrama *as* performative archival encounter. In grappling overtly with loss, love, and the past through textual traces like letters and photographs, *Gertrud* contends with the archive as such. The film also enlists a very particular archival and research sensibility to the film's performance of art melodrama that exists in elaborate relation to what we see represented on screen. Although Dreyer professed to being interested in Hjalmar Söderberg's work for a long time, his inspiration for the film was not exactly Söderberg's 1906 play but rather an entangled collection of published sources circulating around a doctoral thesis written about the play in 1962 titled *Hjalmar Söderberg's "Gertrud": Studies of a Play about Love* (1962), by Swedish doctoral student in literature Sten Rein. *Gertrud*'s epilogue, for instance, which marks the most significant departure from Söderberg's play text, reflects a deep dive into the material in Rein's thesis. Dreyer caught wind of Rein's work after reading a newspaper review of it by Merete Bonnesen in *Politiken*.[2] Bonnesen questions the literary value of Rein's heavy-handed biographical reading of Söderberg's work but admits that its treatment of personal intrigue, literary scandal, and heartbreak "will get your pulse racing"—a rarity for a doctoral thesis.[3] As I show in this chapter, Rein's thesis is both of its time in its casual misogyny and fascinating in that it provides channels of academic legitimacy that allow Dreyer to make a film that effectively queers the research archive by transforming it into a space of desire and performance. The archival fever that Rein's thesis sparked in Dreyer was also personal. Söderberg, Rein, and Dreyer were all captivated by Maria von Platen, the historical woman on whom the character of Gertrud is based.[4] Von Platen lived for extended periods in southern Sweden, not far from where Dreyer's biological mother had spent her short life.

Conducting meticulous research to make a film was nothing new to Dreyer, but *Gertrud* stands out as especially invested in illuminating the performative potential of the academy. This comes across in a short article published in 1989 by a woman named Margit Bergström in the annual publication of the historical society of her small community in southern Sweden, titled "Visit to Remember."[5] Bergström describes how on a sunny day in May 1963, a black limousine unexpectedly pulled up the driveway of her quiet home in the countryside, out of which an elegant older man dressed in black stepped out. He inquired, "Is this Maria von Platen's villa?" to which she replied, "Yes." The man then introduced himself, and Bergström invited him inside to look around. A curious exchange followed, in which "Professor Carl Th. Dreyer," as she refers to him, asked whether she had read a recent doctoral thesis about Hjalmar Söderberg's 1906 play *Gertrud*. Again, she replied, "Yes." Dreyer's subsequent response, she writes, made a deep impression on her. "He looked me straight in the eye and said with great emphasis, 'It was marvelous.'"[6] Bergstöm had read this thesis because Maria von Platen had lived out her final days in the house she inhabited, the house where Dreyer sought to film *Gertrud*'s epilogue.

Although it's not entirely clear exactly why Margit Bergström referred to Dreyer as "professor," if Dreyer had introduced himself as professor, it would have been a familiar role for him. Dreyer engaged with university students about his work on several occasions. In 1943 he led a public discussion hosted by the Student Union at the University of Copenhagen (*Studenterforeningen*) about filming *Day of Wrath*, which he subsequently published as an editorial in *Politiken* under the caption "A Little on Film Style."[7] In 1952 Dreyer had been granted a prestigious license by the Ministry of Justice to operate the Dagmar Theater, later Dagmar Cinema, an honor that affirmed his status as a nationally recognized artist and something like a public intellectual.[8] In 1959 this same organization of university students awarded the title of honorary artist (*æreskunstner*) to Dreyer, the first film director to receive the distinction, and celebrated his achievements in a formal academic ceremony of the kind depicted in *Gertrud*.[9] Dreyer likely also felt a long-standing kinship with his professor friend Ebbe Neergaard, whose scholarship on film history I mention throughout this book. And perhaps most performatively, in an undated photograph in the Dreyer collection, which looks like a publicity still for *Gertrud*,

Figure 25. Dreyer intently reading Sten Rein's thesis on Hjalmar Söderberg's play *Gertrud*. Courtesy of Dreyer Collection, Danish Film Institute.

Dreyer poses professorially in front of his bookshelf, immersed in his copy of Rein's thesis.

This chapter enlists theorizations of performance, research, and the archive with all their paradoxical urges, temporalities, power, and pleasures to read art melodrama in Dreyer's final film. I first consider *Gertrud* as a particularly icy iteration of the woman's film, arguing that the film's formal strategies of reflection and estrangement convey Gertrud's experience as female protagonist restricted within the patriarchal and heteronormative institution of marriage. Drawing on Gertrud's explicit, and queer, rejection of marriage, I then show how the film's estranging aesthetic brings to light a strain of repulsion—including negative feelings, negation, and denial—within canonical melodrama scholarship. This includes Stanley Cavell's "melodrama of the unknown woman" and Peter Brooks's reading of "melodrama refused" in Henry James's late novels—each of which speak to the attraction-repulsion impulse central to Dreyer's art melodrama. Crucially, melodrama refused in *Gertrud* leaves a melodramatic trace: its archive. The second part of the chapter follows this trace quickly through the Freudian impression at the heart of Jacques Derrida's *Archive Fever* and into Rebecca Schneider's discussion of the archive as performance to focus on *Gertrud*'s extraordinary epilogue. *Gertrud* may seem to be Dreyer's most frigid creation, but in many respects, it is his most effusive. Glacial sensibilities bely, unexpectedly, the enflaming passions of the research archive. A cinematic love letter written by an aged man reflecting back on his life work, *Gertrud* blurs the boundaries between the film itself as a contained repository of past memories and the paratexual research conducted to make it. With *Gertrud*, Dreyer imbricates loss and love, attraction and repulsion, in a luminous, affective, and queer performance of archival concerns: preservation, destruction, and memory.

Cooling Down the Woman's Film—
Taking the Temperature of the Unknown Woman

Much like *Ordet*, *Gertrud*'s art melodrama both accentuates and estranges the conventions of the woman's film. Set in the domestic sphere, the film's core conflicts revolve around the experience of its eponymous protagonist, an upper-middle-class, white Swedish woman with uncompromising expectations for love. Throughout the film, the concept of love shows itself to be as much an aspiration for gender equity—the partnership between creative individuals who freely choose and value one another as equals—as a romantic ideal. Each of Gertrud's three failed love affairs in the film marks another encounter with patriarchal inequity that leaves her disappointed and unfulfilled.

Formally, the film's tense, restrained mise-en-scène conveys the pervasive sense that Gertrud's emotional life is constricted, her desires pressed below surfaces, unable to be expressed fully. The opening sequence in Gustav's study in the Kanning's home establishes this baseline freeze. While the expensive furnishings in the room reflect the material comforts of bourgeois life, the pools of light illuminating them imbue everything with a sense of cool detachment. White haze envelops the room's beautiful objects: a vase of flowers, a grandfather clock, a wooden sculpture. Each stands distinctly separated from the next. Paintings in gilded frames hang individually on each wall. As is typical in Dreyer's feature films, the acting and dialogue are highly stylized and stilted.

I read the stylized acting that Dreyer employs in his feature films from *Day of Wrath* on as a deliberate attempt to slow down the supposedly frenetic tempo that he refers to as the inheritance from silent-era cinema. Given that *Gertrud* purports to be a picture from precisely that era, it is as if Dreyer felt compelled to distend the pace of the film even more deliberately. Kanning enters, unpacks his briefcase at his desk, and calls out stiffly to see whether his wife is at home. Gertrud glides into the room with a gentle swish, moving about gracefully, yet doll-like, as if suspended in an invisible yet constrictive mesh of social convention and manners. The camera dollies slowly through the space with an equal languor, gently framing the married couple now sitting at Kanning's desk as they converse, panning back and forth on each of them, and then pulling back to frame them in a two-shot. The odd framing of this couple conveys their estrangement from one another. The characters in *Gertrud*, as is also typical of Dreyer's late work, speak past one another, literally and metaphorically. The slow calmness of their conversation conveys a fundamental lack of connection or intimacy even as the subject matter they're discussing—Gertrud leaving the marriage—grows heated. Their lines of dialogue remain distinct. They never speak over one another; their conversation feels mechanical and rigid. In this room of cold surfaces, even Gertrud's hair, a platinum shell of a turn-of-the-century-cum-1960s updo, shimmers like another of the room's golden frames. She is bound within this life, like the ankle-length skirt cinched tightly around her narrow waist or the satin blouse buttoned up to her chin envelops and constrains her body. Gertrud's statuesque body manifests, at the same time, an unattainable ideal of romantic, heterosexual love and also the fact that she has become yet another pretty thing in her husband's collection. When Gertrud tells Gustav that she is leaving him and he responds that he loves her, she replies coldly that while that may have once been true, now he loves only power, honor, himself, his cleverness, books, and his Cuban cigars. "I won't simply be a thing that you play with once in a while," she retorts. Ultimately, Gertrud will spurn the institution of marriage altogether, reject all romantic relationships with men, and live on her own.

Gertrud's representation of marriage reflected public debates about the institution from around the turn of the century and landed amid the stirrings of second-wave feminism in Denmark in the 1960s. Several reviews of the film in Danish newspapers mentioned the film's treatment of marriage, and even reviewers that panned the film as perplexing or tedious recognized it as saying something about traditional gender roles. Some argued that significant progress had been made when compared to the situation at the beginning of the century. Others questioned whether anything had changed at all in the fifty years since Söderberg wrote the play. Gertrud's decision to abandon her marriage is inflected by turn-of-the-century debates about gender roles in bourgeois marriages sparked by Henrik Ibsen's *A Doll's House*, which premiered in 1879. Gertrud follows the path blazed by Ibsen's Nora, who also leaves her marriage, not to be with another partner but to be on her own. *A Doll's House* was one of many works of the Scandinavian Modern Breakthrough of the 1870s and 1880s that contributed to robust public debates about the double

Figure 26. Gertrud and Gustav speak past one another, trapped in their immaculately decorated bourgeois drawing room. Frame capture, *Gertrud*.

standard of traditional gender expectations that female protagonists experienced.[10] Like Söderberg's play from 1906, Nordisk film texts in the 1910s and 1920s could also be seen as amplifying this cultural movement to the extent that they frequently refuse to align with marriage as the default narrative resolution. Söderberg's play ends with Gertrud departing abruptly, much like Nora, and Gustav calling after her to come back, in vain. Both historical situations through which *Gertrud* was read demonstrate melodrama's penchant for dramatizing contentious social issues by projecting them more or less overtly onto conflict between individuals in the domestic sphere.

Melodrama strives to make evident the feelings of contradiction and inequity in the status quo—this is its critical potential. At the same time that it ruffles feathers, however, it also tends to smooth them down again. Often the longing to return to some prelapsarian equilibrium results in the narrative ultimately reinstating the status quo rather than upending it. Art melodrama, by contrast, tends to display greater tolerance for ambiguity and variation in its inclinations toward nostalgia. Narratively, *Gertrud* takes significant steps to end in a place different than it began. The epilogue that Dreyer adds to Söderberg's play complicates everything by projecting the story thirty years into the future—a temporal shift that melodrama's preference for nostalgia necessarily shies away from—and shows Gertrud as an old woman still living proudly on her own terms. She expresses no regret about leaving her husband, nor does she give up her independence at the very end to be with Axel (Axel Strøbye), her old friend from Paris, when that opportunity presents itself. Yet Dreyer preserves Gertrud's nonnormative decision to leave without romanticizing her choices. While bucking the narrative convention that a female character must be coupled up by the end in order to live a fulfilled life, Gertrud's wish to die alone—unfilled in love but with her ideal of love intact—remains tinged with a hint of sadness. The ambivalence of the epilogue aligns with the constitutive feelings of attraction-repulsion in Dreyer's art melodrama. And to the extent that Gertrud's overtly nonreproductive, nonheteronormative life choices also track as queer, the epilogue reverberates with what Heather Love calls "mixed feelings," the quandary of a queer politics wanting to look forward to a brighter future but also needing to contend seriously with the negative feelings associated with the past and its histories of social exclusion.[11]

Art melodrama also helps name *Gertrud*'s amalgamation of melodramatic subject matter and art cinema's formal trickery. The film disrupts spectator identification with the diegetic world by incorporating formal estrangements that reveal the means by which the fiction is created. The film demonstrates its media reflexivity in perplexing ways. In one flashback scene in which Gertrud arrives at Erland's apartment, instead of editing shots together, cutting, for instance, from a shot of her knocking in the hallway to a reverse shot of her entering the apartment, Dreyer extends the long take and sends the camera around—or through—the wall. The apartment is clearly revealed as a set. Bordwell calls *Gertrud* an "anthology film" for the way that it gathers together an impressive collection of film techniques used in Hollywood continuity editing, albeit in an estranging way, or not for any specific narrative purpose.[12] Seen through Bordwell's structuralist reading, *Gertrud*'s quirky collection of techniques becomes an extended experiment with manipulating the way that film as a medium signifies, or how it undoes meaning. *Gertrud*, then, becomes a film *about* film form, perception, and the experience of watching a film that doesn't construct space and time in normative ways but rather as art cinema. Such estrangement reminds us that art cinema and melodrama alike elicit a corporeal response of body genre in its spectators. Rather than tears or horripilation, *Gertrud* elicits the sensation of time passing, or feelings of boredom and tedium. These, too, are corporeal spectacle that elicit bodily awareness, alerting the spectator that she is observing a fiction rather than being immersed in it.

Bordwell's structuralist reading of *Gertrud* as an intentionally "empty" film, resonates in interesting ways with Peter Brook's formulation of secondary melodrama detailed in chapter 3. In Henry James's late work, signification is purposely interrupted, and matters of life and death remain unsaid or unspoken yet felt in heavy silences and gaps in communication. Brooks recuperates extended, laden silences and emptiness as an excessively reflective kind of melodramatic signification. The condition and signature of *Wings of the Dove*, for instance, "is largely one of semanticizing the abysses of meaning."[13] *Gertrud*, like James's late fiction, uses a lot of verbiage to semanticize emptiness. Characters convey a whole lot of information about all that they're feeling—Gertrud says that she no longer loves her husband, Erland says outright that he will not allow himself to be Gertrud's kept lover—while conveying the profound expanse of emptiness across which they're trying to connect. The tempered, restrained body language of characters in *Gertrud* doesn't align with what they're attempting to communicate to one another.

Put another way, *Gertrud* stylizes familiar melodramatic mechanisms to the point that they function like art cinema's formal estrangements, or secondary melodrama, to put it in Brooks's terms. The pressure with which *Gertrud* represses emotion beneath the play of surfaces is so comprehensive that spectators become aware of it, drawing them out of the fiction. Aesthetic estrangement includes uncomfortable moments when characters ought to react more effusively but remain tense instead, such as when the Kannings' marriage gently explodes before our eyes, or when Gertrud exclaims brutally that love has hooked its claws in her and her expression is captured in a chilly mid-length framing. The film resists the steamy proximity of the close-up. James's intricately stylized, late novels achieve a similar sensibility, according to Brooks. *The Wings of the Dove* (1902), for instance, "is indeed very much about how one can subtilize and complicate the terms of melodrama, their relation to individual character and their conflict, while at the same time preserving their underlying identity and nourishing the drama from their substratum."[14] The direct charge of melodramatic plot or character in James's late work becomes so indirect and reflective that the novel becomes *about* melodramatic epistemology itself. *The Wings of the Dove* "can best be described as the consciousness *of* the melodrama of consciousness."[15] *Gertrud* is art melodrama that is *about* art melodrama. It becomes self-reflexively about self-reflexivity—consciously aware of its art melodrama of consciousness.

The comprehensively nippy chill of *Gertrud*'s form draws attention to its repressions, and the film also overtly plays with psychoanalytic frameworks, with characters discussing psychology and consciousness at length. Axel checks in on Gertrud when she suffers a symptomatic headache at the banquet scene and invites her to go attend psychology lectures with him in Paris where they are currently hypnotizing a woman who claims to have telepathic powers. Then they peer up at a tapestry, and Gertrud puts the dream she has had of being torn apart by hounds up for interpretation. Or in the scene after Gertrud and Erland have made love, she waxes mystically about how the world is but an endless chain of dreams, and even the beautiful mouth she seeks, his, is a dream as well. Dreyer is inordinately sincere in both the stage he sets in *Gertrud* for a psychoanalytically invested reading of the woman's film and melodrama and in extending it so far as to display the film as consciously conscious of such a reading.

The repressive surfaces of *Gertrud* also quiver and then rupture along more conventionally melodramatic lines of the return-of-the-repressed kind that has been extensively theorized in the Hollywood melodrama of Douglas Sirk, Vincente Minnelli, or Nicholas Ray. These are explosively effusive moments of pathos or violence in which the desires roiling beneath a film's veneer can no longer be contained, and instead, they break through in scenes of spectacle like frenzied dance sequences, garishly sexual red objects punctuating the mise-en-scène, or in big tears. Dreyer's sex scene between Erland and Gertrud is a coupling that may happen offscreen, alluded to only through a sensual shadow play of Gertrud undressing, but their copulation is gloriously confirmed in the scene immediately following. The two lovers share a sensual postcoital cigarette, handing it back and forth, Gertrud languidly holding it up to her young lover's mouth, their eyes hungrily locked, before bidding farewell. And although it doesn't come close to the profusion of tears in either *Jeanne d'Arc* or *Ordet*, *Gertrud*, too, shows characters who break down weeping. When Gertrud rejects Gabriel's request to take him back and the tears start flowing, his entire body shudders and his sorrow bursts forth in guttural, inarticulate moans of anguish. Although Gertrud sheds nary a tear in the film, the fury of her passions surfaces in a flashback showing the moment she discovers a fateful note that Gabriel has scribbled: "Woman's love and man's work are enemies from the start." Her disappointment and desperate rage rip forth, and she tears Gabriel's photograph violently to pieces. Gustav will also take this expressive action when Gertrud leaves him, ripping up her photograph. And most magnificently, Gertrud collapses at the banquet when, having just learned of Erland's betrayal, she agrees to sing with him accompanying her. Two lines into Schumann's arrangement of Heine's poem of heartbreak, *Ich grolle nicht*, emotion overtakes her and, chest heaving, she collapses to the ground in a swoon—a quintessentially melodramatic reaction. Verbal registers fail her, but her body conveys her suffering. This swoon, consequently, is an invention of Rein's thesis; it doesn't occur in Söderberg's play.[16] Neither lan-

Figure 27. Gertrud's extraordinary swoon in the middle of her performance. Frame capture, *Gertrud*.

guage, nor even music, suffices to convey the profundity of her experience; it is manifested on and through her body. The iced white satin of her ballgown crumples and melts.

(Art)Melodrama of the Unknown Woman, Melodrama Denied

In exemplifying art melodrama's capacity for emotional estrangement, *Gertrud* also contributes to a conversation about melodrama's potential to engage with bad feelings, or the importance also of negation in theorizing melodrama, when it has been most strongly associated with a spectator's positive overidentification with the fiction. The repulsion undergirding Dreyer's art melodrama archive also highlights this negative pulse. Some scholarship is thinking through the denial of melodrama, or denying melodramatically, without identifying it as an intervention in melodrama studies. Stanley Cavell, for instance, puts melodramatic denial in the service of a philosophical argument in his theorization of the melodramatic rejection of marriage in 1940s Hollywood films in *Contesting Tears: The Hollywood Melodrama of the Unknown Woman*.[17] The female protagonists Cavell analyzes in his American case study follow the path of Nora Helmer, the prototypical "unknown woman" in Ibsen's *A Doll's*

House.[18] The depictions of marriage, partnership, and divorce in the Hollywood films Cavell analyzes illuminate a foundational position of skepticism by considering the question of how one can know another's experience of suffering. In refusing marriage, these unknown women protagonists perform the philosophical position of choosing not to be known by the other. This is analogous to Cavell's main argument that analytical philosophy *melodramatically* refuses to acknowledge that everyday experience can be known at all—a mistake that Wittgenstein's ordinary language philosophy, by contrast, avoids. We might say that Dreyer's performative refusal of Nordisk follows a similar pattern. Through denial of melodrama comes art melodrama. The question of shame or stigma enters in here as well, implicitly. I read Cavell's work as illuminating a parallel between the way that everyday experience is undervalued within analytical philosophy and the way that melodrama is underestimated within high culture. In a lovely convergence between melodrama, epistemology, queer performativity, and shame, Cavell reads Henry James's novella *The Beast in the Jungle* as another parable for this skeptical melodramatic denial of the everyday. Eve Kosofsky Sedgwick's canonical reading of the same story in her essay "The Beast in the Closet" appears in *Epistemology of the Closet,* but she also references it in *Shame, Theatricality and Queer Performativity.* Shame (unmentioned in Cavell, prominent in Sedgwick) and melodrama (unmentioned in Sedgwick, prominent in Cavell) meet—potentially—in the closet.

Shame also initiates another melodramatic refusal of sorts in Raymond Carney's reading of Dreyer's work in *Speaking the Language of Desire,* albeit in reverse of Cavell's. Carney reads through Brooks's *Melodramatic Imagination* to argue for a position antithetical to Wittgenstein's ordinary language philosophy, namely, that Dreyer's films and James's novels each model a radical expressivity that transcends what he sees as the constrictive, banal conventions by which we comprehend everyday reality. As Carney describes it, "At the very moments that Gertrud strives most sublimely to articulate ideals that would rise above the limitations of ordinary expressive realities and the tangled web of human relationships, Dreyer's polite, reserved, sedate social gatherings and dramatic forms embed Gertrud and all of her expressions in contexts that resist her dreams of ideal freedom and love."[19] This description of Gertrud's desires being constricted by the realities of everyday life aligns of course with one of melodrama's fundamental mechanisms, yet Carney refuses to employ the word "melodrama." Carney refuses melodrama, melodramatically, enlisting Brooks's *Melodramatic Imagination* to read Dreyer's main films without explicitly calling Dreyer's films melodramatic. *Gertrud,* in his reading, explores how the banalities of everyday life constrict Gertrud's freedom to express her dreams and ideals, but Carney poses this as an existential or universal problem rather than as a discursive one. The work of masters like Dreyer and James, he claims, transcend the banalities of discourse and are inherently nonideological. Reading Gertrud's "expressive problems" as in any way related to questions of gender equity or political discourse, for instance, is to misinterpret the radical stakes of Dreyer's art.[20] Carney expresses an emphatic skepticism toward feminist critique in particular, writing, "The specific reading I am trying to defend Dreyer and *Gertrud* in particular against is a fashionably 'feminist' one. . . . Gertrud's transcendentalism represents a more radical expressive critique than a political or social analysis of specific institutions and relationships can comprehend."[21] Carney's worldview is of its time—arguing for a position outside of discourse doesn't really make sense any longer. The notion that Carney too, effectively, refuses to use the term "melodrama" also attests to the persistence of melodrama's low culture stigma and demonstrates that Carney's claims to universal humanism or transcendence are still gendered, and not gendered feminine. My point here is that we no longer need to resort to a nonexistent position of objectivity beyond discourse to talk about Dreyer's genius—his work is interesting as a kind of melodrama. Also, Cavell and Carney engage with the performative denial of melodrama to do work in academic discourse: Cavell enlists film to make an argument about philosophy; Carney employs philosophy to make an argument about film. In each case, refusing, melodramatically, remains interesting *as melodrama*.

Melodrama refused, in fact, already figures in Brooks's claim that Henry James's most stylized, cerebral, intricately complex, late novels are secondary melodrama. Referring to *The Golden Bowl* (1904), he writes, "The manners which are preserved through the refusal of melodrama yet bear the imprint of the melodrama refused, the melodrama evoked as possible and thus brought to bear on the scene."[22] Characters resist the urge to yield fully to melodramatic expression—which would violate social propriety—yet its affective force remains palpable and influential. The *trace* of melodrama's refusal remains as well—melodrama is both present and absent at once. The language Brooks uses here echoes with ideas about how the archive functions. Things that are no longer present leave their imprint, their trace. At its most fundamental level, the logic of wanting to preserve something entails actively refusing to acknowledge that it will at some point cease to exist. Denying one's past might still entail evoking it as possible for some future moment. Evoking the terms of Rebecca Schneider's work on performance and historical reenactment introduced in chapter 1, melodrama's refusal can also be multiple. Refusing melodrama may *not* be melodrama, but it is also *not, not* melodrama. Refusal, then, sets up the performative, archival sensibility that I see operating in *Gertrud*'s art melodrama and particularly its epilogue, to which I now turn.

The Epilogue: A Feverish Art Melodrama Archive

Gertrud's eight-minute epilogue opens with a shot of Gertrud, now an old woman, sitting at her desk. It's her birthday, and her friend Axel Nygren pays her an unexpected visit. Axel was briefly introduced earlier in the narrative during the banquet scene. The tender, cerebral friendship between these two people never grew into love. Tragedy was the only legitimate guise for Dreyer's attraction to melodramatic emotion, so it is fitting that when Axel gives Gertrud his latest book as a present, it is about Racine. Gertrud tells him about her simple life as a hermit, occupied with everyday tasks: baking bread, washing her clothing, mending her stockings. Her only help is a lone housekeeper. Listening to the radio and reading the newspaper provide her only contact with the outside world. This is just as she prefers; all she desires is solitude and freedom. When Axel asks why she didn't reply to his last letter, she chides him for using a typewriter—that's no way for old friends to write to one another. He asks for her forgiveness. They talk about Gertrud's lifelong devotion to love. They reminisce and reflect on the past. They also talk about death.

One could write an entire book exploring the intriguing intersections between Dreyer's art melodrama in *Gertrud* and Derrida's *Archive Fever: A Freudian Impression*—their intermingling of Eros and Thanatos and their shared fascinations with memory, authority, and textual traces, with questions of temporality and recording technologies, and with drama. I'll just touch on a few ways that we might think about *Gertrud*'s art melodrama epilogue as a spectacle of archival sensibility. It illuminates, for instance, that the desire to remember constitutes forgetting and that archiving the past is always about foreseeing a future moment, and how the urge to preserve is inseparable from the threat and possibility of destroying. As Derrida writes in the foreword to *Archive Fever*, "As much as and more than a thing of the past, before such a thing, the archive should *call into question* the coming of the future."[23]

In *Gertrud*'s epilogue, Axel and Gertrud are similarly preoccupied with discussing what will be remembered and forgotten, with material and immaterial traces of the past, and with how or whether to preserve these traces or destroy them. We are given an early signal of Gertrud's acutely activated death drive when she refers to herself—somewhat brutally—as forgotten and obliterated (*udslettet*). Axel calls his birthday present to Gertrud a memory of their days in Paris. At another moment, he asks Gertrud whether she remembers that she once said love was everything. In another mid-conversation moment, it occurs to Gertrud to return Axel's letters from over the years. Gesturing toward some future reader that will survive her, she remarks that she can't imagine strange

Figure 28. Gertrud and Axel musing about love and death, sitting in front the fireplace where he will burn his letters. Frame capture, *Gertrud*.

fingers rifling through the heartfelt pages. He takes them and thanks her, asking whether she would object to his burning them. Axel actually tosses them into the fire with a flourish. This burning is reminiscent of Derrida's account of Freud's resistance to writing a book about his discovery of the unconscious (a laborious investment in the archive that can only be justified by its apparent uselessness), in other words, "precisely because its silent vocation is *to burn the archive* and incite amnesia, thus refuting the economic principle of the archive, aiming to ruin the archive as accumulation and capitalization of memory on some substrate and in an exterior place."[24]

Gertrud's epilogue stages archival extremes of love and death. The final lines that Gertrud says to Axel evoke the affective power of remembering, touching things not destroyed but saved, archived as it were, but according to a different economy. Gertrud has just ordered her gravestone upon which no name will be inscribed, instead only "Amor Omnia." Grass and anemones will grow there in the spring, and she says to Axel, if you happen to pass by, pick one and remember her. Take it as words of love that were thought but never spoken, she says. Then they walk primly, arm in arm, toward the door. He ought to leave, she says, lest they end up fleeing to Paris again, as they did once before.

"One day, your visit will be but a memory among all the memories I save [*gemmer på*]. Every so often I pull them out and immerse myself in them [*fordyber mig*]. It feels as though I'm staring into a fire that is about to go out." She sends him on his way, expressing the tantalizing possibility of remembering him in a future moment, by pulling a memory out and touching it. The Eros that pervades *Gertrud*'s epilogue—with its economy of anemones and unnamed graves—invitingly reimagines a different kind of archive, one of noninscription, in which unspoken thoughts remain.

The shifting temporalities reflected in the epilogue also evoke those of the archive. Multiple temporalities intersect and overlap. The gauzy, slightly overexposed lighting scheme that Dreyer uses in the flashbacks in *Gertrud*, the film's other significant moments of temporal displacement, signals that here, too, the sense of time is heightened. The epilogue bolts thirty years into the future so that it's eponymous protagonist can both reflect back on her life and also forward toward her eventual death. Gertrud is not exactly dead, she is youthful and aging at once. "You look so young, your face is smooth and white," Axel remarks. "It will become yellow and wrinkled," Gertrud replies. In the end she waves and closes the door of her vault-like home, as if entombed, preserved, mummified, yet still alive. If this scene offers an ambiguously dispiriting temporality, the epilogue also conveys time as pleasurably ambiguous, extended, and elegantly stalled. Like the slow swerve of the camera tracking through the room that occasionally pauses to frame the two characters when their conversation shifts, time sometimes moves in a curvilinear forward motion, looping slowly around in circles. And sometimes it tracks backward and forward at the same time, ahead of the two friends as they walk, arm in arm, toward the door to say their farewells.

Gertrud's poem at the heart of the epilogue—a document, consequently, that she has preserved for her entire life, further illuminates temporal complexities of the archive. When Axel inquires whether Gertrud has ever thought to write poetry, she fetches the one poem she wrote when she was sixteen and performs it. The film cuts to an insert of the handwritten document, which fills the screen. It is her gospel of love, her manifesto composed of only three short stanzas, "Just look at me. Am I beautiful? No. But I have loved. / Just look at me. Am I young? No. But I have loved. / Just look at me. Do I live? No. But I have loved."[25] Time in the poem is not linear, or at least not exclusively linear. It employs the present perfect tense, *I have loved*, but places this gesture back in time. Confusingly, Gertrud's sixteen-year-old self had inscribed this document for it to be read at some indeterminate moment in the future, when she is no longer living. At that future point in time, however, she will possess knowledge that she will already have loved. Freud will employ a similarly retrospective logic of a future perfect in contending with the archival quandary of whether to try to document in advance the history of a psychoanalytic movement that he hopes will also be so widespread as to be self-evident, making the document irrelevant. Derrida writes, "Freud draws another inference, in the retrospective logic of a future perfect: *he will have to have invented* an original proposition which will make the investment profitable."[26] It makes the head spin, Gertrud's perplexing document from the past, about a young self who is also already old, who has already lived, already aged, already been beautiful, and already loved. The three repeated "no's" that accumulate in a rhythm of negation mark the archival temporality of Gertrud's poem as also an ode to repulsion and attraction.

The perplexingly nonchronological verb tense of *Gertrud*'s epilogue resonates also with the way I read Dreyer's art melodrama archivally—as if he will have to have created his late work in order to illuminate his early work. *Gertrud*'s epilogue casts a retrospective light, for instance, on the ending of Dreyer's Nordisk script "Kniplinger," discussed in chapter 4, in which the suffering protagonist Juliane spends her final days as an ennobled, statuesque hermit. In each film, the protagonist's hair turns gray overnight, making her more statuesque but also making her age ambiguous. Dreyer's script describes Julianne's transformation in the following way: "As concerned her body, she had come into her own. Her beautiful, luxuriant hair had turned entirely gray, giving her youthful face the character of a Rococo bust. Her cheeks had regained their fullness, but her eyes had taken on a particularly melancholy expression, her pupils had grown very wide."[27] As if foreshadowing the young Nina Pens Rode's being aged with makeup to portray Gertrud in the epilogue, Julianne's body also represents two temporal moments at once, an effect of effigy culture: she is young but with a shock of gray hair. The body of each protagonist again becomes a topos for the spectator to decipher. Effectively, Gertrud's hair turns radiantly white in an instant too.[28] Only a quick dissolve separates the scene when we see Gertrud leave her husband for Paris and the moment we encounter her thirty years later, sitting at her desk. Dreyer's fever to depict Gertrud thusly transformed by time impels him to violate his long-standing prohibition of using makeup to age characters. Using wigs and makeup in *Gertrud*'s epilogue marks a significant reversal of the on-set authenticity projects *Jeanne d'Arc* or *Day of Wrath*, in which such costuming practices were deliberately forbidden or dramatically restricted.

Seen from another perspective, Gertrud's performance of her youthful poem resonates as a moment of queer performativity in Sedgwick's theorization. Much like Henry James looks back, late in his life, to engage with his early work in a circuit of self-recognition inflected by shame, Gertrud, too, is another artist, late in her life, reading the work she wrote as an earlier self. And much like for James this circuit of shame becomes a playful, sensual, and erotic engagement with his former texts and self, so Gertrud's reading of her earlier work becomes a performance of textual, archival self-pleasure. While she appreciates the naive audacity of declaring her lifelong devotion to love at age sixteen, she also incorporates any twinge of chagrin this may produce into a strong affirmation of love for her early archive. When Axel asks whether she remembers once saying that nothing in life mattered more than love, and whether she still stood by that still, she adamantly agrees. The gesture is one of embracing her past work unapologetically, with open arms. She regrets nothing. "Looking back on my life at the edge of my grave, I can say, I've suffered a lot and made a lot of mistakes, but I have loved." I imagine transposing Gertrud's sentiments onto Dreyer's as, at the end of his life, he peers back one last time toward his early career with words of love that are thought but never spoken. The epilogue, too, reverberates with the suffering and pleasures of Dreyer's art melodrama archive.

Archive Fever also privileges the epilogue as a dramatic space within which to negotiate archival sensibilities. This is part of Derrida's reading of Yosef Hayim Yerushalmi's book *Freud's Moses: Judaism Terminable and Interminable*, in which Yerushalmi argues that psychoanalysis is a Jewish science. While a majority of Yerushalmi's book is written in the language and authority of the objective scholar, historian, and philologist and draws from memory and archival evidence to do so, *Freud's Moses* concludes on a dramatically different note— a postscript letter titled "Monologue with Freud." This is a letter addressed directly to Freud that conjures forth the dead patriarch and, in so doing, illuminates an entirely different order of knowledge than everything that has come before in the book. Derrida describes the monologue letter as a *coup de théâtre* summoning Freud's ghost:

> Dramatic turn, stroke of theater, *coup de théâtre* within *coup de théâtre*. In an instant which dislocates the linear order of presents, a second *coup de théâtre* illuminates the first. It is also the thunderbolt of love at first sight, a *coup de foudre* (love and transference) which, in a flash, transfixes with light the memory of the first. With another light. One no longer knows what the *time*, what the *tense* of this theater will have been, the first stroke of *theater*, the first *stroke* the *first*. The first period.[29]

Archive Fever and *Gertrud*, in other words, each spotlight an extraordinary epilogue. Several things are striking here. These epilogues present a rich accumulation of many of the archive's temporal concerns—illuminating the moment when what comes second retrospectively illuminates what precedes it. The archive's epistemological concerns also come into play in these moments with the different order of knowledge. Yerushalmi's *coup de théâtre* initiates a different relational truth: "Whether it resembles or pretends to resemble, this postscript undoubtedly carries, in truth, in its very fiction, the truth of the book."[30] The fictionality of Yerushalmi's postscript extends the archive, gesturing toward the future possibility of an enlarged corpus. It also, as I read it, stands as an enthusiastic embrace of a kind of performance of, and in, the archive that raises important questions about the possibility of melodrama as an epistemology. Of interest to me also is the melodramatic turn with which Derrida conveys the spectacle of the postscript. The temporally disorienting flashes of light are cinematic in their way. All of this signals to me something of Dreyer's art melodramatic economy at work in *Archive Fever* as well; at the heart of Yerushalmi's dramatic—and dramatically generative—*coup de théâtre* is a negation not unlike repulsion or some other imprint of melodrama that has perhaps been withheld. And like Yerushalmi's apostrophe addressing the specter of Freud, the art melodrama of *Gertrud*'s epilogue belies similar tensions and pleasures of throwing the authority of academic discourse and emotional discourse together.

James Schamus reads these tensions in Dreyer's work as the conflict between the authority of the written document and that of the cinematic image. Employing a Lacanian framework, Schamus labels this Dreyer's practice of "textual realism." Dreyer, he argues, "always saw the relation between the written and the filmic orders as an agonistic one, as a constant battle of wills."[31] When Dreyer sought to transmute the authority of texts into cinematic images, thereby vivifying the "real," historical person underlying the fictional character on screen, characters then struggle to transcend their status as representation and become real consciousness. In Schamus's reading, this left Dreyer torn between his allegiance to text and to image—and obsessed with restaging a gendered battle between the two, hence the prevalence of a particular kind of feminine suffering in Dreyer's films: "Dreyer's heroines are constantly doing battle with authorial figures—their 'transcendence' is almost always a martyrdom at the hands of a textual regime."[32]

I understand the archival regime animating *Gertrud*, and especially its epilogue, a bit differently for a couple of reasons. While the epilogue undoubtedly reanimates the real (Maria von Platen, the character of Gertrud), it also reanimates literary critic and scholar John Landquist, as the Axel character. As I imagine it, the textual regime operating in *Gertrud*, and especially the film's epilogue, is expansive enough to be Dreyer's passionate love letter to the archive, created in a flush of archival fever, suffused with snippets of text drawn from a multitude of literary and academic sources. This reanimation of text doesn't martyr Gertrud; it sustains her as an elegant archive, preserving and performing her. Resurrecting ghosts may have signaled Yerushalmi's shift away from his expertise as a scholar and academic, but for Dreyer, dramatic fictional resurrection was his bread and butter. By contrast, Dreyer's *coup de théâtre* within the *coup de théâtre* of *Gertrud*, the epilogue of his final film, dramatizes the affective truths of the academy.

Dreyer's Dramatic Research, Archive as Performance

The intriguing tangle of paratextual sources related to *Gertrud*—which I include under the umbrella term "archive"—attests to Dreyer's fever for research. *Gertrud* reveals his practice of art melodrama at its most archival, most meta-reflexive, and also most performative. In her chapter "In the Meantime: Performance Remains," Rebecca Schneider argues that the archive be considered another kind of performance. The distinctions commonly drawn between *archive* (understood as material traces of history or text) and *performance* (often defined as ephemerality, liveness that necessarily disappears) don't suffice to account for the encounter between the researcher and archival object or text. This is the moment that Gertrud describes, bringing forth memories and immersing herself in them. Schneider references the theatricality of phrasing in *Archive Fever*, such as the *coup de théâtre*, as indicative of Derrida's actual point that "archives are, first and foremost, *theatres* for repertoires of preservation, leaning toward and into a promise of the coming 'liveness' of encounter."[33] Like the script of a play is understood to remain for some future production, Schneider argues, "materials in the archive are given too, for the *future* of their (re)enactment. . . . The performative bases [*sic*] of the archive, is that it is a house of and for performative repetition, not stasis."[34] The self-contradictory logic of the archive, in other words, proposes to hold the traces of the past still but necessarily relies on some future researcher to engage with these materials, much like an actor performing a scripted role. This entails repetition, and in this repetition, the historical past is not only fundamentally not still; it is only ever legible through a kind of touch or animated encounter with it. The archival trace is no longer of the past but necessarily also belongs to the present moment when it is being touched or reenacted. Schneider puts this another way in a challenge to Diana Taylor's distinction between archive and repertoire, arguing that archive is *"another kind of performance, . . . also* part of an embodied repertoire—a set of live practices of access given to take place in a house (the literal archive) built for live encounter with privileged remains, remains that, ironically, *script*, the encountering body as disappearing even as the return of the body is assumed by the very logic of preservation that assumes disappearance."[35] The point is that any textual archive requires the performative touch of interaction to be meaningful. Gertrud's epilogue, then, reanimates not only historical people but also Dreyer's bodily encounter with their archival traces. Dreyer's research becomes performative cinema.

But backing up a moment, there's something unexpectedly feverish about Dreyer's research process. His fascination with Sten Rein's thesis, mentioned briefly at the beginning of the chapter, is but the tip of the iceberg. Dreyer took copious research notes and typed citations from various books that he cut into strips and then would sort and put into envelopes. He collected a detailed performance history of Söderberg's play and as much information as he could on Maria von Platen, including interviewing her nephew and contacting Söderberg's children about his relationship with their father's ex-lover. Dreyer had clipped a large number of newspaper reviews from various productions of the play, both from when it premiered in 1907 and from later productions in 1953 and 1958. The research materials also make evident that Dreyer was conscious of documenting the process of research, as if imagining them being touched by some future researcher. He documented the institutional traces of his own research practice: checklists of articles to look up in the library, a letter to the university library in Lund, Sweden, requesting to check out their materials, as well as the library receipts for books he checked out from the Royal Library in Copenhagen. Dreyer's archive demonstrates a self-archiving consciousness. Amid his carefully labeled boxes and envelopes of research materials are some intriguingly labeled "KASS," likely an abbreviation for *kassere*— to delete or throw away. In a repetition of Gertrud's tender impulses both to destroy and to save, Dreyer carefully retained these envelopes of scraps that were supposed to be thrown away. Certainly, there were practical reasons for Dreyer to organize his materials in this way, but the system also suggests the immense care with which he undertook this work. It also gestures toward Dreyer's desire to document something of the institutional legitimacy of his research process. He drew extensively from academic sources that would have lent authority to the project—another attempt to elevate the cinema's legitimacy as an art form.

Among these materials is Dreyer's physical copy of Sten Rein's thesis. It stands as another interesting archival artefact bearing the traces of Dreyer's research—the text is heavily underlined and full of notes scrawled in the margins. Dreyer also looked up many of the sources that Rein consults for his reconstruction of key events. In a section titled "Background," Rein lays out a year-by-year account of the affair between Maria von Platen and Hjalmar Söderberg (who was unhappily married at the time), which lasted off and on for about five years. It was during this time that von Platen had an affair with Gustaf Hellström, a cocky young writer who, like the Erland character he inspired in Dreyer's film, openly bragged about his romantic conquest. This affair destroyed Söderberg, on whom the Gabriel Lidman character is based, and he fled to Copenhagen in 1906, where he wrote his play *Gertrud* in the flush of heartbreak about the scandal. As other sections in the thesis, such as "Maria von Platen in Her Own Eyes and Through Others" and "Characteristics of Maria in the Role of Gertrud," suggest, Rein took an expansive approach to exploring the intersections between biography and fiction. So much so that Rein's approach looks a lot like Dreyer's process of "creative adaptation" that Morten Egholm sees in *Gertrud*.[36] Egholm has written extensively on Dreyer's career-long interest in adapting literary texts for the cinema and his balancing of the desire to remain faithful to the authority of an original text with the goal of creating a piece of art that reflected his own personal vision. In conceiving *Gertrud*, Dreyer combined elements of the play with details drawn from Söderberg's biography in much the same way that Rein intertwines the two in his thesis.

But Rein's analysis also establishes a quite sensational model of academic research for Dreyer to emulate. Like the intriguing tangle of paratextual sources undergirding *Gertrud*, Rein blends a variety of academic and literary sources related to Söderberg's play text in undertaking his analysis. This approach reflects the tiny, tightly knit intellectual milieu of the fin-de-siècle literary scene in Stockholm in which artists, writers, literary critics, and academics intermingled and wrote lots of letters to one another. The thesis reads like a cultural who's who of the milieu of the time, in which intellectual production was inextricable from love affairs and literary intrigues. As a translator from French with an astute sense for literature, Maria von Platen played an interesting role in these literary circles of fin-de-siécle Stockholm. She had relationships (epistolary and otherwise) with many central figures, including Swedish author Oscar Levertin, whose lectures on literature she had attended. As recently as 2006, journalist and scholar Kurt Mälarstedt wrote a biography of von Platen titled *Ett liv på egna vilkor* (A life on her own terms). Because everyone knew everyone's business in the tiny Swedish capital city, literary production of the period often included scarcely disguised references to actual people and other self-referential inside jokes. In one instance, when Levertin encountered von Platen out on the town, he smugly "asked her how Martin Birck was," referencing the main character in Söderberg's autobiography and nodding to their not entirely secret affair. In another instance, Söderberg signals the knowledge of von Platen's affair with John Landquist, the inspiration for the Axel Nygren character, when one of the characters in his play *Aftonstjärnan* sits in a café reading Landquist's doctoral thesis on free will titled *Viljan* (Volition). The point is that Rein incorporated all this intrigue under the auspices of academic research.

Gertrud's art melodrama extends and reenacts this pulsing cultural moment, exuding an understated passion for a dramatic kind of academic research. It's worth mentioning, too, that the configuration of passion, love, scandal, and academic research was not a new one for Dreyer. *Gertrud* is another instantiation of the same conflicts that Dreyer depicted years earlier when he pits the authority of academic discourse—literally figured as academic theses, literary scholarship, and the final product—against love in the 1945 Swedish film *Två Människor* (*Two People*). This would be the only film in his archive that Dreyer actively renounced, largely in response to casting decisions over which he had little control. The love triangle in *Two People* revolves around a young woman, her thesis-writing husband, and his academic advisor, whose plagiarism of the thesis in question (on schizophrenia) leads to murder and the double suicide of the lovers. Something about *Gertrud* not only evokes but inspires research. Jonathan Rosenbaum opens his essay "*Gertrud* as Nonnarrative: The Desire for the Image" by remarking that his review of the film took an unusually long time to write (a year) because of the research he undertook to write it. This included, among other things, researching Dreyer's interest in von Platen and the biological mother who gave him up for adoption. Not having access to sources in Swedish or Danish, Rosenbaum consulted Martin Drouzy's 1982 psychobiography of Dreyer, *Carl Th. Dreyer, født Nilsson* (Carl Th. Dreyer, Born Nilsson), and Söderberg's play text in French translation.

Rein's thesis models surprisingly performative and gender-queer possibilities for academic and archival work, in part because he establishes Söderberg's creative process as also a precedent. Responding to love and heartbreak, Söderberg engages with past moments in order to re-represent them in different ways in future work, productively blurring of the lines between fictional representation and historical events. Söderberg refigured his affair with von Platen in a number of literary works, including his 1912 novel *Den allvarsamma leken* (*The Serious Game*), in which the character of Lydia Stille becomes a somewhat less sympathetic Gertrud. In his notebooks, Söderberg referred to von Platen by the names of the many female characters she inspired: Gertrud, Lydia, and Helga Gregorius (from his 1905 novel written before the scandal, *Doktor Glas*).[37]

Söderberg's process also included projecting himself into his fictional characters, particularly his female characters, which Rein describes in terms that range from deep curiosity with femininity to cross-gender performance, or drag. Rein devotes an entire chapter to "Söderberg and the Feminine" and spends considerable time musing about Söderberg's performances of femininity: "Hjalmar Söderberg's interest in the roles assigned to women in the drama of life has resulted in a strange expression in his production."[38] At school, Söderberg used his older sister's books, prompting his classmates to nickname him Frida. He readily embraced this feminine role, according to Rein, even giving a young female character in his autobiographical 1901 novel, *Martin Bircks ungdom* (*Martin Birck's Youth*), his own physical features.[39] Söderberg penned one short story along with several pieces in Nordisk Revy under a feminine pseudonym, Mary Ekeblad.[40] Söderberg also apparently began writing a novel that Rein compares to Virginia Woolf's *Orlando*, the plot of which he describes as a male protagonist choosing to inhabit a woman's body to see the world through her eyes.[41] In another section, Rein draws attention to a sketch that Söderberg included in the fourth edition of his first novel, *Förvillelser* (*Delusions*) (1895), which shows a two-headed body with one male head and one female, their faces turned in opposite directions. Rein suggests that it bears a symbolic relationship to Gertrud's motto in the play, "I believe in the desire of flesh, and the soul's incurable loneliness," which Dreyer will transmute into Gertrud's desire for connection and refusal to compromise. Given Dreyer's professed and lifelong interest in feminine suffering and embodiment, it's not difficult to imagine him identifying with Söderberg's empathy for female experience, which Rein describes: "A male Swedish author who feels an intimacy with the thoughts and feelings of the female psyche, who sees a woman simply as a human being, is actually something quite rare."[42] As I discussed in relation to *Day of Wrath*, Dreyer could also describe his ambition as an auteur in terms of self-projection: his own face onto the body of his film. Söderberg's process, at least in Rein's reading, goes beyond the *coup de théâtre* of the heartfelt letter to a dead patriarch in *Archive Fever* and toward a kind of cross-gender, intermedial reenactment—all within the auspices of academic discourse.

From the perspective of the archive, much of the academic gravitas of *Gertrud*'s epilogue—as well as its sensuality—gathers around the Axel Nygren character. A minor and amiable, though largely forgettable, character from the banquet scene earlier in the film, Axel plays a disproportionately large role in the epilogue. This is because a letter written by John Landquist, the Swedish scholar and literary critic on whom he is modeled, plays a crucial role in Rein's thesis. Landquist and von Platen had an intimate relationship early in his career. He first encountered her name as the translator of a collection of short stories by Anatole France but only met her later in Scandinavian expat circles in Paris, where she had fled following the premiere of Söderberg's *Gertrud* play. He was a student. They socialized and attended lectures on psychology together, and she shared her perspective about the scandal. Landquist would only ever refer to von Platen in platonic and egalitarian terms, as a collaborator, insightful critic of his work, and source of intellectual inspiration, but the two lived together as a couple for a year and a half in Stockholm beginning in 1908. Landquist wrote his doctoral thesis on free will during this period. All these details—apart from the romantic intimacy that their relationship likely entailed—come across in the letter that Landquist wrote to Rein when Rein requested information from him for his thesis.[43] Rein relies heavily on this letter when he elaborately reconstructs the personality of the real-life Maria von Platen through the imaginative inter-reading of Söderberg's novels, plays, scraps of notes, and three letters that von Platen wrote to Oscar Levertin—in one of which she relates her version of the affair with Söderberg. Sources on von Platen were scant, in other words. Just as Gertrud allows Axel to burn his letters in the epilogue, Maria von Platen, too, protected her privacy by destroying most of her correspondence. She asked her lovers and acquaintances to do the same—particularly after her affair with Söderberg became a public secret with the double premiere of the play in Stockholm and Copenhagen in 1907. One letter to Levertin explicitly asks him to burn it after reading, which he clearly did not.

Nestled within the long letter that Rein solicited from Landquist is a short missive that von Platen wrote to him before she died. Here she describes the quotidian detail of her life as a hermit and chides Landquist for writing to her on the typewriter, all of which Dreyer incorporates into *Gertrud*'s dialogue. Von Platen refers to Landquist as the love of her youth, not a cherished friend. It is a beautiful, archival *mis-en-abîme* of textual performance: von Platen's letter within Landquist's letter, nestled in the epilogue to a film that also presents itself as a missive sent from the past. The epistles Axel throws into the fire in *Gertrud*'s epilogue are resurrected by the epilogue itself, via the appendix in the thesis. Rein's approach activates archival materials in a performative repetition for a future (re)enactment that will include his thesis and, eventually, Dreyer's film.

It's not difficult to imagine, as Martin Drouzy and others have done, that Dreyer resurrects Maria von Platen, whether consciously or not, as a way of dealing with the traumatic loss of his biological mother—a kind of attraction. To this I would also add that Maria von Platen, as Rein portrays her in the thesis, also affords Dreyer an intriguing model for breaking with the past—a kind of repulsion. Part of von Platen/Gertrud's appeal is precisely her archival sensibility as a character, and a performing character. In a letter to Levertin, von Platen describes herself as a "child of the moment" with little concern for the future, someone who knows that while she may have memories she loves, these will inevitably fade. "All we have is the present," she writes. "The present is mine, and when I feel something strongly, whether admiration, gratitude or something more, I have difficulty denying myself the pleasure of sharing it, even if I'm not at all sure how it will be received."[44] In his letter, Landquist reiterates von Platen's capacity to live in the moment, emphasizing it as a crucial aspect of her independent spirit. "She was always alone and free. The past was dead to her, and the future could come as it liked. The present was alive."[45] In a move that can perhaps be considered *of its time*, Rein casually pathologizes von Platen as "hysteroid," a designation that he claims, along with the term "hysterical," to be simply descriptive rather than pejorative. "There are psychological designations for an emotional life, the 'strength' of which is equal to its 'intensity' but not its 'duration' and hardly therefore with 'depth.' The most prevalent is *hysterical*, or better, given that it's a completely normal psychological phenomenon: *hysteroid*."[46] Von Platen's impulsiveness, combined with her unusually strong will, gifted intellect, and artistic talents, as Rein describes her, posed a greater problem for those around her, who fell victim to her impetuous charms, than for her personally. Interestingly, Rein emphasizes performance to link von Platen's strong feelings to her temporal variability. Her artistic gifts and capacity to shift from moment to moment or "now to now" coincided with her ambitions to train as an actor, something that Landquist describes in his letter, but which ultimately also came to naught.[47] Rein speculates that a debut in that profession would have been difficult in her late thirties.

Ultimately, von Platen's "hysteroid" status derives from her ultimate inability or unwillingness to negotiate between past and present. Rein disparages von Platen for discarding her past emotions, contacts, and experiences too easily, for breaking off relationships with her (male) lovers. Interwoven in this portrait of von Platen is Rein's implicit reiteration of traditional gender roles against which von Platen appears strange or abnormal. I would reframe the refusal of both von Platen and Gertrud to organize their lives according to conventional benchmarks of success, including marriage and procreation, as contributing to queer critiques of patriarchal institutions and norms that would restrain them. Given Dreyer's fascination with hysteria, which I discussed in the previous chapter, von Platen's "hysteroid" nature certainly would have intrigued him. When this pathological overinvestment in the present moment reemerges in the figure of Gertrud in the epilogue, however, Dreyer tempers it by conveying this dignified old-young woman as more temporally ambiguous. She remains elegantly unknown, embodying the past, future, and present all at once.

I imagine Dreyer projecting himself into Gertrud, a female protagonist who, like so many populating Dreyer's archive, is a complex and radiantly fallible character. But I also imagine Dreyer projecting himself into the character of Axel, as professor, intellectual confident, and equal of this peculiar woman—her secret lover. Landquist describes socializing almost exclusively with von Platen during the joyous period around 1907 when he wrote his thesis and remarks that she exerted a calming effect on his work—nothing like the contentious and gendered conflict between man's work and a woman's love figured in *Gertrud*. He considered von Platen a valuable collaborator who inspired him but also critiqued his work soundly, pulling no punches, as an equal. Von Platen's love and way of being in the world influenced Landquist's doctoral work in psychology, which sought to observe the concrete fluctuations of interiority with all its push and pull between being constrained and being free, between repetition and invention, as a way of grappling with the question of free will. In this, his thesis—which Dreyer also read in researching *Gertrud*—reflects a creative impulse that, as I see it, approximates something of the attraction-repulsion of Dreyer's art melodrama.

When Landquist refers to von Platen's propensity for temporal incongruity, calling her "alone and free," and "a woman for whom the past was dead, the present moment was alive, and the future might come as it may" (which Rein would interpret as hysterical), it is actually part of a larger passage in which Landquist reflects back on his early academic work.[48] Like James peers back at his early work, or Dreyer looks back at Nordisk, Landquist reflects that as a young man, he couldn't look within himself without also seeing his female companion within him—von Platen was an integral part of his work. He follows this by citing a poetic and somewhat mystical passage from his thesis fifty years earlier in which he describes how the love of one's feminine essence—as a source of light, pride, incomprehensibility, inimitability, in its incomparability—becomes will and ego. This performative moment for Landquist reads a bit like Gertrud's manifesto to love that she wrote at age sixteen. He peers back at his earlier work not feeling shame at its callow idealism but with the realization that for fifty years he has resisted revealing experience fully. "That was written by a person I hadn't wanted to acknowledge," he writes.[49] Again, critical reflection and emotion give spark to each other. And in another *coup de théâtre* revealing the affective truths of academic discourse, Landquist describes his doctoral thesis as inflected by his experience of the ethereal helplessness of love—a consequence of spending all his time with von Platen. Only retrospectively would he comprehend that the language of an academic thesis was not supposed to evidence the flush of love.

As other chapters have demonstrated, Dreyer's films each stage an encounter with his past by reworking moments in his own art melodramatic archive, from Nordisk onward. Declaring itself explicitly as an artifact from the past, *Gertrud* stages the past overtly and effusively. Like *The Parson's Widow* or *La Passion de Jeanne d'Arc*, which trace some aspect of an on-set performance event, *Gertrud* traces Dreyer's encounter with the archive itself. The film stages a highly affective, performative encounter not only with a personal archive but also with the public discourse surrounding the academic research archive. As such, *Gertrud* places itself within a line of impassioned and imperfect academic research that takes issue with the distinction between reason and emotion, showing the two to be inextricably charged together. Within the film's complex enmeshments, research becomes cinema performance, and cinema facilitates the further touch of the archive. *Gertrud* thus contributes to a body of scholarship working at the intersection of artistic and archival practices and raises questions about the archival sensibility of narrative film.

Gertrud's art melodrama draws attention to the emotional impact of engaging with traces of the past that persist into the present. It gestures toward the potential pleasures of archival work—Eros as well as Thanatos. With *Gertrud*, Dreyer reflects wholeheartedly back on his youth and proclaims, above all else, that he *has loved*.

Conclusion

In 1963 Dreyer wrote a preface for the revised edition of *The Story of Danish Film*, which he framed as a letter to its author, Ebbe Neergaard, his old friend who had passed away a few years earlier. Most of Dreyer's life and career lay behind him—he would have been about seventy-four—and the apostrophe dedicated to his deceased friend allows him the opportunity to reflect on his earlier work, on his past self. Rather that adulatory praise of the contributions Neergaard's scholarship had made to the study of Danish cinema—which Dreyer claims Neergaard wouldn't have appreciated—Dreyer delves into his archive of memories to reflect fondly on their encounters in Paris, where they shared meals and talked about cinema. Dreyer had just completed *Jeanne d'Arc*, and conversation one night revolved around Falconetti's performance in the film. Dreyer describes a scene on set in which he watches Falconetti as she watches dailies of herself from the previous day's filming. He observes her reacting to the almost supernatural beauty that radiated from her image on film, describing it as something that happened to her during her performance that even she couldn't explain. Dreyer and Neergaard agree, here, that Falconetti had lived the part of *Jeanne d'Arc* in a mysterious, otherworldly way. In these moments of inspiration, Dreyer remarks, Falconetti drew upon hidden feelings deep within that were foreign and unknown, even to her. She watched herself without recognizing herself. This capacity to draw forth something entirely opposite to yet incorporated within her becomes a source of empathy and inspiration for Falconetti. As Dreyer writes, "Maybe an actor can only understand another person, if he has this other person—*and also his opposite nature*—within him."[1] It is possible that in the back of his mind, Dreyer was also recalling Neergaard's review of the film in *Politiken* in 1928, the closing passage of which also portrays the charge of opposites as essential to the lessons *Jeanne d'Arc* might impart to other filmmakers. Neergaard's review reads: "*Jeanne d'Arc* is one of the most peculiar films that has ever been shown; as with all works created by a single-mindedly determined, distinctly monomaniacal psyche, it is unforgettable—unforgettable in its combination of spectacular results and almost pathetic-seeming deficiencies. There's no doubt that our film people will be able to reap knowledge, both positive and negative, by studying this above-all untraditional film."[2] Importantly, in the line immediately following opposite natures in the preface, Dreyer reframes this opposition as also popular culture: "This explains at any rate that Falconetti, who at night was shining in the light frivolous acting of the Boulevard theatres, could in the mornings find the sublime expression of what Jeanne felt, as her life was running down."[3] Dreyer's description of Falconetti's boulevard acting as "frivolous" work belies the continued presence of melodrama's low culture stigma in his imagination. Decades had passed since he began his film career working in the popular culture powerhouse Nordisk Films Kompagni during the Golden Age of Danish melodrama. But long after his reputation as an international auteur had been secured, the urge persists to denigrate *varieté* in order to articulate *Jeanne d'Arc* as extraordinary. Performing this denial of melodrama produced a charge for Dreyer throughout his career and clearly remained relevant to the way that he positioned himself publicly as a director, to the end.

The preface also illuminates the complexities of Dreyer's dismissal of popular culture in important ways. The pressure that Dreyer felt to elevate cinema as an art—the motivating factor behind disparaging melodrama—also comes through clearly. The task of challenging cinema's stigma as popular entertainment remained central to Dreyer's self-understanding as a director. In the preface Dreyer thanks Neergaard for taking up this same fight and championing both film's status as an art and the idea that film directors ought to be seen as creative artists responsible for imprinting works of art with their individual personality. He refers to Neergaard's sentiment expressively as "words spoken out of my own heart."[4] Dreyer's dismissal of the boulevard theater is also complicated performatively. Dispensing with what is effectively melodrama, as superficial, theatrical, and uncinematic, necessarily entails reviving it, bringing it up yet again and thus affirming its continued relevance through negation. Nordisk *varieté* is still at play, so to speak, in relation to Dreyer's theorizations about film.

Much in Dreyer's preface resonates with key arguments I have made in *Visions and Victims*, most centrally that Dreyer's simultaneous attraction to, and repulsion of, his melodramatic past, combined with the pressure he felt to make art, resulted in his innovations of the melodramatic mode that I call art melodrama. The main contribution of *Visions and Victims* to melodrama scholarship is in defining the contours of art melodrama, a subgenre and critical category within the melodramatic mode to help explain how the bodies

and big feelings in Dreyer's work coexist with the cerebral, estranging styliza-
tions and reflection. As a critical category, art melodrama is a dramatic form
that focuses on dramatizing expressivity and reflexivity more explicitly than
other generic iterations of the melodramatic mode—although it also draws
subgenres like the domestic melodrama into its orbit. As we've seen in moments of extreme corporeality in Dreyer's films, art melodrama can push pathos to its sadistic and masochistic extremes. The ways in which art melodrama frames bodies in extremis prompts spectators to feel corresponding
forms of extremis in their own bodies, while also prompting reflection on
representation itself in ways that inhibit identification with the fiction. Crucially, art melodrama allows us to expand what we imagine when we think of
cinematic reflexivity by also including extreme affects as they have been pejo-
ratively associated with feminized, infantilized, or queer bodies: embodied
awareness and sympathy for others conveyed through shock, pain, and emotional intensities such as anger, grief, confusion, and elation. Art melodrama
also expands reflexivity through its intermediality. Dreyer's art melodrama
draws attention to cinema as a medium by juxtaposing it with theater, the
pictorial arts, music, literature, and print media, among other forms of aesthetic representation.

Dreyer's capacity to convey heartfelt affect and sentiment comes across subtly in the preface, but as I have sought to convey in this book, it comes across
forcefully in Dreyer's films. *Visions and Victims* has questioned Dreyer's reputation as a reserved, intense, and demure filmmaker, arguing that he in fact made
films that pay significant attention to conveying emotions and corporeality—
the hearts of others. More pointedly, as a feminist project, *Visions and Victims*
has challenged the implicit gender bias undergirding Dreyer's received reception as a director. A great deal of earlier scholarship on Dreyer actively resisted
using the term "melodrama" to talk about Dreyer's persistent representations of
pathos because of the term's association with genres deemed feminine. In terms
of spectatorship, challenging gender bias has meant challenging the notion that
a spectator of art cinema is inherently a matter of masculine critical distance,
while being a spectator of melodrama entails feminization, or the effusive
overidentification with, and relinquishing of, critical control of the self in consuming the fictional world. Dreyer's art melodrama demands that spectators
both think and feel, expanding what reflexivity and medium consciousness
look like. Art melodrama helps name an array of traditionally feminized elements operating in a traditionally masculinized form and vice versa.

Visions and Victims has also shown that Dreyer's work exhibited a persistent
engagement with performance, acting, and the theater even as he actively
distanced his film work from such influences. Dreyer and Neergaard, for

instance, discussed Stanislavsky over their meals in Paris, where Neergaard set Dreyer straight when Dreyer expressed the opinion that the extensive process of acting was "exaggerated and somewhat affected."[5] Dreyer's work also reveals art melodrama to be deeply invested in the intellectual, inherently reflective thrills of performance, particularly to the extent that it interrogates the tensions between the live performance of actors and the traces of their performance on film. Suffering is one example of Dreyer's many representations of the body in extremis that involved exerting pressure on the performing bodies of his actors. Other examples, including scenes of birthing, death, madness, and hysteria, abound in Dreyer's work. Dreyer's art melodrama exploits such performance situations and their combinations of *embodiment*—the body as functioning as a tangible or visible form of an idea, quality, feeling, or character—and *corporeality*, relating to the physical, acting, material body (that is, in contrast to the spirit). Exploring liveness, which also resonates with performance studies, allows Dreyer to explore the ontological specificities of film as a medium as well as its aesthetics. Dreyer could disparage live performance as theatrical, melodramatic, and inauthentic in the same breath that he imbued the photographic medium of film with a privileged ontological access to reality. But this underplays his persistent investments in exploring live performance and the way that this liveness is transferred or altered through the process of capturing it on film. The materiality of the performing body functions as a site of pathos or thrill that is intertwined with ontological and epistemological inquiry. Feeling, imagining, and thinking about the broader circumstances underlying scenes of peril or suffering automatically raises questions about the ethics of capturing, aestheticizing, and consuming such experience on film. Seen more broadly, Dreyer's art melodrama achieves its full expression in the embodied performativity of the tensions between art cinema and melodrama. *Visions and Victims* has shown that while Dreyer's work has not typically been regarded as experimenting with performance and performing bodies, it ought to be.

Part of the pressure Dreyer felt to distinguish film from theater derives from the teleological understanding of film's development that he had internalized. Dreyer's preface to Neergaard illuminates this as well when he remarks that Falconetti's performance is all the more incredible because it came about in a moment when film had not yet "freed itself from the theatre," implying the coming of some future moment when cinema will have developed away from its theatrical past.[6] Part of the queer intervention of *Visions and Victims* is to read imaginatively against this normative teleology to position Dreyer's film work as imagining low with high, old with new, early with late in diverse ways. This is to reconsider the teleological origin story that undergirds Dreyer's development as a director as having been instigated by a decisive break with Nordisk melodrama. *Visions and Victims* has read Dreyer's major films as, instead, reflecting his attraction-repulsion to the titillating and controversial Danish film melodrama in which he was immersed early in his career at Nordisk. This has meant exploring the intriguing continuities between Dreyer's Nordisk scripts and his "mature" films as well as their differences. Another part of this intervention involves acknowledging that the melodramatic imagination operating at Nordisk was more intriguing than is often held. *Visions and Victims* has argued that early Danish cinema was already exploring art melodrama and traced this to the aesthetic, ontological, and epistemological inquiry into the body prevalent at the time, what Mark Sandberg has called effigy culture. This historical revision of Dreyer's career trajectory has implications for unsettling the narrative of cinema's development from the silent era into the present, by which Danish film history is understood to have moved from primitive to advanced, childish to mature. Reframing Dreyer as one of the key figures of both Danish cinema and the canon of European art cinema, as being as invested in melodramatic practices as in art cinema ones, goes hand in hand with showing early Danish melodrama to be more media reflexive, ambiguous, expressive, and artistic than previously thought.

Visions and Victims has also sought to open avenues for further research. In exploring the way that Dreyer's attraction to melodrama remains performatively intertwined with bad feelings and negative affect evocative of queer shame, I have theorized art melodrama in relation to conversations about queer historiography and affect, but there is much more that could be said about these connections given that these scholarly discussions in queer theory are extensive. *Visions and Victims* has only scratched the surface. Similarly, *Visions and Victims* has examined how melodrama's stigma impacted Dreyer's work, by looking at how the term functioned rhetorically to construct Dreyer's historical persona. This opens the door for further exploration of how melodrama as a term of lowbrow othering might also function as the slot substitution for racialized Others. A subtext in my book, which I hope will lead to more research on Dreyer's corpus and beyond, is that the term "melodrama" functions discursively as an umbrella category or slot substitution for other Others, for instance, queer or racialized subjectivities. The discourse of taming, disciplining, or otherwise eradicating melodramatic excesses runs problematically adjacent to discourse on racial and ethnic purity. My hope is that thinking of melodrama as a category by which nonnormative ways of being in the world have been openly disparaged will contribute to critical discussions about how notions of purity, sincerity, and authenticity employed to canonize figures of European art cinema, like Dreyer, are also imbricated with constructions of whiteness, and white supremacy. Again, there is much more important work to be done.

My primary encounter with Dreyer's work was through his personal archive and collection, which sparked my ideas about how his art melodrama emerges through affective engagement with his own oeuvre as a personal archive. *Visions and Victims* activates a process of viewing and reading that parallels the way that Dreyer's early work at Nordisk functions as a reservoir of past textual encounters for him to grapple with as he creates his later work. Dreyer's film work extends the reach of the melodramatic mode—into the (research) archive itself. Dreyer's research archive and practices have been enlisted to bolster his reputation for extreme realism and authenticity. *Visions and Victims* shows the archive to be a creatively performative space as well—making the textual archive also space of intellectual thrills, ambivalent bodies, and melodrama. I am excited about the possibilities that this approach might contribute to questions of aesthetic and affective performance related to the archive. Dreyer's art melodrama achieves its full expression in the embodied performativity of the tensions between art cinema and melodrama. Reading Dreyer's career and work as archive, I argue, becomes a valuable methodological approach to thinking about melodrama and art cinema differently.

Visions and Victims has explored art melodrama in the particular context of Dreyer and Danish melodrama in hopes of providing another conceptual tool to talk not only about European art cinema auteurs like Pedro Almodóvar, Michael Haneke, and Lars von Trier as melodrama auteurs but also to inspire scholarship on the productive tensions between emotion and reflection in film histories around the world. Dreyer's archive provides a stepping-off point for further research into moments in which mass culture and high culture become intimately—if not always harmoniously—entwined. *Visions and Victims* thus contributes to scholarly conversations on both melodrama and art cinema that are intent on generating new personal and institutional histories, conceptualizations of cinema spectatorship, questions about national versus international film cultures, and interest in film form more expansively. The hope is that *Visions and Victims* might function as a model for reexamining historical trajectories of film in contexts well beyond Denmark and Europe.

Returning to Dreyer's preface, I want to end with the possibility of reading Dreyer's intriguing scene of watching Falconetti watching herself on screen as embodying something of art melodrama's affective complexity. I imagine it as a moment of intense identification for both Falconetti and Dreyer—with multiple narcissistic circuits happening at once. I imagine Dreyer captivated by the miraculous conflict going on within and outside of Falconetti. I also imagine Falconetti experiencing the moment in a more conflicted, a less idealized way—perhaps through her body, deeply fatigued after a late night on stage followed by an early morning on set. Instead of fully banishing Falconetti's boulevard performance from his mind, it is the lens through which Dreyer watches Falconetti watching her transformation as *Jeanne d'Arc* on screen. He again puts oppositions into productive tension, projecting his attraction-repulsion onto Falconetti's stage acting life. Like Falconetti, Dreyer, too, carries his "opposite nature," both positive and negative, within him. Falconetti acts out melodrama but carries an otherworldly "real" Jeanne with her; Dreyer acts out realized mysticism while carrying the melodrama of boulevard theater within him. The scene elaborates art melodrama's combination of art cinema and melodrama as a productively hybrid and tense one. Its energy derives from the various ways it integrates sensibilities commonly deemed to be binary opposites of one another: popular and elite, mainstream and independent, obvious and ambiguous, feminine and masculine, passive and active. Art melodrama articulates the discursive space of high culture within low, and low culture within high. It's only a short step to seeing Dreyer's melodrama or Nordisk or both as part of the "opposite nature" working within him, animating his work, already within him, in ways that he was not always able to recognize or acknowledge.

Appendix
Carl Th. Dreyer's Filmography

Dreyer's full filmography, including a wealth of digitalized materials, is available online through *Carl Th. Dreyer—Liv og Værk* (*Carl Th. Dreyer—The Man and His Work*), http://www.carlthdreyer.dhk/Filmene.aspx. Scripts are listed here in chronological order. The title in quotes is the working title written on the script. The number following indicates the catalog number corresponding to each film and script designated by the Nordisk Films Collection housed at the Danish Film Institute. Most of the programs for these films are digitalized and available online through *Filmdatabasen*, the National Database of Danish Film, https://www.dfi.dk/viden-om-film/filmdatabasen.

Early Scripts

Bryggerens Datter (*Dagmar* [UK]) (Rasmus Ottesen, Denmark, 1912). No longer extant.

Dødsridtet (*The Leap to Death* [UK]) (Rasmus Ottesen, Denmark, 1912). No longer extant.

Balloneksplosionen (*The Hidden Message* [UK]) (Kay van der Aa Kühle, Denmark, 1913). No longer extant.

Chatollets Hemmelighed (*The Secret of the Bureau* [UK]) (Hjalmar Davidsen, Denmark, 1913). "Chatollets Hemmelighed," Nordisk Collection, DFI, 164b.

"Döden Forener" (Death Unites). Dreyer's script sent to the Swedish Film Institute ca. 1913.

Elskovs Opfindsomhed (Love's Ingenuity, Sofus Wolder, Denmark, 1913). "Hans og Grethe," Nordisk Collection, DFI, 1062.

Krigskorrespondenter (*War Correspondents* [UK]) (Vilhelm Glückstadt, Denmark, 1913). No longer extant.

Juvelerernes Skræk (*The Skeleton Hand* [UK]) (Alexander Christian, Denmark, 1915). "Skelethaanden," Nordisk Collection, DFI, 1335.

Ned med Vaabnene! (*Lay Down Your Arms!* [UK/US]) (Holger-Madsen, Denmark, 1915). "Ned med Vaabnene," Nordisk Collection, DFI, 1163a.

Den Hvide Djævel (*The Devil's Protegé* [UK]) (Holger-Madsen, Denmark, 1916). "Esther," Nordisk Collection, DFI, 1352a.

Den Skønne Evelyn (*Evelyn the Beautiful* [UK]) (A. W. Sandberg, Denmark, 1916). "Den Skønne Evelyn," Nordisk Collection, DFI, 1371b.

En Forbryders Liv og Levned (*A Criminal's Diary* [UK]) (Alexander Christian, Denmark, 1916). "En Forbryders Memoirer," Nordisk Collection, DFI, 1366b.

Guldets Gift (*The Temptation of Mrs. Chestney* [UK]) (Holger-Madsen, Denmark, 1916). "Lerhjertet," Nordisk Collection, DFI, 1405.

Pavillonens Hemmelighed (*The Mystery of the Crown Jewels* [UK]) (Karl Mantzius, Denmark, 1916). "Guldkuglen," Nordisk Collection, DFI, 1200.

Penge (*Money* [UK]) (Karl Mantzius, Denmark, 1916), "Penge," Nordisk Collection, DFI, 1236b.

Rovedderkoppen (*The Spider's Prey* [UK]) (August Blom, Denmark, 1916). "Den Røde Enke," Nordisk Collection, DFI, 1350.

Den Mystiske Selskabsdame (*The Mysterious Companion* [UK]) (August Blom, Denmark, 1917). "Legationens Gidsel," Nordisk Collection, DFI, 1488a.

Fange Nr. 113 (*Convict No. 113* [UK]) (Holger-Madsen, Denmark, 1917). "Fange No. 113," Nordisk Collection, DFI, 1551.

Glædens Dag (*Misjudgement* [UK]) (Alexander Christian, Denmark, 1917). "Miskendt," Nordisk Collection, DFI, 1595a.

Hans Rigtige Kone (*Which Is Which?* [UK]) (Holger-Madsen, Denmark, 1917). "Hans Rigtige Kone," Nordisk Collection, DFI, 1591.

Herregaards-Mysteriet (*The Hands* [UK]) (Alexander Christian, Denmark, 1917). "Hænderne," Nordisk Collection, DFI, 1557.

Hotel Paradis (*Hotel "Paradise"* [UK]) (Robert Dinesen, Denmark, 1917), "Hotel Paradis," Nordisk Collection, DFI, 1621.

Lydia (*The Music-hall Star* [UK]) (Holger-Madsen, Denmark, 1918). "Lydia," Nordisk Collection, DFI, 1479c.

Gillekop (August Blom, Denmark, 1919). "Gillekop," Nordisk Collection, DFI, 1509c.

Grevindens Ære (*Lace* [UK]) (August Blom, Denmark, 1919). "Kniplinger," Nordisk Collection, DFI, 1732b.

Films Directed

Præsidenten (*The President*, Carl Th. Dreyer, Denmark, 1919)

Blade af Satans Bog (*Leaves from Satan's Book*, Carl Th. Dreyer, Denmark, 1921)

Prästänkan (*The Parson's Widow*, Carl Th. Dreyer, Sweden, 1921)

Die Gezeichneten (*Love One Another*, Carl Th. Dreyer, Germany, 1922)

Der var engang (*Once Upon a Time*, Carl Th. Dreyer, Denmark, 1922)

Michael (*Michael*, Carl Th. Dreyer, Germany, 1924)

Du skal ære din Hustru (*Master of the House*, Carl Th. Dreyer, Denmark, 1925)

Glomdalsbruden (*The Bride of Glomdal*, Carl Th. Dreyer, Norway, 1926)

La Passion de Jeanne d'Arc (*The Passion of Joan of Arc*, Carl Th. Dreyer, France, 1928)

Vampyr (Carl Th. Dreyer, France/Germany, 1932)

Mødrehjælpen (*Good Mothers*, Carl Th. Dreyer, Denmark, 1942)

Vredens Dag (*Day of Wrath*, Carl Th. Dreyer, Denmark, 1943)

Två människor (*Two People*, Carl Th. Dreyer, Sweden, 1945)

Vandet paa Landet (*Water from the Land*, Carl Th. Dreyer, Denmark, 1946)
Landsbykirken (*The Danish Village Church*, Carl Th. Dreyer, Denmark, 1947)
Kampen mod Kræften (*The Fight against Cancer*, Carl Th. Dreyer, Denmark, 1947)
De nåede færgen (*They Caught the Ferry*, Carl Th. Dreyer, Denmark, 1948)
Thorvaldsen (Carl Th. Dreyer, Denmark, 1949)
Storstrømsbroen (*The Storstrøm Bridge*, Carl Th. Dreyer, Denmark, 1950)
Et slot i et slot (*A Castle within a Castle*, Carl Th. Dreyer, Denmark, 1954)
Ordet (Carl Th. Dreyer, Denmark, 1955)
Gertrud (Carl Th. Dreyer, Denmark, 1964)

Nordisk *Offer* (Victim/Sacrifice) Films and Scripts

Lægens Offer (The doctor's victim/sacrifice, director unknown, 1909), Nordisk Collection, DFI, 541. No extant scenario.

Paul Wangs Skæbne (Paul Wang's destiny; alternative title: *Storbyens Offer*/The victim of the big city, Viggo Larsen, 1909), Nordisk Collection, DFI, 492. No extant script.

Massøsens Offer (To save a son, Alfred Lind, 1910). No extant scenario.

Krigens Ofre (Victims of war, director unknown). No extant scenario.

Mormonens Offer (*A Victim of the Mormons*, August Blom, 1911). "Offeret" (The victim/sacrifice), Nordisk Collection, DFI, 843c.

Shanghai'et (alternative title: *Mænd som Ofre for Slavehandel*/Men as victims of the slave trade, Eduard Schnedler-Sørensen, 1912). "Shanghai'et" (Shanghaied), Nordisk Collection, DFI, 920b.c.

Barfodsdanserindens Offer (The victim/sacrifice of the barefoot dancer, director unknown, 1912). No extant script.

Strejken paa den gamle Fabrik (The strike at the old factory; alternative distribution titles in the UK: *The Sacrifice*, *His Sacrifice*, Robert Dinesen, 1913), Nordisk Collection, DFI, 987. No extant script.

Princesse Elena (*The Princess's Dilemma*; alternative distribution title in Germany: *Opfer einer hohen Frau*, Holger-Madsen, 1913). "Princesse Elena" (Princess Elena), Nordisk Collection, DFI, 1073.

Privatdetektivens Offer (Sofus Wolder, 1913). "Privatdetektivens Offer" (The private detective's victim/sacrifice), Nordisk Collection, DFI, 1045.

Moderen (The mother; alternative distribution title in the UK: *A Mother's Sacrifice*, Robert Dinesen, 1914). "Moderen" (The Mother), Nordisk Collection, DFI, 1079.

Et Kærlighedsoffer (A victim/sacrifice of love, *I Shall Revenge*, Robert Dinesen, 1914). "Kærlighedens Offer" (Love's sacrifice), Nordisk Collection, DFI, 1129.

En Skæbne (alternative title: *Den hvide Slavehandels sidste Offer*/The white slave-trade's last victim, Robert Dinesen, 1915). "En Skæbne" (A destiny), Nordisk Collection, DFI, 1249b.

Hvor Sorgerne glemmes (Where sorrows are forgotten, Holger-Madsen, 1916). "Søster Cecilies offer" (Sister Cecilie's sacrifice), Nordisk Collection, DFI, 1389.

Børsens Offer (The victim of the stock exchange, Alexander Christian, 1916). "Børsen" (The stock exchange), Nordisk Collection, DFI, 1312d.

Kornspekulantens Forbrydelse (The crime of the speculative grain trader; alternative title: *Kornspekulantens Offer*/The victim of the speculative grain trader, Robert Dinesen, 1916). "De To Verdener" (The two worlds), Nordisk Collection, DFI, 1334c.

Viljeløs Kærlighed (Involuntary love; alternative distribution title in the UK: *Hypnotist's Victims*, Hjalmar Davidsen, 1916). "En fremmed Vilje" (A foreign will), Nordisk Collection, DFI, 1385b.

Selskabsdamen (The companion, Martinius Nielsen, 1916). "En Kvindes Offer" (A woman's sacrifice), Nordisk Collection, DFI, 1395b.

Stakkels Meta (alternative distribution title in the UK: *Cora's Sacrifice*, Martinius Nielsen, 1916). "Stakkels Meta" (Poor Meta), Nordisk Collection, DFI, 1409b.

Livets Genvordigheder (Life's hardships; alternative distribution title in the UK: *The Bowl of Sacrifice*, Alexander Christian, 1916). "I Kamp med Skæbnen" (Battling with destiny), Nordisk Collection, DFI, 1460.

Mand mod Mand (Man against man, Alexander Christian, 1917). "Offer for sin egen Hævn" (Victim of his own revenge), Nordisk Collection, DFI, 1481b.

Krigens Fjende (*The Munition Conspiracy*, Holger-Madsen, 1917). "Acostatets første Offer" (The first victim/sacrifice of the acostate [*sic*]), Nordisk Collection, DFI, 1367a.

Notes

Introduction

1. Hilde Doolittle, "The Passion of Joan of Arc," in *American Movie Critics: An Anthology from the Silents until Now*, ed. Phillip Lopate, Library of America (New York: Library of America, 2006), 39.

2. Doolittle, "Joan of Arc," 39.

3. Doolittle, "Joan of Arc," 41.

4. Doolittle, "Joan of Arc," 39.

5. As I return to presently, "impurity" is the term Rosalind Galt and Karl Schoonover use to delineate art cinema as a complex and ambiguous discursive space in their volume *Global Art Cinema: New Theories and Histories* (New York: Oxford University Press, 2010), 6.

6. This is in the vein of Miriam Hansen's theorization of cinema as vernacular modernism or David Andrews's discussion of the "high zones" within disparaged genres like soft core pornographic cinema. See Miriam Hansen, "The Mass Production of the Senses: Classical Cinema as Vernacular Modernism," *Modernism/Modernity* 6, no. 2 (1999): 59–77; David Andrews, "Toward an Inclusive, Exclusive Approach to Art Cinema," in *Global Art Cinema*, New Theories and Histories (New York: Oxford University Press, 2010), 62–74.

7. For a discussion of the interrelation of pathos, victimization, and "lower" forms historically associated with the feminine, see Mary Ann Doane, "Pathos and Pathology: The Cinema of Todd Haynes," *Camera Obscura* 19, no. 57 (2004): 1–20.

8. Scholars now see melodrama as a pervasive cultural mode that encompasses distinct signifying practices and interpretive codes for meaning-making, which informs numerous genres and is present in a wide array of aesthetic media, including theater, music, literature, the pictorial arts, silent film, sound film, and television as well as politics and psychology. The melodramatic mode, as it has been theorized by scholars Linda Williams and Christine Gledhill among others, typically includes images of virtuous suffering (often, but not exclusively, of female characters) and expresses characters' interiority through the language of embodiment and gesture (ranging from the intimacy of a teardrop to large-scale spectacles). Formally, it incorporates an array of narrative devices designed to generate emotion, including peripetia (reversals),

anagnorisis (recognition), coincidence (fate), *coup-de-théâtre, scènes-à-faire* (explosive climaxes). Typically, the protagonists' feelings, rather than narrative logic, drive the drama. The veritable explosion of melodrama scholarship in the academy that began in the 1960s and 1970s continues to expand melodrama's global as well as semantic and conceptual reach. The collection *Melodrama after the Tears* (2016), edited by Scott Loren and Jörg Mettelmann, for instance, explores melodrama as imbricated in a much broader politics of victimhood, which raises questions ranging from race and colorism to the Holocaust and contemporary notions of self-formation. See Scott Loren and Jörg Metelmann, *Melodrama after the Tears: New Perspectives on the Politics of Victimhood* (Amsterdam: Amsterdam University Press, 2016).

9. Peter Brooks, *The Melodramatic Imagination: Balzac, Henry James, Melodrama, and the Mode of Excess* (1976; repr., New Haven, CT: Yale University Press, 1995). See, for example, Richard Murphy's chapter "The Poetics of Hysteria: Expressionist Drama and the Melodramatic Imagination," in *Theorizing the Avant-Garde: Modernism, Expressionism, and the Problem of Postmodernity* (Cambridge: Cambridge University Press, 1999), 142–79.

10. Thomas Elsaesser, "Tales of Sound and Fury: Observations on the Family Melodrama," in *Imitations of Life: A Reader on Film & Television Melodrama*, ed. Marcia Landy (Detroit: Wayne State University Press, 1992), 68–91, originally published in *Monogram*, no. 4 (1972): 2–15. Sirk, drawing on his background in Brechtian theater practice, played a significant role in retrospectively positioning these films as ideological critique. See Douglas Sirk, *Sirk on Sirk: Interviews with Jon Halliday*, Cinema One 18 (London: Secker and Warburg for the British Film Institute, 1971). See also Barbara Klinger, *Melodrama and Meaning: History, Culture, and the Films of Douglas Sirk* (Bloomington: Indiana University Press, 1994).

11. Linda Williams, "Melodrama Revised," in *Refiguring American Film Genres: History and Theory*, ed. Nick Browne (Berkeley: University of California Press, 2000), 45.

12. See, for instance, Brigitte Peucker, "Violence and Affect: Haneke's Modernist Melodramas," in *The Material Image: Art and the Real in Film* (Stanford, CA: Stanford University Press, 2007), 130–58. In addition to new extremism in European cinema, there are several "other traditions" that I don't explicitly discuss in the book but that might be fruitful to explore in relation to art melodrama, including, in the US, the postwar queer avantgarde cinema and, a few decades later, the new queer cinema, both of which draw on melodramatic tropes.

13. Galt and Schoonover, *Global Art Cinema*, 8. Galt and Schoonover also argue that art cinema designates an impure spectator address that combines high and low. Early "foreign" art film in the postwar period, for instance, was often consumed by spectators enjoying its camp and its relatively risqué depictions of sexuality as well as its artfulness.

14. See Barbara Klinger, "The Art Film, Affect and the Female Viewer: *The Piano* Revisited," *Screen* 47, no. 1 (2006): 19–41; John David Rhodes, "Art Cinema's Immaterial Labors," *Diacritics* 46, no. 4 (2018): 96–116.

15. This parallels the revisionist trajectory of melodrama studies represented in Christine Gledhill and Linda Williams, *Melodrama Unbound: Across History, Media, and National Cultures*, Film and Culture (New York: Columbia University Press, 2018). Gledhill and Williams track sweeping aesthetic shifts in the meaning of the term while

also attempting "to historicize melodrama in relation to its past intermedial forms and diverse cultural contexts." Gledhill and Williams, *Unbound*, 2. Similarly, David Andrews defines art cinema broadly as combining ideas of quality, authorship, and anti-commercialism. See David Andrews, *Theorizing Art Cinemas: Foreign, Cult, Avant-Garde, and Beyond* (Austin: University of Texas Press, 2013).

16. Andrews, "Toward an Inclusive, Exclusive Approach to Art Cinema," 64. *Visions and Victims* is fully invested in the paradoxical project that Andrews describes as redefining art cinema "in a contextual, value-neutral way so that it is truly inclusive, capable of covering all permutations, past and present." This revised theory, he argues, "does not dismiss the genre's old myths and ideals, for these mystifications are basic to the genre's commercial perseverance" (64). For a book-length expansion of art cinema, see Andrews, *Theorizing Art Cinemas*.

17. For a theorization of melodrama as between realism and modernism, see Christine Gledhill, "Christine Gledhill on 'Stella Dallas' and Feminist Film Theory," *Cinema Journal* 25, no. 4 (1986): 45. For a discussion of the recuperation of early cinema by the avant-garde, see Tom Gunning, "The Cinema of Attraction[s]: Early Film, Its Spectator and the Avant-Garde," in *The Cinema of Attractions Reloaded*, ed. Wanda Strauven (Amsterdam: Amsterdam University Press, 2006), 381–88. For a discussion of Scandinavian genre and art film hybrids as "medium concept" films, see Andrew K. Nestingen, *Crime and Fantasy in Scandinavia: Fiction, Film and Social Change*, New Directions in Scandinavian Studies (Seattle: University of Washington Press; Copenhagen: Museum Tusculanum Press, University of Copenhagen, 2008).

18. A few notable exceptions include Benjamin Kohlmann's discussion of Bertolt Brecht and melodrama in "Awkward Moments: Melodrama, Modernism, and the Politics of Affect," *PMLA: Publications of the Modern Language Association of America* 128, no. 2 (2013): 337–52; and Antonin Artaud's admiration of the scale of spectacle in the romantic theater in *The Theater and Its Double*, Evergreen Original E-127 (New York: Grove Press, 1958).

19. David Bordwell, "The Art Cinema as a Mode of Film Practice," *Film Criticism* 4, no. 1 (1979): 56–64.

20. John Mercer and Martin Shingler, *Melodrama: Genre, Style and Sensibility* (New York: Columbia University Press, 2013), 96–97. The other traditions outside of Hollywood they discuss are popular Hindi or "Bollywood" cinema and Chinese cinema from the People's Republic of China.

21. Mercer and Shingler, *Genre, Style and Sensibility*, 97.

22. Steve Neale, "Art Cinema as Institution," *Screen (London)* 22, no. 1 (1981): 15. Dreyer's name occurs again in Neale's passage noting art cinema's perpetuation of an ideology of personal expression (i.e., the auteur) as a strategy of resistance that sets it apart from mainstream commercial cinema. "And hence at a broader cultural level, the overwhelming association of Art Cinema as a whole with a set of individual names: Antonioni, Bergman, Bertolucci, Bresson, Buñuel, Chabrol, Dreyer, Fassbinder, Fellini, Herzog, Truffaut, Visconti, Wenders, etc." Neale, "Art Cinema as Institution," 36.

23. For the most comprehensive and authoritative collection of materials about Dreyer's life and work, see the Danish Film Institute's website: "Carl Th. Dreyer," https://www.carlthdreyer.dk/en/carlthdreyer.

24. For a discussion of the reception of *Day of Wrath* as it was released in occupied Denmark, see Casper Tybjerg, "Helvedesildens genskær: Allegori og frigørelsevilje i besættelsetidens film," *Kosmorama* 233 (Summer 2004): 93–115.

25. Dreyer's films are often understood as intended for initiated audiences who bring a critical distance to their viewing experience, spectators who consume film in order to be edified rather than entertained. As the British Film Institute writes in its introduction to Dreyer's work, "Dreyer stripped away everything he saw as superfluous to his goal [of achieving psychological realism], resulting in an abstract, minimalist aesthetic which often breaks with the rules of conventional filmmaking. It's no wonder his work can feel alienating to the uninitiated." "Where to Begin with Carl Dreyer," British Film Institute, accessed October 27, 2020, https://www2.bfi.org.uk/news-opin ion/news-bfi/features/fast-track-fandom-where-begin-carl-dreyer.

26. Richard Abel, *French Cinema: The First Wave, 1915–1929* (Princeton, NJ: Princeton University Press, 1984). This French context overlaps, in turn, with Christophe Wall-Romana's reading of avant-garde melodrama in the work of Jean Epstein. See Christophe Wall-Romana, *Jean Epstein* (Manchester: Manchester University Press, 2013).

27. Many of Dreyer's films are period pieces adapted from plays. For analysis of Dreyer as a "visionary interpreter of the thoughts of others," see Morten Egholm, *En visionær fortolker af andres tanker: Om Carl Th. Dreyers brug af litterære forlæg*, PhD diss. (Copenhagen: Det Humanistiske Fakultet, Københavns Universitet, 2009).

28. Linda Williams, *Playing the Race Card: Melodramas of Black and White from Uncle Tom to O. J. Simpson* (Princeton, NJ: Princeton University Press, 2001), 16.

29. Ebbe Neergaard, Beate Neergaard, and Vibeke Steinthal, *[En filminstruktørs arbejde.] Ebbe Neergaards bog om Dreyer, i videreført og forøget udgave ved Beate Neergaard og Vibeke Steinthal* (Copenhagen: Dansk Videnskabs Forlag, 1963), 103.

30. See, for instance, Tom Gunning, "The Horror of Opacity: The Melodrama of Sensation in the Plays of André de Lorde," in *Melodrama: Stage, Picture, Screen*, ed. Jacqueline Susan Bratton et al. (London: British Film Institute, 1994), 50–64.

31. See Laura Mulvey, "Visual Pleasure and Narrative Cinema," *Screen* 16, no. 3 (October 1, 1975): 6–18; Mary Ann Doane, *The Desire to Desire: The Woman's Film of the 1940s*, Theories of Representation and Difference (Bloomington: Indiana University Press, 1987).

32. Being essentially expressive, melodrama represents interiority through what Peter Brooks calls "an aesthetics of embodiment," likening it to hysteria, which also externalizes psychic conflict in symptoms to be deciphered. Peter Brooks, "Melodrama, Body, Revolution," in *Melodrama: Stage, Picture, Screen*, ed. Jacqueline Susan Bratton et al. (London: British Film Institute, 1994), 17.

33. In several instances, Dreyer's on-set production accounts describe how he *actually* put his actors in harm's way. In *Glomdalsbruden* (*The Bride of Glomdal*, 1926), the protagonist Tore (Einar Sissener) purportedly nearly drowned during the film's climactic action scene filmed in river rapids. And when filming *Vredens dag* (*Day of Wrath*, 1943), Dreyer reportedly left actress Anna Svierkier, who played Herlofs-Marthe, tied to a ladder as the crew ate lunch. Such moments of bodily peril have been used by scholars to consolidate Dreyer's directorial persona and his personal film stamp as a director intent on pursuing filmic realism that is assumed to be antithetical to either

popular culture or melodrama. See Jean Drum and Dale Drum, *My Only Great Passion: The Life and Films of Carl Th. Dreyer*, Filmmakers Series 68 (Lanham, MD: Scarecrow, 2000). As Ben Singer has argued, realism can be a key element of popular culture melodrama. See Ben Singer, *Melodrama and Modernity: Early Sensational Cinema and Its Contexts*, Film and Culture (New York: Columbia University Press, 2001).

34. For a psychobiographical reading of Dreyer's work and career, see Martin (Maurice) Drouzy, *Carl Th. Dreyer, født Nilsson, 3 3* (København: Gyldendal/Reitzel, 1982).

35. The idea that melodrama is incompatible with either realism or subtilty remains tenacious. To cite an emblematic example from outside film studies, Paul C. Ha, in his introduction to a 2017 art exhibition at MIT, writes that "*An Inventory of Shimmers* addresses the recent turn toward affect—variously defined as forces of encounter, sensations, even emotions. But the work shown is neither sentimental nor melodramatic; instead, it reveals affect to be a part of daily life." Paul C. Ha, "Inventory of Shimmers: Objects of Intimacy in Contemporary Art," in *An Inventory of Shimmers: Objects of Intimacy in Contemporary Art*, ed. Henriette Huldisch (Cambridge, MA: MIT List Visual Arts Center, 2017), 6. Film scholars working on melodrama have done much to redeem melodrama, but its stigma as incompatible with the nuance or critical potential of art continues to resonate.

36. Melodrama is sometimes the elephant in the room in scholarship on Dreyer. In comparing Dreyer's films to the work of Henry James, Raymond Carney draws explicitly from Peter Brooks's melodramatic reading of the author, without ever using the word "melodrama" to describe Dreyer's work. See Raymond Carney, *Speaking the Language of Desire: The Films of Carl Dreyer* (New York: Cambridge University Press, 1989).

37. Using the term "universal" here is not to imply that all suffering is the same or equivalent. Neither do I contend that the representation of young white women suffering under patriarchy might be representative of all women's experience under patriarchy. I do, however, believe that being human involves a shared vulnerability for suffering in some form. I gesture toward the universal here with the same tentative gesture that Galt and Schoonover do when they carefully retain the potential for art cinema to speak meaningfully to audiences around the globe. This involves also maintaining critical distance to the claim of art cinema's universal language of humanism to the extent that it also operates as shorthand for Eurocentrism. Dreyer's work has, of course, inspired art cinema well beyond the Danish or European context. Mexican experimental filmmaker Carlos Regadas, for instance, remade Dreyer's *Ordet* (1955) as *Stellet Licht (Silent Light)* in 2007, setting it in a Mennonite community in northern Mexico.

38. Carl Th. Dreyer, "Lidt om filmstil," in *Om filmen: Artikler og Interviews*, ed. Erik Ulrichsen (Copenhagen: Gyldendals Uglebøger, 1964), 75.

39. Doolittle, "Joan of Arc," 40.

40. Doolittle, "Joan of Arc," 41. Luis Buñuel's writing on *Jeanne d'Arc* offers another version of spectatorship that highlights the sadomasochistic potential of art melodrama. "And the humanity of the Maid of Orleans spills forth from this work of Dreyer's more than from any other performance we have seen. We all wanted to give her a little thrashing just to be able to hand her a sweet right after. Not letting her have dessert to punish her childish integrity, her transparent stubbornness—that we could

see; but why burn her? Spotted with tears, licked by flames, hair cropped short, dirty as a street urchin, she stops crying for one moment to watch pigeons alight on the church cupola. Then she dies." Luis Buñuel, *An Unspeakable Betrayal: Selected Writings of Luis Buñuel*, trans. Garrett White (Berkeley: University of California Press, 2002), 122. Drawn to images of Jeanne's suffering, Buñuel condones Jeanne's diminutive thrashing, hinting at the potential sadism enlisted to bring them forth. He also bears witness to their pathos while questioning their ultimate purpose. Buñuel created both melodrama and avant-garde films, providing another example, along with Abel Gance's work, for combining the two. Buñuel's question, "Why burn her?" gives Dreyer his own little thrashing. This capacity for eliciting strong affect and shock, incorporating reflective breaks in the diegesis, and exploring ethical boundaries is typical of Dreyer's art melodrama.

41. Doolittle, "Joan of Arc," 41.

42. Harry M. Benshoff, "The Monster and the Homosexual," in *The Dread of Difference*, 2nd ed. (Austin: University of Texas Press, 2021), 119.

43. Williams, "Melodrama Revised," 45.

44. For an overview of feminist critique of melodrama in the 1970s, see Pam Cook, "Melodrama and the Women's Picture," in *Gainsborough Melodrama*, ed. Sue Aspinall, Robert Murphy, and British Film Institute (London: British Film Institute, 1988), 248–62. Other works that contribute to the debate about the woman's film include Linda Williams, "'Something Else besides a Mother': 'Stella Dallas' and the Maternal Melodrama," in *Imitations of Life: A Reader on Film & Television Melodrama*, ed. Marcia Landy (Detroit: Wayne State University Press, 1991), 307–30; Doane, *The Desire to Desire*; Tania Modleski, "Time and Desire in the Woman's Film," *Cinema Journal* 23, no. 3 (1984): 19–30; and E. Ann Kaplan, "Mothering, Feminism and Representation: The Maternal Melodrama and the Woman's Film, 1910–1940," in *Home Is Where the Heart Is: Studies in Melodrama and the Woman's Film*, ed. Christine Gledhill (London: British Film Institute, 1987), 113–37.

45. Christine Gledhill notes the prominent role that feminist criticism plays in melodrama scholarship, writing: "The significance of feminist analysis of melodrama is not simply that it brings a 'woman's area' into critical view, but that it poses wider questions about gender and culture. At stake are the categories used to demarcate art from entertainment, the serious from the trivial, the tragic and the realist from the melodramatic— demarcations which determine how the relationship between ideology, popular culture and pleasure is conceptualised." Christine Gledhill, ed., *Home Is Where the Heart Is: Studies in Melodrama and the Woman's Film* (London: British Film Institute, 1987), 2.

46. Linda Haverty Rugg's article, "A Tradition of Torturing Women," in *A Companion to Nordic Cinema*, ed. Mette Hjort and Ursula Lindqvist (Hoboken, NJ: John Wiley & Sons, 2016), 351–69, in which Dreyer figures prominently, does just that.

47. In one sense, my work argues that there is perverse pleasure in continuing to subject oneself to what Girish Shambu in his manifesto "For a New Cinephilia" calls "the cinema of male pathology" in order to interrogate and rework it. Depending on one's ideological take, *Visions and Victims* either expands or falls outside of new cinephilia, by which "the new cinephile feels no desire to continue subjecting herself to the cinema of male pathology." See Girish Shambu, *Film Quarterly* 72, no. 3 (March 1, 2019): 34.

48. In this sense his work resembles the distanced pathos that Doane theorizes in the cinema of Todd Haynes, but whereas the strength of Haynes's cinema is his open rejection of the fear of combining intellectuality, pathos and logos, suffering and its analysis, feeling and its articulation, the body and speech, Dreyer's embrace of genre or melodrama is never openly accomplished in this way. I would definitely call Haynes's cinema art melodrama, although the mechanism by which it comes into being is different. See Doane, "Pathos and Pathology," 18.

49. See Amanda Doxtater, "Perilous Performance: Dreyer's Unity of Danger and Beauty," August 17, 2010, https://www.carlthdreyer.dk/en/carlthdreyer/about-dreyer/working-method/perilous-performance-dreyers-unity-danger-and-beauty.

50. This is a key element of Williams's argument in "Melodrama Revised." The question of vulnerability, femininity, and femme-ininity has opened up new perspectives on feminine, suffering, and the body. See, for instance, Ann Cvetkovich, *An Archive of Feelings: Trauma, Sexuality, and Lesbian Public Cultures*, Series Q (Durham, NC: Duke University Press, 2003); Anu Koivunen, Katariina Kyrölä, and Ingrid Ryberg, *The Power of Vulnerability: Mobilising Affect in Feminist, Queer and Anti-Racist Media Cultures* (Manchester: Manchester University Press, 2018); Adriana Margareta Dancus, *Exposing Vulnerability: Self-Mediation in Scandinavian Films by Women* (Bristol, UK: Intellect, 2019); and Ulrika Dahl, "Femmebodiment: Notes on Queer Feminine Shapes of Vulnerability," *Feminist Theory* 18, no. 1 (2017): 35–53.

51. Matthew Buckley, "Unbinding Melodrama," in *Melodrama Unbound: Across History, Media, and National Cultures*, ed. Christine Gledhill and Linda Williams (New York: Columbia University Press, 2018), 16.

52. Eve Kosofsky Sedgwick, "Shame, Theatricality, and Queer Performativity: Henry James's *The Art of the Novel*," in *Touching Feeling: Affect, Pedagogy, Performativity* (Durham, NC: Duke University Press, 2003), 35–65.

53. Other sources of shame include James's earlier bouts of depression and his failed ambitions to write for the theater. See Sedgwick, "Shame," 40.

54. Sedgwick, "Shame," 39.

55. "The Art Film, Affect and the Female Viewer: *The Piano* Revisited," *Screen* 47, no. 1 (Spring 2006): 20.

56. Rebecca Schneider, *Performing Remains: Art and War in Times of Theatrical Reenactment* (Florence: Taylor & Francis, 2011), 109.

57. Heather Love, *Feeling Backward: Loss and the Politics of Queer History* (Cambridge, MA: Harvard University Press, 2007).

58. For a discussion of Lars von Trier's *Dancer in the Dark* (2000) as arthouse musical in conversation with "smart" melodrama, see Charles Burnetts, *Improving Passions: Sentimental Aesthetics and American Film* (Edinburgh: Edinburgh University Press, 2017), 145–51.

59. David Bordwell, *The Films of Carl-Theodor Dreyer* (Berkeley: University of California Press, 1981), 9. Bordwell's influential monograph on Dreyer in English, *The Films of Carl-Theodor Dreyer*, and Edvin Kau's monograph in Danish, *Dreyers filmkunst* (Copenhagen: Akademisk Forlag, 1989), did much to establish Dreyer's reputation as a hyper-attuned formalist and uncompromising aesthete who imposed his own singular, auteur vision on each film project. Bordwell's reading of Dreyer, and particularly *Gertrud* (1964), has evolved over the years, as evidenced in his blog post "Dreyer

Re-Reconsidered," Observations on Film Art (blog), June 14, 2010, http://www.davidbor dwell.net/blog/2010/06/14/dreyer-re-reconsidered/.

60. Jack Halberstam, *The Queer Art of Failure* (Durham, NC: Duke University Press, 2011), 3.

Chapter 1. Reading Dreyer's Early Archive

1. She is also referred to as "The Predator Spider" in Danish Film Institute's (hereafter, DFI) translation or the Red Widow in the script. According to the *Rovedderkoppen* program, the film is a "Criminal Novel in 3 Acts and 50 Sections" (Kriminalroman i 3 Akter) by "the famous Norwegian author Stein Riverton," a pseudonym for one of Dreyer's collaborators, Sven Elvestad, who wrote the novel on which the screenplay was based. Dreyer is likely responsible for the screenplay. Thank you to Casper Tybjerg for bringing this detail to my attention. The DFI launched its website devoted to Dreyer's life and work, http://carlthdreyer.dk, in 2010. This expanded Dreyer's oeuvre to include early scripts that he wrote before he began directing films. In some cases, he is explicitly acknowledged as the writer, sometimes he receives a writer's credit, and in other cases, they are identifiable as Dreyer's because the company's records show that he received payment for writing them. When possible, I use the typed versions of scripts, particularly if they include written indications that they had actually been used during shooting. Sometimes the names of characters vary between script and program. In these cases, I refer to the character names listed in the program.

2. The scene with Valentine's hand is available in the fragmentary footage of the film digitalized on the DFI's website. "Danish Silent Film," accessed November 1, 2023, https://www.stumfilm.dk/en/stumfilm/streaming/film/rovedderkoppen.

3. Dreyer script, "Rovedderkoppen," 1, DFI Dreyer website, accessed November 1, 2023, https://www.carlthdreyer.dk/carlthdreyer/filmene/rovedderkoppen.

4. Nordisk offered the possibility of innovation within constraint in ways that resonate with Thomas Elsaesser's assessment of Douglas Sirk's melodrama in the 1950s as having benefited from the creative obstructions that the Hollywood studio system placed on it. Commercial necessities, political censorship, and the various morality codes impinging on Hollywood melodrama in the 1940s–1950s, he argues, actually benefited Sirk's melodramatic style by providing thematic parameters for artistic expression that "encouraged a conscious use of style-as-meaning, which is a mark of what I would consider to be the very condition of a modernist sensibility working in popular culture." Elsaesser, "Tales of Sound and Fury," 77.

5. The full list of genre designation in English reads: "Drama, Erotic melodrama, Crime film, Detective movies, Gangster film, Silent films." "The Spider's Prey," accessed November 1, 2023, https://www.dfi.dk/en/viden-om-film/filmdatabasen/film /rovedderkoppen?_ga=2.136688496.1596052323.1684621303-1363815405.1635963199#Ma terials.

6. Mark B. Sandberg, *Living Pictures, Missing Persons: Mannequins, Museums and Modernity* (Princeton, NJ: Princeton University Press, 2005), 5.

7. Dreyer script, "Rovedderkoppen," 33, DFI Dreyer website, accessed November 1, 2023, https://www.carlthdreyer.dk/carlthdreyer/filmene/rovedderkoppen.

8. There is also an intellectual pleasure in looking at Valentine's fingers alongside the phenomenologically laden "sensible scene" experience that Vivian Sobchack describes in

her reading of the art film *The Piano* (Jane Campion, 1993). In her canonical chapter, "What Her Fingers Knew," Sobchack reads key moments in the film as first perceivable through her own fingers. See Vivian Carol Sobchack, *Carnal Thoughts: Embodiment and Moving Image Culture* (Berkeley: University of California Press, 2004).

9. The company established a story department in 1911. For a comprehensive account of scriptwriting at Nordisk, see Stephen Michael Schröder, "Screenwriting for Nordisk 1906–1918," in *100 Years of Nordisk Film*, ed. Lisbeth Richter Larsen and Dan Nissen (Copenhagen: Danish Film Institute, 2006). Schröder also manages an extensive database of authors of Danish film scripts, accessible at http://danlitstummfilm .uni-koeln.de/.

10. Ebbe Neergaard, *Historien om dansk film* (Copenhagen: Gyldendal, 1960), 94.

11. For a comprehensive account of the company's rise to dominance and its subsequent decline, see Isak Thorsen, "Nordisk Films Kompagni 1906–1924: The Rise and Fall of the Polar Bear," in *100 Years of Nordisk Film*, ed. Lisbeth Richter Larsen and Dan Nissen (Copenhagen: Danish Film Institute, 2006), 53. For a comprehensive business history of the company, see Christian Isak Thorsen, "Isbjørnens anatomi: Nordisk Films Kompagni som erhvervsvirksomhed i perioden 1906–1928" (PhD diss., Copenhagen University, 2009); and also Isak Thorsen, "Surviving a Crisis: Nordisk Films Kompagni as a World Player," in *A History of Danish Cinema*, ed. C. Claire Thomson, Isak Thorsen, and Pei-Sze Chow (Edinburgh: Edinburgh University Press, 2021), 21–29.

12. See Stephen Michael Schröder, "Screenwriting for Nordisk, 1906–1918," in *100 Years of Nordisk Film*, ed. Lisbeth Richter Larsen and Dan Nissen (Copenhagen: Danish Film Institute, 2006), 96–113.

13. Marguerite Engberg, *Dansk stumfilm. De store år [Bind] 2* (Copenhagen: Rhodos, 1977), 439.

14. For an analysis of Nordisk's savvy ability to alter names and costumes to sell films to competing markets, including those supporting opposing sides of a war, see Casper Tybjerg, "The Spy Who Loved Me: Benjamin Christensen and the Danish Silent Spy Melodrama," *Journal of Scandinavian Cinema* 9, no. 3 (2019): 253–76.

15. See Isak Thorsen, "Filmsfabrikken i Valby," in *Dansk film i krydsfeltet mellem samarbejde og konkurrence*, ed. Chris Mathieu and Jesper Strandgaard Pedersen (Lund: Ariadne Förlag, 2009), 93–111.

16. Kau, *Dreyers filmkunst*, 38. Dreyer's retraction actually concedes that a smaller, more modest production would have more dramatic impact than an expensive epic. Kau includes the entire flurry of correspondence between Dreyer and Nordisk in the filmography. See Kau, *Dreyers filmkunst*, 392–94.

17. Isak Thorsen has since thrown light on the relationship between Dreyer and Nordisk by describing how several directors left Nordisk in the decline following World War I, a fact that likely contributed to Dreyer's getting the chance to direct in the first place, noting that Dreyer actually maintained a friendly relationship with company executives.

18. Peter Schepelern, "Danish Film History, 1910–1920," accessed May 21, 2023, https://www.dfi.dk/en/english/danish-film-history/danish-film-history-1910-1920.

19. Buckley, "Unbinding Melodrama," 16.

20. Ebbe Neergaard, *The Story of Danish Film*, trans. Elsa Gress (Copenhagen: Det Danske Selskab / The Danish Institute, 1963), 23.

21. Neergaard, *Historien*, 39. The films Neergaard analyzes as social melodrama do not actually advertise themselves as such; the program for *Evangeliemandens Liv* (*The Candle and the Moth*, Holger-Madsen, 1915), for instance, which Neergaard calls a quintessential "social melodrama," refers to it as a "folk play" (*Folkeskuespil i 3 Akter*) in three acts.

22. For a book-length analysis of practices of normalization and Othering in early Danish cinema, including questions of gender and race, see Constanze Gestrich, "Die Macht der dunklen Kammern: Die Faszination des Fremden im frühen dänischen Kino" (PhD diss., Humboldt-Universität, 2008).

23. Neergaard, *Historien*, 54.

24. Neergaard, *Historien*, 55. Neergaard associates the artfulness of Nordisk's social melodrama with the short, but wildly successful, international career of actor Valdemar Psilander, whose talents were showcased in such early artistic successes as *Evangeliemanden* (*The Candle and The Moth*, Holger-Madsen, 1915). At the same time, Neergaard uses the term "melodrama" to refer to the artistic deficiencies in *Klovnen* (*The Clown*, A.W. Sandberg, 1917), which he sees as inferior to Psilander's earlier efforts. He associates the melodramatic exaggeration of an earlier time with the presumably unrealistic clasping of one's heart or forehead or collapsing completely to express sorrow. See Neergaard, *Historien*, 53.

25. Neergaard, *Historien*, 93.

26. Ron Mottram, *The Danish Cinema before Dreyer* (Metuchen, NJ: Scarecrow, 1988), 81. Mottram characterizes Nordisk, or Danish social melodrama during the period from 1910 to 1914, as taking place mainly indoors, in realistic sets, often with actual furniture and photographed in deep focus. Often mirrors functioned to expand playing space by reflecting characters who were not directly visible in the action of the frame. Nordisk's naturalism is ultimately not enough to save the company from its decline around World War I. Mottram enlists the same teleology to argue that Nordisk's production solidified into formulas rather than developing. See Mottram, *Danish Cinema*, 213. The title of Mottram's book also reinforces the rhetoric of a break in the history of Danish cinema as well as the central role that Dreyer plays in conceptualizations of this small-nation cinema history.

27. E. Deidre Pribram, "Melodrama and the Aesthetics of Emotion," in *Melodrama Unbound: Across History, Media, and National Cultures*, ed. Christine Gledhill and Linda Williams (New York: Columbia University Press, 2018), 243–44.

28. See, for instance, the discussion of Nora's tarantella scene in *A Doll's House* in Toril Moi, *Henrik Ibsen and the Birth of Modernism: Art, Theater, Philosophy* (New York: Oxford University Press, 2006), 236–37. For an analysis of masculinity and emotion in the work of Ola Hansson, August Strindberg, and Knut Hamsun, see Anna Jörngården, *Tidens tröskel: Uppbrott och nostalgi i skandinavisk litteratur kring sekelskiftet 1900* (Höör: Brutus Östlings Bokförlag Symposion, 2012).

29. John Mercer and Martin Shingler liken elements of Ibsen and Strindberg's work to the Hollywood family melodramas of the 1950s. See Mercer and Shingler, *Genre, Style and Sensibility*, 95–96.

30. Neergaard, *Historien*, 85.

31. Neergaard, Neergaard, and Steinthal, *Bog om Dreyer*, 16.

32. For a discussion of *Terje Vigen*'s impact on the Swedish production model, see Bengt Forslund, *Victor Sjöström: His Life and His Work* (New York: New York Zoe-

trope, 1988), 54–63. Ebbe Neergaard attributes Nordisk's eventual failure to compete on the international market to its misguided attempts to internationalize its melodrama rather than highlight its Danishness. Instead of following the Swedish model, which highlighted the Swedishness of its literary material and films, according to Neergaard, Nordisk mistakenly put its efforts into a series of clumsy Danish adaptations of Dickens, and several semi-fiasco projects such as *Atlantis* (August Blom, 1913) and *Himmelskibet* (*A Trip to Mars*, Holger-Madsen, 1918). See Neergaard, *Historien*, 81–82. Of course, with the coming of sound technology, even the Swedish model eventually succumbed to competition from Hollywood. Leif Furhammar has complicated the high culture (Swedish)–low culture (Danish) binary from the Swedish perspective, arguing that the golden age of Swedish cinema, largely epitomized in scholarship by Mauritz Stiller and Victor Sjöström, was actually a more diverse, popular culture period than scholars have usually assumed. See Leif Furhammar, *Filmen i Sverige: En historia i tio kapitel och en fortsättning* (Stockholm: Dialogos Filminstitutet, 2003), 11–89.

33. I take the English phrase "Count and Countess films" from an uncredited translator of Dreyer's article in Carl Theodor Dreyer, *Dreyer in Double Reflection: Translation of Carl Th. Dreyer's Writings about the Film (Om Filmen)*, ed. Donald Skoller (New York: Da Capo Press, 1973), 22. Unless otherwise noted, all translations from Danish are my own. The public debate in Denmark about the status of its film industry, in which Dreyer was participating, boiled down to the question of whether quality or quantity would better allow Denmark to compete internationally. Nordisk's collected newspaper clippings surrounding the release of Dreyer's second and last feature film with the company, *Leaves from Satan's Book*, demonstrate a lively public newspaper discussion about whether Nordisk's artistic merits (or often its lack thereof) would allow the company to compete on the international film market. Debates about film as an art form and Dreyer's role as an artist were part of public discourse in Denmark and not limited to film industry publications. Dreyer was not the only director thought capable of being Denmark's artistic hope. A. W. Sandberg, who filmed several Dickens adaptations in the 1920s, is also considered in the same discussion.

34. Thorsen, "Rise and Fall," 56.

35. Dreyer, "Swedish Film," in *Double Reflection*, 22. Dreyer does cite Benjamin Christensen as an important exception to his widespread aspersion of early Danish film direction. Interesting also, Dreyer credits Griffith (as emblematic of American film) with advancing film technique (realism, the close-up, etc.) but at the expense of its soul. These English translations are from Dreyer, *Double Reflection*.

36. For a discussion of the impact of Swedish Golden Age films on Nordic film industries, see Casper Tybjerg, "Searching for Art's Promised Land: Nordic Silent Cinema and the Swedish Example," in *A Companion to Nordic Cinema*, ed. by Mette Hjort and Ursula Lindqvist (Hoboken, NJ: John Wiley & Sons, Inc, 2016), 271–90. While not considered a melodramatic author in her day, recent scholarship on Selma Lagerlöf has treated melodramatic aspects of her work. Lagerlöf received the Nobel Prize for Literature in 1909, suggesting that her work was both melodramatic and culturally respectable. See Elizabeth Ann DeNoma, "Multiple Melodrama: The Making and Remaking of Three Selma Lagerlöf Narratives in the Silent Era and the 1940s" (PhD diss., University of Washington, 2000).

37. Dreyer, "Svensk film," in *Double Reflection*, 19. Uncredited English translation.

38. Dreyer, "Svensk film," 23. Uncredited English translation.

39. Bordwell, *Films of Carl-Theodor Dreyer*, 24.

40. Tytti Soila, Astrid Söderbergh-Widding, and Gunnar Iversen, *Nordic National Cinemas* (New York: Routledge, 1998), 9.

41. In his monograph on Dreyer, Edvin Kau links Nordisk with melodrama in a way that leaves open the possibility that Dreyer's mastery of everything from the action of a chase seen to melodrama's "high-voltage emotion" contributed to his competence as a director. See Kau, *Dreyers filmkunst*, 17. Casper Tybjerg uses the term "melodrama" to refer to films that include a "love plot" or romantic triangle in an attempt to appeal to female spectators. See Tybjerg, "The Spy," 260.

42. See Marguerite Engberg, "The Erotic Melodrama in Danish Silent Films, 1910–1918," *Film History* 5, no. 1 (1993): 63–67. The breakthrough film was *The Abyss* (1910), starring Asta Neilsen and directed by Urban Gad, technically a film produced by Fotorama, not Nordisk, although Nordisk would end up incorporating Fotorama.

43. Engberg, *Dansk stumfilm*, 440. For a discussion about how melodramatic endings didn't suit every market, see 456.

44. Engberg, *Dansk stumfilm*, 441. The entire discussion of melodrama can be found here: Engberg, *Dansk stumfilm*, 439–64.

45. For a nuanced and insightful analysis of the complex interrelationship between national identity and the film industry in Denmark, see C. Claire Thomson, Isak Thorsen, and Pei-Sze Chow, "Introduction," in *A History of Danish Cinema*. ed. C. Claire Thomson, Isak Thorsen, and Pei-Sze Chow (Edinburgh: Edinburgh University Press, 2021), 1–18. This collection also includes a chapter by Casper Tybjerg reading Dreyer's career and its relation to national identity as "entangled history." See Casper Tybjerg, "The European Principle: Art and Border-Crossings in Carl Theodor Dreyer's Career," in *A History of Danish Cinema*, ed. C. Claire Thomson, Isak Thorsen, and Pei-Sze Chow (Edinburgh: Edinburgh University Press, 2021), 41–50.

46. Henning Carlson, "Excerpt from an Obituary of Carl Th. Dreyer," in *Carl Th. Dreyer: Danish Film Director, 1889–1968*, ed. Søren Dyssegaard, Presentation Books Ministry of Foreign Affairs (Copenhagen: Van Rasmussens Litografiske Trykkeri, 1969), 4.

47. Neergaard, *Historien*, 98.

48. Dreyer script, "Esther/Djævelens Protégé," 1, DFI Dreyer website, accessed November 1, 2023, https://www.carlthdreyer.dk/carlthdreyer/filmene/den-hvide-djaevel.

49. See P. Adams Sitney, "Moments of Revelation: Dreyer's Anachronistic Modernity," in *Modernist Montage: The Obscurity of Vision in Cinema and Literature* (New York: Columbia University Press, 1990), 53–80.

50. Dreyer, "Lidt om Filmstil," 74.

51. Sandberg, *Living Pictures*.

52. Most studies of melodrama in Scandinavia follow a similar logic and recognize melodrama as a response to the reduced (moral) legibility caused by social upheavals consequent with Scandinavia's relatively late modernization and industrialization in the latter half of the nineteenth century. Maria Karlsson situates melodrama in Selma Lagerlöf's novels as responding to modernization. See Maria Karlsson, *Känslans röst: Det melodramatiska i Selma Lagerlöfs romankonst*, Brutus Östlings bokförl (Stockholm:

Symposion, 2002). Christine Hamm reads Amalie Skram's novels and critical writings as a melodramatic response to artistic and social debates of the Modern Breakthrough. See Christine Hamm, "Medlidenhet og melodrama: Amalie Skrams litteraturkritikk og ekteskapsromaner" (PhD diss., University of Bergen, 2002). Hamm draws a further parallel between Skram's work about the changing role of women in society during this period and Stanley Cavell's genre designation, "the melodrama of the unknown woman," which references Henrik Ibsen's character Nora Helmer from *A Doll's House*—the play that opened the floodgates of Modern Breakthrough debates in Scandinavia—as an archetypical "unknown woman." I discuss Cavell's work in chapter 6.

53. For a discussion of on-set death when Dreyer visits Abel Gance's *Napoleon*, see Amanda Doxtater, "Perilous Performance: Dreyer's Unity of Danger and Beauty," August 17, 2010, https://www.carlthdreyer.dk/en/carlthdreyer/about-dreyer/working-method/perilous-performance-dreyers-unity-danger-and-beauty.

54. Sandberg, *Living Pictures*, 5.

55. Mark B. Sandberg, "Mastering the House: Performative Inhabitation in Dreyer's *The Parson's Widow*," in *Northern Constellations: New Readings in Nordic Cinema*, ed. C. Claire Thomson (Norwich, UK: Norvik Press, 2006), 23–42.

56. Stolid matriarchal characters recur throughout Dreyer's oeuvre, as formidable forces, whether the no-nonsense mother-in-law in *Master of the House* or Merete in *Day of Wrath*. Even Marguerite Chopin (Henriette Gérard), the vampire in *Vampyr*, bears a striking resemblance to these matriarchs in her bodily comportment and Lutheran clothing.

57. Sandberg, "Mastering the House," 37.

58. Schneider, *Performing Remains*, 43.

59. Quoted in Daniel Gerould, "Russian Formalist Theories of Melodrama," in *Imitations of Life: A Reader on Film & Television Melodrama*, ed. Marcia Landy (Detroit: Wayne State University Press, 1992), 129.

60. Neergaard, *Historien*, 38.

61. Christine Gledhill, "Signs of Melodrama," in *Stardom: Industry of Desire*, ed. Christine Gledhill (London: Routledge, 1991), 207–29.

62. Elizabeth Freeman, *Time Binds: Queer Temporalities, Queer Histories, Perverse Modernities* (Durham, NC: Duke University Press, 2010).

63. Tom Milne, "Carl Theodor Dreyer: The Early Works," in *Cinema: A Critical Dictionary: The Major Film-Makers*, ed. Richard Roud (New York: Viking Press, 1980), 291.

Chapter 2. *La Passion de Jeanne d'Arc*

1. Neergaard, Neergaard, and Steinthal, *Bog om Dreyer*, 51.

2. David Bordwell, *Filmguide to La Passion de Jeanne d'Arc* (Bloomington: Indiana University Press, 1973), 18.

3. Paul Moor. "The Tyrannical Dane." *Theatre Arts* (April 1951): 35–36.

4. *Lydia* was distributed as *The Music-Hall Star* (UK), as *Der Flammentanz* (Germany), and as *Trahida no amor* (Portugal), with various spellings of the name "Lydia."

5. Carl Th. Dreyer, "Swedish Film," in Dreyer in Double Reflection: Translation of Carl Th. Dreyer's Writings about the Film (Om Filmen), ed. Donald Skoller (New York: Da Capo Press, 1973), 22–23.

6. Dreyer's interest in the spectacle of sacrificial or persecuted female characters perishing by fire (*bål* in Danish) reoccurs throughout his oeuvre, both before and after *Jeanne d'Arc*. In *Day of Wrath* (1943), Herlofs-Marthe will be tied to a ladder and burnt as a witch. Anne will face the same fate. In *Leaves from Satan's Book* (1921), an episode set during the Spanish Inquisition ends as the innocent Isabella is condemned and carried out in a swoon to be burned, a scene to which the audience is not actually privy.

7. Throughout this chapter, I ascribe femininity to both Jeanne d'Arc and Falconetti's bodies. As Maxine Savage has suggested in their paper "Something Trans about the Archive: Dreyer's *Jeanne d'Arc*," given at the Committee on LGBT History Queer History Conference, 2022, there is much to be gained in trans* readings of this character and film.

8. Jeremy Maron and André Loiselle, *Stages of Reality: Theatricality in Cinema* (Toronto: University of Toronto Press, 2017), 4. In establishing this baseline definition of theatricality, Loiselle and Maron draw on work by Tracy Davis and Thomas Postlewait, Patrice Pavis, Samuel Weber, Laura Mulvey, Michael Fried, Erika Fischer-Lichte, and Roland Barthes, among others, in their introduction.

9. Maron and Loiselle, *Stages of Reality*, 4. The authors draw from work by Roland Barthes to talk about sensuous acknowledgment.

10. For a discussion of Vesterbro's development as an entertainment district for museological, theatrical, and cinematic spectatorship, see Sandberg, *Living Pictures*, 9–17. For a discussion of the European tradition of variety theater and adjacent film practices, without specific reference to Denmark, see Joseph Garncarz, "The European Fairground Cinema: (Re)Defining and (Re)Contextualizing the 'Cinema of Attractions,'" in *A Companion to Early Cinema*, ed. André Gaudreault, Nicolas Dulac, and Santiago Hidalgo (Oxford: Wiley-Blackwell, 2012), 317–33.

11. Gledhill, "On 'Stella Dallas,'" 44–48.

12. Gledhill, "On 'Stella Dallas,'" 46. In a similar vein, Peer Sørensen explores pathos and irony in Danish author Herman Bang's literary melodrama. For a discussion of Bang's novella *Mikaël* that Dreyer filmed in 1924, see Peer E. Sørensen, *Vor tids temperament: Studier i Herman Bangs forfatterskab* (Copenhagen: Gyldendal, 2009), 319–26.

13. Heide Schlüpmann, *The Uncanny Gaze: The Drama of Early German Cinema* (Urbana: University of Illinois Press, 2010), 13.

14. Heide Schlüpmann, "Asta Nielsen and Female Narration: The Early Films," in *A Second Life: German Cinema's First Decades*, ed. Thomas Elsaesser with Michael Wedel (Amsterdam: Amsterdam University Press, 1996), 119.

15. Schlüpmann, "Asta Nielsen," 119.

16. Ebbe Neergaard. *En filminstruktørs arbejde: Carl Th. Dreyer og hans ti film* (Copenhagen: Atheneum Dansk Forlag. 1940), 19.

17. As discussed in the previous chapter, Neergaard does also praise Nordisk cinema for its capacity for emotional expressivity but not its melodrama. Neergaard wrote the first history of Danish cinema. Published posthumously in 1960, the volume included a preface by Dreyer to his friend.

18. Klaus Rifbjerg, "Om Neergaard om Dreyer," *Vindrosen, Gyldendals Litterære Magasin* 11 (1964): 67.

19. Carl Th. Dreyer, "Realiseret mystik," in *Om filmen: Artikler og Interviews*, ed. Erik Ulrichsen (Copenhagen: Gyldendals Uglebøger, 1964), 31.

20. For a counterpoint to the rhetoric of makeup as disingenuous, see Alice Maurice, "Making Faces: Character and Makeup in Early Cinema," in *Corporeality in Early Cinema: Viscera, Skin, and Physical Form*, ed. Marina Dahlquist et al. (Bloomington: Indiana University Press, 2018), 206–17. Maurice discusses how facial makeup in early American cinema is disguising, additive, and transforming while also remaining an extension of the face contiguous with facial features and expression, making it a body part.

21. Carl Th. Dreyer, "Den virkelige talefilm," in *Om filmen: Artikler og Interviews*, ed. Erik Ulrichsen (Copenhagen: Gyldendals Uglebøger, 1964), 32.

22. See Dreyer, *Double Reflection*.

23. Fischer-Lichte redefines performance in terms of its phenomenology rather than hermeneutics, drawing a sharp distinction between film and performance; filming or otherwise recording performance negates it as performance. My reading of Dreyer's desire for film to be as interactive as live theater clearly blurs this distinction. See Erika Fischer-Lichte, *The Transformative Power of Performance: A New Aesthetics* (London: Routledge, 2008).

24. As I have explored elsewhere, Dreyer's interest in extreme performance included traditions of mass spectacle such as the ritualized danger and beauty of the bullfight. See Doxtater, "Perilous Performance."

25. David Bordwell, "Nordisk and the Tableau Aesthetic," in *100 Years of Nordisk Film*, ed. Lisbeth Richter Larsen and Dan Nissen (Copenhagen: Danish Film Institute, 2006), 82–83.

26. Dreyer's Nordisk script "Den skønne Evelyn" also features a very similar scene, complete with camera setups and a "Wild West" cowboy show at "Variete Grandville." Dreyer's script sets up a shot first from the point of view of the audience, and then, by means of a physical prop-bridge, the perspective is reversed and the camera is in the position of the orchestra. See Dreyer script, "Den skønne Evelyn," division/scene 35, DFI Dreyer website, accessed November 1, 2023, https://www.carlthdreyer.dk/carlth dreyer/filmene/den-skoenne-evelyn.

27. Elsewhere in *Michael*, Dreyer includes POV shots from the perspective of paintings hanging on the wall.

28. Wall-Romana, *Jean Epstein*.

29. Carl Th. Dreyer "Dreyer 1950," unpublished introduction to *Jeanne d'Arc* (Dreyer Collection, Danish Film Institute, 1950).

30. Michel Delahaye, "Entretien avec Carl Theodor Dreyer," in *La Politique des Auteurs: Les Entretiens* (Paris: Cahiers du cinema, 2001), 234.

31. Rob Edelman, "Variete," accessed July 2, 2023, http://www.filmreference.com /Films-Tw-Vi/Variete.html. As Kristen Thompson points out in her video essay, the French had been working with the "detached camera" for some time before this film. See Kristin Thompson, "Kristin Thompson on Variety (1925, dir. E. A. Dupont)," https://www.youtube.com/watch?v=X4TovIvgoVI.

32. Rob Edelman, "Variete."

33. Quoted in Gerould, "Russian Formalist Theories of Melodrama," 128–29.

34. Galt and Schoonover, *Global Art Cinema*, 6.

35. As Linda Williams writes, "Sympathy for another grounded in the manifestation of that person's suffering is arguably a key feature of all melodrama." Williams, *Playing the Race Card*, 16.

36. Dreyer script, "Esther/Djævelens Protégé," 1.

37. Neergaard, *Historien*, 126.

38. Drum and Drum, *Great Passion*, 128.

39. Dreyer, "Dreyer 1950."

40. See Fischer-Lichte, *Transformative Power*, 11–23, for a discussion of harm in work by Marina Abramović.

41. Drum and Drum, *Great Passion*, 139.

42. Singer, *Melodrama and Modernity*, 185. Nordisk also included its share of spectacularly performative stunt work, including the fantastic aerial acrobatics of Emilie Sannom.

43. I am grateful to Casey Shoop for this formulation.

44. Jean Renoir describes the experience of *Jeanne d'Arc*, and particularly the haircut scene, in terms that approach religious ritual. "This shaven head was the purity of Joan of Arc. It was her faith. . . . It was and remains the abstraction of the whole epic of Joan of Arc. What is miraculous is that this is also the case with the spectators who continue to come and purify themselves in the pure waters of Dreyer's *Joan of Arc*." Jean Renoir, "Dreyer's Sin," in *Carl Th. Dreyer: Danish Film Director, 1889–1968*, ed. Søren Dyssegaard (Presentation Books Ministry of Foreign Affairs, Copenhagen: Van Rasmussens Litografiske Trykkeri, 1969), 45.

45. Bodil Thomsen and David Bordwell have each read *Jeanne d'Arc*'s naked physiognomy, conveyed particularly in close-up, as evidence that it is not melodrama. For Thomsen, the film becomes "real," haptic flesh, which she sees as antithetical to melodrama. For Bordwell, the film's corporeality is trumped by psychology of an order that is incommensurate with melodrama's corporeal legibility and narrative goals. For Charles Affron, as well, the naturalism of the close-up is automatically incompatible with melodramatic type. See Bodil Marie Thomsen, "On the Transmigration of Images: Flesh, Spirit and Haptic Vision in Dreyer's *Jeanne d'Arc* and von Trier's Golden Heart Trilogy," in *Northern Constellations: New Readings in Nordic Cinema*, ed. C. Claire Thomson (Norwich, UK: Norvik Press, 2006), 43–47; Bordwell, *Films of Carl-Theodor Dreyer*; Charles Affron, *Cinema and Sentiment* (Chicago: University of Chicago Press, 1982).

46. Bordwell, *Filmguide*, 19.

47. Schneider, *Performing Remains*, 14.

48. Buñuel, "Carl Dreyer's The Passion of Joan of Arc (1928)," in *An Unspeakable Betrayal*, 122.

Chapter 3. *Vampyr*

1. "Carmilla" is one of four short stories in volume 3 of the 1872 collection *In a Glass Darkly*. See a subsequent edition, Joseph Sheridan Le Fanu, *In a Glass Darkly* (London: R. Bentley and Son, 1897), 358–467. Johannes Weber reads *Vampyr* as actually drawing from several of the stories, including "The Room in the Dragon Volant"—which includes a scene in which a man meets his corpse. See Johannes Weber, "'Doctor! I'm losing blood!' 'Nonsense! Your blood is right here': The Vampirism of Carl

Theodor Dreyer's Film *Vampyr*," in *Vampires and Zombies*, ed. Dorothea Fischer-Hornung and Monika Meuller (Jackson: University Press of Mississippi, 2016), 192.

2. Weber, "Your blood," 195.

3. Weber, "Your blood," 195. He goes on to say that Chopin needs a cane and has to be supported by the doctor. The most recognizable vampire element of the story is her final staking and her metamorphosis from fresh corpse to skeleton.

4. Allan Gray is called David Gray in the French version.

5. Williams, *Playing the Race Card*, 15.

6. See Elsaesser, "Tales of Sound and Fury," 68–91; Loren and Metelmann, *Melodrama after the Tears*.

7. These include *Den Hvide Slavehandels Sidste Offer* (The White Slave Trade's Last Victim/Sacrifice in the hands of impostors [No. 2], August Blom, 1911), *Barfodsdanserindens Offer* (The Barefoot Dancer's Victim/Sacrifice, not distributed internationally, director unknown, 1912), *Børsens Offer* (The Victim of the Stock Exchange, Alexander Christian, 1912), *Privatdetektivens Offer* (The Private Detective's Victim/Sacrifice, Sophus Wolder, 1913), *Hvor Sorgerne Glemmes* (*Søster Cecilies Offer/Sister Cecilia/*Sister Cecilie's Victim/Sacrifice, Holger-Madsen, 1915), *Kornspekulantens Forbrydelse* (*Kornspekulantens Offer/*The Victim of The Speculative Grain Trader, Robert Dinesen, 1916), and *En Kvindes Offer* (A Woman's Victim/Sacrifice, Martinius Nielsen, 1916). Apart from one "Fi and Bi film" (a Danish Laurel and Hardy duo) from 1924, potentially a parody of Nordisk melodrama, all the *Offer* films I found were made between 1910 and 1916. The Fi and Bi film is called *Ole Opfinders Offer* (Lau Lauritzen, Denmark, 1924). No program, script, or stills exist for this film, only posters held in the DFI's Stills and Posters Archive.

8. Program for *Mormonens Offer*, DFI.

9. Robert Bechtold Heilman, *The Iceman, the Arsonist, and the Troubled Agent; Tragedy and Melodrama on the Modern Stage* (Seattle: University of Washington Press, 1973), 57.

10. Heilman also argues that melodramatic and tragic modes are often combined in various configurations, sometimes as if the two struggle against one another rather than having tragedy replace melodrama as a presumably more sophisticated form. Consider, for instance, that "the tragedy of Oedipus is the melodrama of Thebes." Heilman, *The Iceman*, 58.

11. Program for *Vampyrdanserinden*, DFI, accessed October 5, 2021, https://video .dfi.dk/filmdatabasen/20140/Vampyrdanserinden_20140_Filmprogram.pdf?_ga=2.27 16720.1231899898.1633477019-1470532686.1633477019.

12. For a brilliant reading of how sound, voice, and multilingualism in *Vampyr* contribute to its aesthetic of visual obfuscation, see Benjamin Bigelow, "Lurking in the Blind Space: *Vampyr* and the Multilinguals," *Journal of Scandinavian Cinema* 5, no. 3 (September 1, 2015): 223–39.

13. Carl Th. Dreyer and Christen Jul, *Writing Vampyr* (New York: Criterion Collection, 2008), 46.

14. Dreyer and Jul, *Writing Vampyr*, 66.

15. Dreyer and Jul, *Writing Vampyr*, 38.

16. Harold Bloom, *The Anxiety of Influence: A Theory of Poetry* (New York: Oxford University Press, 1997).

17. Brooks, *Melodramatic Imagination*, 157.

18. Brooks, *Melodramatic Imagination*, 157.

19. Brooks, *Melodramatic Imagination*, 154.

20. Brooks, *Melodramatic Imagination*, 157.

21. Brooks, *Melodramatic Imagination*, 158.

22. Brooks, *Melodramatic Imagination*, 196.

23. Brooks, *Melodramatic Imagination*, 195.

24. Sigmund Freud, "Screen Memories," in *On Freud's "Screen Memories,"* ed. Howard B. Levine and Gail S. Reed, Contemporary Freud: Turning Points and Critical Issues (London: Routledge, 2015), 3–24.

25. Brooks, *Melodramatic Imagination*, 201.

26. Dreyer and Jul, *Writing Vampyr*, 39, 62, 63.

27. Dreyer and Jul, *Writing Vampyr*, 71. Interestingly, the screenplay refers to Niklas's ego, that is, the actor's rather than the character Gray whom he plays in the film.

28. The script reads: "The landscape is bathed in a gray, dim twilight; every object has a tinge of unreality." Dreyer and Jul, *Writing Vampyr*, 4. Representing "death" continued to be a key topos of effigy culture that allowed Dreyer the opportunity to test the limits, potential, and differences between theater and film as media. This is evident in his 1939 review of Betty Nansen's production of Capek's play, titled *The Mother* (1938), featuring a mother character who is visited by the spirits of her dead sons (an inverse victim constellation to the one in *Ordet*). The article reveals Dreyer's early musings about the limits of staging ethereal bodies, figures whom the other characters on stage are not supposed to see but whom the audience (along with the mother) are to see as dead, but which risk being perceived as too material. Dreyer writes, "Fru Nansen's dead were lacking the mark of unreality [*uvirkelighedspræget*] and consequently failed to produce that peculiar ambiance that the playwright imagined as the background for the drama. Many of the play's scenes became embarrassing as opposed to producing release and liberation." Carl Th. Dreyer, "To skuespil, der faldt," in *Om filmen: Artikler og Interviews*, ed. Erik Ulrichsen (Copenhagen: Gyldendals Uglebøger, 1964), 62. Nansen's dead, according to Dreyer, were living and only living. Dreyer laments that at one point during the performance he glimpsed one of the supposed apparitions wearing socks.

29. Dreyer and Jul, *Writing Vampyr*, 50, 60, 40, 39.

30. Dreyer and Jul, *Writing Vampyr*, 88.

31. Carol J. Clover, "Her Body, Himself: Gender in the Slasher Film," *Representations*, no. 20 (1987): 189.

32. Linda Williams, "Film Bodies: Gender, Genre, and Excess," *Film Quarterly* 44, no. 4 (1991): 4. For a revised version of Clover's body genre argument, see Carol J. Clover, *Men, Women, and Chain Saws: Gender in the Modern Horror Film*, Princeton Classics (1992; repr., Princeton, NJ: Princeton University Press, 2015). To reiterate, I treat melodrama as an expansive mode that informs art melodrama, a genre.

33. For a study of the interrelationship between art cinema and horror films, see Joan Hawkins, *Cutting Edge: Art-Horror and the Horrific Avant-Garde* (Minneapolis: University of Minnesota Press, 2000).

34. Sharon L. Snyder and David T. Mitchell, *Cultural Locations of Disability* (Chicago: University of Chicago Press, 2006), 158. See also Rosemarie Garland-Thomson,

"The Politics of Staring: Visual Rhetorics of Disability in Popular Photography," in *Disability Studies: Enabling the Humanities*, ed. Sharon L. Snyder, Brenda Jo Brueggemann, and Rosemarie Garland-Thomson (New York: Modern Language Association of America, 2002), 56–75.

35. Snyder and Mitchell, *Cultural Locations*, 162.

36. Dreyer and Jul, *Writing Vampyr*, 65.

37. Dreyer and Jul, *Writing Vampyr*, 66–67.

38. Dreyer and Jul, *Writing Vampyr*, 67.

39. Benshoff, "The Monster and the Homosexual," 117. See also Jack Halberstam, *Skin Shows: Gothic Horror and the Technology of Monsters* (Durham, NC: Duke University Press, 1995).

40. Sue-Ellen Case, "Tracking the Vampire," *Differences* 3, no. 2 (1991): 3.

41. Heilman, *The Iceman*, 57.

Chapter 4. *Day of Wrath* and "Kniplinger"

1. Andrew Webber, "Cut and Laced: Traumatism and Fetishism in Luis Buñuel's *Un Chien Andalou*," in *Projected Shadows: Psychoanalytic Reflections on the Representation of Loss in European Cinema*, ed. Andrea Sabbadini (New York: Routledge, 2007), 93–94.

2. The second version (b) of the "Kniplinger" scenario deviates substantially from version (c), which has different page numbers and scene numbers. I use version (b) in my analysis because its plot aligns most closely with the plot description in the film's program.

3. See "Grevindens Ære," DFI Dreyer website, accessed July 4, 2023, https://www.carlthdreyer.dk/carlthdreyer/filmene/grevindens-aere.

4. Dreyer script, "Kniplinger," 37, DFI Dreyer website, accessed November 1, 2023, https://www.carlthdreyer.dk/carlthdreyer/filmene/grevindens-aere.

5. See Mercer and Shingler, *Genre, Style and Sensibility*.

6. Between *Vampyr* in 1932 and *Day of Wrath*, Dreyer would complete only one short film. Reviews of the film were mixed, but as typically happened with Dreyer's career, public discussions about the viability of the Danish film industry often drew on Dreyer's career to serve as a kind of bellwether. Releasing *Day of Wrath* in 1943 in occupied Denmark raised these stakes even higher.

7. Christian Jul, *Day of Wrath* Program, Dreyer Collection, DFI: 1A Vredens Dag, 20–21, accessed July 4, 2023, https://www.carlthdreyer.dk/carlthdreyer/filmene/vredens-dag.

8. Dreyer, "Lidt om filmstil," 72.

9. Dreyer, "Lidt om filmstil," 74.

10. Dreyer, "Lidt om filmstil," 76.

11. Dreyer, "Lidt om filmstil," 75.

12. Brooks, *Melodramatic Imagination*. Carney cites Brooks in a footnote. See Raymond Carney, *Speaking the Language of Desire: The Films of Carl Dreyer* (New York: Cambridge University Press, 1989), 68.

13. Bordwell, *Films of Carl-Theodor Dreyer*, 117.

14. See David Bordwell, "The Art Cinema as a Mode of Film Practice," *Film Criticism* 4, no. 1 (1979): 56–64.

15. David Bordwell and Kristen Thompson, *Film Art: An Introduction*, 9th ed. (New York: McGraw-Hill, 2010), 249–50. In the same section, Bordwell and Thompson

describe how visual parallels such as shadows filtering across the faces of Anne and Herlofs-Marthe might link the fates of the two characters, but "however clear such parallel relations may seem, the chains of narrative cause and effect lead us straight to ambiguities. The uncertainty revolves around the problem of witchcraft" (250).

16. Program for *Grevindens Ære*, DFI Dreyer website, accessed July 4, 2023, https://www.carlthdreyer.dk/carlthdreyer/filmene/grevindens-aere. This proposal to live separate lives as a married couple will echo Gustav's proposal in *Gertrud* when she confronts him with her intention to leave him.

17. Dreyer script, "Kniplinger," 14.

18. Dreyer script, "Kniplinger," 63.

19. Dreyer, "Lidt om Filmstil," 75.

20. Elsaesser, "Tales of Sound and Fury," 68.

21. Sirk, *Sirk on Sirk*. See also Klinger, *Melodrama and Meaning*.

22. Elsaesser, "Tales of Sound," 75.

23. Elsaesser, "Tales of Sound," 79.

24. Elsaesser, "Tales of Sound," 76.

25. Elsaesser, "Tales of Sound," 76.

26. Elsaesser, "Tales of Sound," 79.

27. Mercer and Shingler, *Genre, Style and Sensibility*, 15.

28. Elsaesser, "Tales of Sound," 86.

29. François Truffaut, *The Films in My Life* (New York: Simon and Schuster, 1985), 48.

30. Dreyer, "Lidt om Filmstil," 78.

31. Williams, "Film Bodies," 4.

32. Brooks, *Melodramatic Imagination*, 205.

33. Dreyer script, "Kniplinger," 40.

34. Dreyer script, "Kniplinger," 40.

35. Dreyer, "Lidt om Filmstil," 72.

36. Dreyer, "Lidt om Filmstil," 71.

37. Dreyer, "Lidt om Filmstil," 71–72.

38. Dreyer, "Lidt om Filmstil," 76–77.

39. Sandberg, "Mastering the House," 39.

Chapter 5. *Ordet*

1. The convention in scholarly work on Dreyer written in English is to use the Danish title for the film, in other words, *Ordet*, rather than its English translation, *The Word*. I have opted to follow this tradition.

2. Bordwell, *Films of Carl-Theodor Dreyer*, 144.

3. Paul Schrader, *Transcendental Style in Film* (Berkeley: University of California Press, 2018), 153.

4. Schrader, *Transcendental Style*, 40.

5. Schrader, *Transcendental Style*, 143.

6. Schrader, *Transcendental Style*, 156.

7. Drouzy, *Carl Th. Dreyer*, 18.

8. C. Claire Thomson, "The Slow Pulse of the Era: Carl Th. Dreyer's Film Style," in *Slow Cinema*, ed. Tiago de Luca and Nuno Barrados Jorge (Edinburgh: Edinburgh University Press, 2022), 47–58.

9. See also Amanda Doxtater, "The Word (Ordet, 1955)," in *Lexicon of Global Melodrama*, vol. 1, ed. Katharina Gerund et al. (Bielefeld: Transcript Verlag, 2022), 103–6.

10. Kaplan, "Mothering, Feminism and Representation," 126.

11. Williams, "Melodrama Revised," 59.

12. The pity we feel at this woman's maternal sacrifice is compounded by its utter lack of recognition by her daughter. One might contrast this to Sirk's climactic ending to *Imitation of Life* (1959), which culminates in the "ungrateful" daughter's tearful recognition of her mother's sacrifice that comes too late.

13. Drum and Drum, *Great Passion*, 233.

14. Brooks, "Melodrama, Body, Revolution," 19.

15. For a sense of how important this project was to Dreyer, see Jes Nysten, "An Unrealized Lifelong Dream—Dreyer's Jesus Film," DFI Dreyer website, accessed July 4, 2023, https://www.carlthdreyer.dk/en/carlthdreyer/about-dreyer/themes/unrealised-lifelong-dream-dreyers-jesus-film. *Leaves from Satan's Book* (*Blade af Satans Bog*, 1921), discussed in chapter 1, also featured an episode depicting Jesus's betrayal by Judas.

16. Dreyer had seen Munk's play performed in 1932 and approached the playwright about acquiring the rights to film it, but they were too expensive. Only some twenty years later, after Swedish director Gustaf Molander made a version in Sweden, did the rights eventually become available. In the 1950s, Dreyer's hopes of filming *Jesus of Nazareth* were stoked by an American producer named Blevins Davis. Initially he also imagined that if he could make *Ordet* in the US rather than in Europe, it might pave the way for financing the Jesus project, but it remained unrealized. Dreyer's dreams of American financing never came to fruition.

17. Jan B. Wahl, *Carl Theodor Dreyer and Ordet: My Summer with the Danish Filmmaker*, Screen Classics (Lexington: University Press of Kentucky, 2012), 13–14.

18. Carl Theodor Dreyer, *Jesus* (New York: Dell, 1973), 67, my emphasis.

19. Dreyer, *Jesus*, 67–68.

20. Dreyer, *Jesus*, 73–74.

21. Dreyer also elegantly disperses identification among the participants and witnesses with whom the spectator might also identify, whether the men carrying their son and father on their shoulders to the temple, their hopeful anticipation balanced by their aching backs, or in the faith of the crowd as the man walks away on his own accord, or perhaps even with Jesus, the quintessential figure of suffering.

22. Dreyer, *Jesus*, 292.

23. Dreyer, *Jesus*, 292.

24. Two soldiers garrisoned in a household fall in love with the same young woman. Høfft is poor and cannot afford to propose to her, while Fang inherits a fortune from his aunt, the countess de la Garde. Ripping the document out of Høfft's hand, Fang initiates a treacherous cat-and-mouse chase in pursuit of the document. At one moment, vicious dogs chase Høfft up the lone tree growing along a steep ocean cliff. Seeing his chance, Fang proceeds to saw the tree down. The script reads, "The actor should be equipped with the kinds of boots that workers use when they climb telephone poles. . . . The tree falls, but in the direction out over the water. He sees v. Høffts figure, possibly a manikin, clinging tightly to a branch." Dreyer script, "Chatollets Hemelighed" (version 2), 20–21, DFI Dreyer website, accessed November 4, 2023, https://www.carlthdreyer.dk/carlthdreyer/filmene/chatollets-hemmelighed.

25. Høfft is, however, five years younger than Dreyer.

26. Dreyer script, "Chatollets Hemelighed," 2.

27. See Peter Schepelern. "Biograf-problemer—Refleksioner over den Psykobiografiske Metode i Martin Drouzys Dreyer Monografi," in *Sekvens Filmæstetik & Billedhistorie*, Filmvidenskabelig årbog Institut for Film & Medievidenskab (Copenhagen: Copenhagen University Press, 1983), 123–48. For Drouzy's response to Schepelern's critique in the same volume, see Martin (Maurice) Drouzy, "For og Imod Psykobiografien—Svar til Peter Schepelern," in *Sekvens Filmæstetik & Billedhistorie*, Filmvidenskabelig årbog Institut for Film & Medievidenskab (Copenhagen: Copenhagen University Press, 1983), 149–64.

28. Williams, "Melodrama Revised," 58.

29. Bordwell, *Films of Carl-Theodor Dreyer*, 151.

30. Williams, "Melodrama Revised," 74.

31. Franco Moretti. "Kindergarten," in *Signs Taken for Wonders: Essays in the Sociology of Literary Forms*, trans. Susan Fischer, David Forgacs, and David Miller (London: Verso, 1983), 162.

32. Moretti, "Kindergarten," 162.

Chapter 6. *Gertrud*

1. The working title for *The Parson's Widow* (1921) referred to it as a "time picture from the 1700s" in an unpublished script at the DFI, referenced in a note in Sandberg, "Mastering the House," 42. "Tidsbillede" could also be translated as "time image," evoking work by Gilles Deleuze, *Cinema*, trans. Hugh Tomlinson, Barbara Habberjam, and Robert Galeta (Minneapolis: University of Minnesota Press, 1986). Dreyer's use of the term resonates more closely with Andre Bazin's ontological conceptualization of the photographic image as mummified, preserved bodies: objectivity in time. See Andre Bazin, "The Ontology of the Photographic Image," trans. Hugh Gray, *Film Quarterly* 13, no. 4 (Summer 1960): 4–9. Consequently, the last line of Bazin's piece reads as a possible *coup de théâtre* reversal: "On the other hand, of course, cinema is also a language."

2. Sten Rein, *Hjalmar Söderbergs Gertrud: Studier kring ett karleksdrama* (Stockholm: Bonniers, 1962); Merete Bonnesen, "Den alvorlige leg: Historien om Gertrud og Hjalmar Söderberg," *Søndags Politiken*, December 6, 1964.

3. Bonnesen, "Den alvorlige leg."

4. See Drouzy, *Carl Th. Dreyer*; Jonathan Rosenbaum, "Gertrud as Nonnarrative: The Desire for the Image," in *Placing Movies* (Berkeley: University of California Press, 2020), 105–16.

5. Margit Bergström, "Besök att minnas," *Föreningen Gamla Christanstads årskrift*, 1989, 140–43. I am grateful to Kurt Mälarstedt for sharing this source with me.

6. Bergström, "Besök att minnas," 140.

7. Dreyer, "Lidt om filmstil."

8. For an account of Dreyer's work at Dagmar Cinema, see DFI Dreyer website, accessed July 4, 2023, https://www.carlthdreyer.dk/en/carlthdreyer/about-dreyer/work places/dagmar-cinema.

9. Drum and Drum, *Great Passion*, 247.

10. See, for instance, J. P. Jakobsen's *Marie Grubbe* (1876) and Amalie Skram's novels, including *Constance Ring* (1885).

11. Love, *Feeling Backward*, 27. Other interesting examples of nonpositivity at the intersection of queer theory and melodrama are Lauren Berlant's use of impasse and Jonathan Goldberg's discussion of impossibility. See Lauren Gail Berlant, *Cruel Optimism* (Durham, NC: Duke University Press, 2011); Jonathan Goldberg, *Melodrama: An Aesthetics of Impossibility*, Theory Q (Durham, NC: Duke University Press, 2016).

12. Bordwell, *Films of Carl-Theodor Dreyer*.

13. Brooks, *Melodramatic Imagination*, 186.

14. Brooks, *Melodramatic Imagination*, 180.

15. Brooks, *Melodramatic Imagination*, 192–93.

16. This is according to a review of Rein's doctoral thesis. See Herbert Friedländer, "Sten Rein: Hjalmar Söderbergs Gertrud. Studier kring ett kärleksdrama," *Samlaren: Tidskrift för svensk litteraturhistorisk forskning* 83 (1962): 301.

17. Stanley Cavell, *Contesting Tears: The Hollywood Melodrama of the Unknown Woman* (Chicago: University of Chicago Press, 1996).

18. Melodrama of the unknown woman stands in contrast to the Hollywood comedy of remarriage, a genre he had treated earlier in Stanley Cavell, *Pursuits of Happiness: The Hollywood Comedy of Remarriage*, Harvard Film Studies (Cambridge, MA: Harvard University Press, 1981).

19. Carney, *Language of Desire*, 284.

20. Carney, *Language of Desire*, 277.

21. Carney, *Language of Desire*, 279.

22. Brooks, *Imagination*, 195–96.

23. Jacques Derrida, *Archive Fever: A Freudian Impression*, Religion and Postmodernism (Chicago: University of Chicago Press, 1996), 33–34.

24. Derrida, *Archive Fever*, 12, my emphasis.

25. The inserted shot shows the third verse of the poem, which reads: "Lever jeg." ("Do I live."). The question mark is missing. This translation is from the British Film Institute's DVD release of the film.

26. Derrida, *Archive Fever*, 9.

27. Dreyer script, "Kniplinger," 44, DFI Dreyer website, accessed November 1, 2023, https://www.carlthdreyer.dk/carlthdreyer/filmene/grevindens-aere.

28. As Jonathan Rosenbaum notes in "Gertrud as Nonnarrative," apparently there were verses separating the end of the film and the epilogue—but at some point, Dreyer removed them.

29. Derrida, *Archive Fever*, 37.

30. Derrida, *Archive Fever*, 55.

31. James Schamus, "Dreyer's Textual Realism," in *Rites of Realism*, ed. Ivone Margulies (Durham, NC: Duke University Press, 2020), 316.

32. Schamus, "Textual Realism," 320.

33. Schneider, *Performing Remains*, 109.

34. Schneider, *Performing Remains*, 108.

35. Schneider, *Performing Remains*, 108. Schneider objects to Taylor's distinction between repertoire and archive by describing the performing body as marked by syncopated time, allowing it to function like I discussed in chapter 1, as a kind of recording device.

36. Morten Egholm, "The Innovative and Wilful [*sic*] Adaptor—What Carl Th. Dreyer Did to Hjalmar Söderberg's 'Gertrud,'" *Tijdschrift Voor Skandinavistiek* 27, no. 2 (2006): 163.

37. Dreyer had expressed interest in Söderberg's work much earlier in his career and had even sought to film *Doktor Glas*. Drum and Drum, *Great Passion*, 249–50.

38. Rein, *Hjalmar Söderbergs Gertrud*, 55.

39. Rein, *Hjalmar Söderbergs Gertrud*, 47.

40. Rein, *Hjalmar Söderbergs Gertrud*, 51.

41. Rein, *Hjalmar Söderbergs Gertrud*, 56–57.

42. Rein, *Hjalmar Söderbergs Gertrud*, 44–45.

43. In the letter included as an appendix in Rein's thesis, Landquist refers to their relationship rather coolly as an acquaintance (*bekantskap*), but according to Kurt Mälarstedt's biography of Maria von Platen, they lived practically as husband and wife for a period. Landquist recounts this in a private letter he writes to Ellen Keys, which differs significantly from the letter he wrote to Rein. Mälarstedt had access to this letter; Rein did not. See Kurt Mälarstedt, *Ett liv på egna villkor: Om Maria von Platen* (Stockholm: Wahlström & Widstrand, 2006).

44. Rein, *Hjalmar Söderbergs Gertrud*, 283–84.

45. Rein, *Hjalmar Söderbergs Gertrud*, 288.

46. Rein, *Hjalmar Söderbergs Gertrud*, 218.

47. Rein, *Hjalmar Söderbergs Gertrud*, 218.

48. Rein, *Hjalmar Söderbergs Gertrud*, 288.

49. Rein, *Hjalmar Söderbergs Gertrud*, 289.

Conclusion

1. Carl Th. Dreyer, "Preface," in Ebbe Neergaard, *The Story of Danish Film*, trans. Elsa Gress (Copenhagen: Det Danske Selskab / The Danish Institute, 1963), 4.

2. Neergaard, Neergaard, and Steinthal, *Bog om Dreyer*, 51.

3. Dreyer, "Preface," 4.

4. Dreyer, "Preface," 4.

5. Dreyer, "Preface," 4.

6. Dreyer, "Preface," 4.

Bibliography

Abel, Richard. *French Cinema: The First Wave, 1915–1929*. Princeton, NJ: Princeton University Press, 1984.

Affron, Charles. *Cinema and Sentiment*. Chicago: University of Chicago Press, 1982.

Andrews, David. "Toward an Inclusive, Exclusive Approach to Art Cinema." In *Global Art Cinema*, 62–74. New Theories and Histories. New York: Oxford University Press, 2010.

Andrews, David. *Theorizing Art Cinemas: Foreign, Cult, Avant-Garde, and Beyond*. Austin: University of Texas Press, 2013.

Artaud, Antonin. *The Theater and Its Double*. Evergreen Original E-127. New York: Grove Press, 1958.

Barrett, Alex. "Where to Begin with Carl Dreyer." British Film Institute, February 3, 2016. https://www2.bfi.org.uk/news-opinion/news-bfi/features/fast-track-fandom-where -begin-carl-dreyer.

Bazin, Andre. "The Ontology of the Photographic Image." Translated by Hugh Gray. *Film Quarterly* 13, no. 4 (Summer 1960): 4–9.

Benshoff, Harry M. "The Monster and the Homosexual." In *The Dread of Difference*, 116–42. 2nd ed. Austin: University of Texas Press, 2021.

Bergström, Margit. "Besök att minnas." *Föreningen Gamla Christanstads årskrift*, 1989, 140–43.

Berlant, Lauren Gail. *Cruel Optimism*. Durham, NC: Duke University Press, 2011.

Bigelow, Benjamin. "Lurking in the Blind Space: *Vampyr* and the Multilinguals." *Journal of Scandinavian Cinema* 5, no. 3 (September 1, 2015): 223–39.

Bloom, Harold. *The Anxiety of Influence: A Theory of Poetry*. New York: Oxford University Press, 1997.

Bonnesen, Merete. "Den alvorlige leg: Historien om Gertrud og Hjalmar Söderberg." *Søndags Politiken*, December 6, 1964.

Bordwell, David. "The Art Cinema as a Mode of Film Practice." *Film Criticism* 4, no. 1 (1979): 56–64.

Bordwell, David. "Dreyer Re-Reconsidered." *Observations on Film Art* (blog), June 14, 2010. http://www.davidbordwell.net/blog/2010/06/14/dreyer-re-reconsidered/.

Bordwell, David. *Filmguide to La Passion de Jeanne d'Arc.* Filmguide Series FG-1. Bloomington: Indiana University Press, 1973.

Bordwell, David. *The Films of Carl-Theodor Dreyer.* Berkeley: University of California Press, 1981.

Bordwell, David. "Nordisk and the Tableau Aesthetic." In *100 Years of Nordisk Film*, edited by Lisbeth Richter Larsen and Dan Nissen, 81–95. Copenhagen: Danish Film Institute, 2006.

Bordwell, David, and Kristin Thompson. *Film Art: An Introduction.* 9th ed. New York: McGraw-Hill, 2010.

Brooks, Peter. "Melodrama, Body, Revolution." In *Melodrama: Stage, Picture, Screen*, edited by Jacqueline Susan Bratton, Jim Cook, Christine Gledhill, and British Universities Film Council, 11–24. London: British Film Institute, 1994.

Brooks, Peter. *The Melodramatic Imagination: Balzac, Henry James, Melodrama, and the Mode of Excess.* 1976. Reprint, New Haven, CT: Yale University Press, 1995.

Buckley, Matthew. "Unbinding Melodrama." In *Melodrama Unbound: Across History, Media, and National Cultures*, edited by Christine Gledhill and Linda Williams, 15–29. Film and Culture. New York: Columbia University Press, 2018.

Buñuel, Luis. *An Unspeakable Betrayal: Selected Writings of Luis Buñuel.* Translated by Garrett White. Berkeley: University of California Press, 2000.

Burnetts, Charles. *Improving Passions: Sentimental Aesthetics and American Film.* Edinburgh: Edinburgh University Press, 2017.

Carlson, Henning. "Excerpt from an Obituary of Carl Th. Dreyer." In *Carl Th. Dreyer: Danish Film Director, 1889–1968*, edited by Søren Dyssegaard, 4. Presentation Books, Ministry of Foreign Affairs. Copenhagen: Van Rasmussens Litografiske Trykkeri, 1969.

Carney, Raymond. *Speaking the Language of Desire: The Films of Carl Dreyer.* New York: Cambridge University Press, 1989.

Case, Sue-Ellen. "Tracking the Vampire." *Differences* 3, no. 2 (1991): 1–20.

Cavell, Stanley. *Contesting Tears: The Hollywood Melodrama of the Unknown Woman.* Chicago: University of Chicago Press, 1996.

Cavell, Stanley. *Pursuits of Happiness: The Hollywood Comedy of Remarriage.* Harvard Film Studies. Cambridge, MA: Harvard University Press, 1981.

Clover, Carol J. "Her Body, Himself: Gender in the Slasher Film." *Representations*, no. 20 (1987): 187–228.

Clover, Carol J. *Men, Women, and Chain Saws: Gender in the Modern Horror Film.* Princeton Classics. 1992. Reprint, Princeton, NJ: Princeton University Press, 2015.

Cook, Pam. "Melodrama and the Women's Picture." In *Gainsborough Melodrama*, edited by Sue Aspinall, Robert Murphy, and British Film Institute, 248–62. London: British Film Institute, 1988.

Cvetkovich, Ann. *An Archive of Feelings: Trauma, Sexuality, and Lesbian Public Cultures.* Series Q. Durham, NC: Duke University Press, 2003.

Dahl, Ulrika. "Femmebodiment: Notes on Queer Feminine Shapes of Vulnerability." *Feminist Theory* 18, no. 1 (2017): 35–53.

Dancus, Adriana Margareta. *Exposing Vulnerability: Self-Mediation in Scandinavian Films by Women.* Bristol, UK: Intellect, 2019.

Danish Film Institute. "Carl Th. Dreyer." Accessed July 4, 2023. https://www.carlth dreyer.dk/en/carlthdreyer.

Delahaye, Michel. "Entretien avec Carl Theodor Dreyer." In *La Politique des Auteurs: Les Entretiens*, 233–65. Paris: Cahiers du cinema, 2001.

Deleuze, Gilles. *Cinema*. Translated by Hugh Tomlinson, Barbara Habberjam, and Robert Galeta. Minneapolis: University of Minnesota Press, 1986.

De Noma, Elizabeth Ann. "Multiple Melodrama: The Making and Remaking of Three Selma Lagerlöf Narratives in the Silent Era and the 1940s." PhD diss., University of Washington, 2000.

Derrida, Jacques. *Archive Fever: A Freudian Impression*. Religion and Postmodernism. Chicago: University of Chicago Press, 1996.

Doane, Mary Ann. *The Desire to Desire: The Woman's Film of the 1940s, Theories of Representation and Difference*. Bloomington: Indiana University Press, 1987.

Doane, Mary Ann. "Pathos and Pathology: The Cinema of Todd Haynes." *Camera Obscura* 19, no. 57 (2004): 1–20.

Doolittle, Hilde [H.D.]. "The Passion of Joan of Arc." In *American Movie Critics: An Anthology from the Silents until Now*, edited by Phillip Lopate, 39–44. Library of America. New York: Library of America, 2006.

Doxtater, Amanda. "Perilous Performance: Dreyer's Unity of Danger and Beauty." August 17, 2010. https://www.carlthdreyer.dk/en/carlthdreyer/about-dreyer/working-method/perilous-performance-dreyers-unity-danger-and-beauty.

Doxtater, Amanda. "*The Word (Ordet*, 1955)." In *Lexicon of Global Melodrama*, vol. 1, edited by Katharina Gerund, Heike Paul, Sarah Marak, and Marius Henderson, 103–6. Bielefeld: Transcript Verlag, 2022.

Dreyer, Carl Th. "Den virkelige talefilm" (1933). In *Om filmen: Artikler og Interviews*, edited by Erik Ulrichsen, 31–36. Copenhagen: Gyldendals Uglebøger, 1964.

Dreyer, Carl Th. "Dreyer 1950." Unpublished introduction to screening of *La Passion de Jeanne d'Arc* at Danish Film Museum. In Dreyer's *Udklips mapper*, Dreyer Collection, Danish Film Institute. 1950.

Dreyer, Carl Theodor. *Dreyer in Double Reflection: Translation of Carl Th. Dreyer's Writings about the Film (Om Filmen)*. Edited by Donald Skoller. Da Capo Paperback. New York: Da Capo Press, 1973.

Dreyer, Carl Theodor. *Jesus*. New York: Dell, 1973.

Dreyer, Carl Th. "Lidt om filmstil" (1943). In *Om filmen: Artikler og Interviews*, edited by Erik Ulrichsen, 71–80. Copenhagen: Gyldendals Uglebøger, 1964.

Dreyer, Carl Th. *Om filmen: Artikler og Interviews*. Edited by Erik Ulrichsen. Copenhagen: Gyldendals Uglebøger, 1964. First published by Ny Nordisk Forlag, Arnold Busck (Copenhagen), 1959.

Dreyer, Carl Th. "Preface." In Ebbe Neergaard, *The Story of Danish Film*, translated by Elsa Gress, 3–5. Copenhagen: Det Danske Selskab / The Danish Institute, 1963.

Dreyer, Carl Th. "Realiseret mystik" (1929). In *Om filmen: Artikler og Interviews*, edited by Erik Ulrichsen, 30–31. Copenhagen: Gyldendals Uglebøger, 1964.

Dreyer, Carl Th. "To skuespil, der faldt" (1939). In *Om filmen: Artikler og Interviews*, edited by Erik Ulrichsen, 60–63. Copenhagen: Gyldendals Uglebøger, 1964.

Dreyer, Carl Th., and Christen Jul. *Writing Vampyr*. New York: Criterion Collection, 2008.

Drouzy, Martin (Maurice). *Carl Th. Dreyer, født Nilsson. 3 3*. Copenhagen: Gyldendal/ Reitzel, 1982.

Drouzy, Martin (Maurice). "For og Imod Psykobiografien—Svar til Peter Schepelern." In *Sekvens Filmæstetik & Billedhistorie*, 149–64. Filmvidenskabelig årbog Institut for Film & Medievidenskab. Copenhagen: Copenhagen University Press, 1983.

Drum, Jean, and Dale Drum. *My Only Great Passion: The Life and Films of Carl Th. Dreyer*. Filmmakers Series 68. Lanham, MD: Scarecrow, 2000.

Edelman, Rob. "Variete." Accessed July 2, 2023. http://www.filmreference.com/Films -Tw-Vi/Variete.html.

Egholm, Morten. *En visionær fortolker af andres tanker: Om Carl Th. Dreyers brug af litterære forlæg*. PhD diss. Copenhagen: Det Humanistiske Fakultet, Københavns Universitet, 2009.

Egholm, Morten. "The Innovative and Wilful [*sic*] Adaptor—What Carl Th. Dreyer Did to Hjalmar Söderberg's 'Gertrud.'" *Tijdschrift Voor Skandinavistiek* 27, no. 2 (2006): 157–77.

Elsaesser, Thomas. "Tales of Sound and Fury: Observations on the Family Melodrama." In *Imitations of Life: A Reader on Film & Television Melodrama*, edited by Marcia Landy, 68–91. Detroit: Wayne State University Press, 1992. [Originally published in *Monogram*, no. 4 (1972): 2–15.]

Engberg, Marguerite. *Dansk stumfilm. De store år [Bind] 2*. Copenhagen: Rhodos, 1977.

Engberg, Marguerite. "The Erotic Melodrama in Danish Silent Films, 1910–1918." *Film History* 5, no. 1 (1993): 63–67.

Fischer-Lichte, Erika. *The Transformative Power of Performance: A New Aesthetics*. London: Routledge, 2008.

Forslund, Bengt. *Victor Sjöström: His Life and His Work*. New York: New York Zoetrope, 1988.

Freeman, Elizabeth. *Time Binds: Queer Temporalities, Queer Histories, Perverse Modernities*. Durham, NC: Duke University Press, 2010.

Freud, Sigmund. "Screen Memories." In *On Freud's "Screen Memories,"* edited by Howard B. Levine and Gail S. Reed, 3–24. Contemporary Freud: Turning Points and Critical Issues. London: Routledge, 2015.

Friedländer, Herbert. "Sten Rein: Hjalmar Söderbergs Gertrud. Studier kring ett kärleksdrama." *Samlaren: Tidskrift för svensk litteraturhistorisk forskning* 83 (1962): 298–302.

Furhammar, Leif. *Filmen i Sverige: En historia i tio kapitel och en fortsättning*. Stockholm: Dialogos Filminstitutet, 2003.

Galt, Rosalind, and Karl Schoonover. *Global Art Cinema: New Theories and Histories*. New York: Oxford University Press, 2010.

Garland-Thomson, Rosemarie. "The Politics of Staring: Visual Rhetorics of Disability in Popular Photography." In *Disability Studies: Enabling the Humanities*, edited by Sharon L. Snyder, Brenda Jo Brueggemann, and Rosemarie Garland-Thomson, 56–75. New York: Modern Language Association of America, 2002.

Garncarz, Joseph. "The European Fairground Cinema: (Re)Defining and (Re)Contextualizing the 'Cinema of Attractions.'" In *A Companion to Early Cinema*, edited by André Gaudreault, Nicolas Dulac, and Santiago Hidalgo, 317–33. Oxford: Wiley-Blackwell, 2012.

Gerould, Daniel. "Russian Formalist Theories of Melodrama." In *Imitations of Life: A Reader on Film & Television Melodrama*, edited by Marcia Landy, 118–34. Detroit:

Wayne State University Press, 1992. [Originally published in *Journal of American Culture* 1, no. 1 (1978): 152–68.]

Gestrich, Constanze. "Die Macht der dunklen Kammern: Die Faszination des Fremden im frühen dänischen Kino." PhD diss., Berliner Beiträge zur Skandinavistik, 0933-4009, Bd. 15. Nordeuropa-Institut der Humboldt-Universität, Berlin, 2008.

Gledhill, Christine. "Christine Gledhill on 'Stella Dallas' and Feminist Film Theory." *Cinema Journal* 25, no. 4 (1986): 44–48.

Gledhill, Christine. "Introduction." In *Home Is Where the Heart Is: Studies in Melodrama and the Woman's Film*, edited by Christine Gledhill, 1–4. London: British Film Institute, 1987.

Gledhill, Christine. "Signs of Melodrama." In *Stardom: Industry of Desire*, edited by Christine Gledhill, 207–29. London: Routledge, 1991.

Gledhill, Christine, and Linda Williams. *Melodrama Unbound: Across History, Media, and National Cultures*. Film and Culture. New York: Columbia University Press, 2018.

Goldberg, Jonathan. *Melodrama: An Aesthetics of Impossibility*. Theory Q. Durham, NC: Duke University Press, 2016.

Gunning, Tom. "The Cinema of Attraction[s]: Early Film, Its Spectator and the Avant-Garde." In *The Cinema of Attractions Reloaded*, edited by Wanda Strauven, 381–88. Amsterdam: Amsterdam University Press, 2006.

Gunning, Tom. "The Horror of Opacity: The Melodrama of Sensation in the Plays of André de Lorde." In *Melodrama: Stage, Picture, Screen*, edited by Jacqueline Susan Bratton, Jim Cook, Christine Gledhill, and British Universities Film Council, 50–64. London: British Film Institute, 1994.

Ha, Paul C. "Inventory of Shimmers: Objects of Intimacy in Contemporary Art." In *An Inventory of Shimmers: Objects of Intimacy in Contemporary Art*, edited by Henriette Huldisch, 6. Cambridge, MA: MIT List Visual Arts Center, 2017.

Halberstam, Jack. *The Queer Art of Failure*. Durham, NC: Duke University Press, 2011.

Halberstam, Jack. *Skin Shows: Gothic Horror and the Technology of Monsters*. Durham, NC: Duke University Press, 1995.

Hamm, Christine. "Medlidenhet og melodrama: Amalie Skrams litteraturkritikk og ekteskapsromaner." PhD diss., University of Bergen, 2002.

Hansen, Miriam. "The Mass Production of the Senses: Classical Cinema as Vernacular Modernism." *Modernism/Modernity* 6, no. 2 (1999): 59–77.

Hawkins, Joan. *Cutting Edge: Art-Horror and the Horrific Avant-Garde*. Minneapolis: University of Minnesota Press, 2000.

Heilman, Robert Bechtold. *The Iceman, the Arsonist, and the Troubled Agent; Tragedy and Melodrama on the Modern Stage*. Seattle: University of Washington Press, 1973.

Jörngården, Anna. *Tidens Tröskel: Uppbrott Och Nostalgi i Skandinavisk Litteratur Kring Sekelskiftet 1900*. Höör: Brutus Östlings Bokförlag Symposion, 2012.

Jul, Christian. *Day of Wrath* Program, Dreyer Collection, Danish Film Institute: 1A Vredens Dag. Accessed July 4, 2023. https://www.carlthdreyer.dk/carlthdreyer/filmene /vredens-dag.

Kaplan, E. Ann. "Mothering, Feminism and Representation: The Maternal Melodrama and the Woman's Film, 1910–1940." In *Home Is Where the Heart Is: Studies in*

Melodrama and the Woman's Film, edited by Christine Gledhill, 113–37. London: British Film Institute, 1987.

Karlsson, Maria. *Känslans röst: Det melodramatiska i Selma Lagerlöfs romankonst.* Brutus Östlings bokförl. Stockholm: Symposion, 2002.

Kau, Edvin. *Dreyers filmkunst.* Denmark: Akademisk Forlag, 1989.

Klinger, Barbara. "The Art Film, Affect and the Female Viewer: The Piano Revisited." *Screen* 47, no. 1 (2006): 19–41.

Klinger, Barbara. *Melodrama and Meaning: History, Culture, and the Films of Douglas Sirk.* Bloomington: Indiana University Press, 1994.

Kohlmann, Benjamin. "Awkward Moments: Melodrama, Modernism, and the Politics of Affect." *PMLA: Publications of the Modern Language Association of America* 128, no. 2 (2013): 337–52.

Koivunen, Anu, Katariina Kyrölä, and Ingrid Ryberg. *The Power of Vulnerability: Mobilising Affect in Feminist, Queer and Anti-Racist Media Cultures.* Manchester: Manchester University Press, 2018.

Landy, Marcia, ed. *Imitations of Life: A Reader on Film & Television Melodrama.* Contemporary Film and Television Series. Detroit: Wayne State University Press, 1991.

Le Fanu, Joseph Sheridan. "Carmilla." In *In a Glass Darkly,* 358–467. London: R. Bentley and Son, 1897.

Loren, Scott, and Jörg Metelmann. *Melodrama after the Tears: New Perspectives on the Politics of Victimhood.* Film Culture in Transition. Amsterdam: Amsterdam University Press, 2016.

Love, Heather. *Feeling Backward: Loss and the Politics of Queer History.* Cambridge, MA: Harvard University Press, 2007.

Mälarstedt, Kurt. *Ett liv på egna villkor: Om Maria von Platen.* Stockholm: Wahlström & Widstrand, 2006.

Maron, Jeremy, and André Loiselle. *Stages of Reality: Theatricality in Cinema.* Toronto: University of Toronto Press, 2017.

Maurice, Alice. "Making Faces: Character and Makeup in Early Cinema." In *Corporeality in Early Cinema: Viscera, Skin, and Physical Form,* edited by Marina Dahlquist, Doron Galili, Jan Olsson, and Valentine Robert, 206–17. Bloomington: Indiana University Press, 2018.

Mercer, John, and Martin Shingler. *Melodrama: Genre, Style and Sensibility.* New York: Columbia University Press, 2013.

Milne, Tom. "Carl Theodor Dreyer: The Early Works." In *Cinema: A Critical Dictionary, The Major Film-Makers,* edited by Richard Roud, 291–96. New York: Viking Press, 1980.

Modleski, Tania. "Time and Desire in the Woman's Film." *Cinema Journal* 23, no. 3 (1984): 19–30.

Moi, Toril. *Henrik Ibsen and the Birth of Modernism: Art, Theater, Philosophy.* New York: Oxford University Press, 2006.

Moor, Paul. "The Tyrannical Dane." *Theatre Arts,* April 1951, 35–38.

Moretti, Franco. "Kindergarten." In *Signs Taken for Wonders: Essays in the Sociology of Literary Forms,* translated by Susan Fischer, David Forgacs, and David Miller. London: Verso, 1983.

Mottram, Ron. *The Danish Cinema before Dreyer.* Metuchen, NJ: Scarecrow, 1988.

Mulvey, Laura. "Visual Pleasure and Narrative Cinema." *Screen* 16, no. 3 (October 1, 1975): 6–18.

Murphy, Richard (John). *Theorizing the Avant-Garde: Modernism, Expressionism, and the Problem of Postmodernity.* Cambridge: Cambridge University Press, 1999.

Neale, Steve. "Art Cinema as Institution." *Screen* 22, no. 1 (1981): 11–40.

Neergaard, Ebbe. *En filminstruktørs Arbejde: Carl Th. Dreyer og hans ti film.* Copenhagen: Atheneum Dansk Forlag, 1940.

Neergaard, Ebbe. *Historien om dansk film.* Copenhagen: Gyldendal, 1960.

Neergaard, Ebbe. *The Story of Danish Film.* Translated by Elsa Gress. Copenhagen: Det Danske Selskab / The Danish Institute, 1963.

Neergaard, Ebbe, Beate Neergaard, and Vibeke Steinthal. *[En filminstruktørs Arbejde.] Ebbe Neergaards bog om Dreyer, i videreført og forøget udgave ved Beate Neergaard og Vibeke Steinthal.* Copenhagen: Dansk Videnskabs Forlag, 1963.

Nestingen, Andrew K. *Crime and Fantasy in Scandinavia: Fiction, Film and Social Change.* New Directions in Scandinavian Studies. Seattle: University of Washington Press; Copenhagen: Museum Tusculanum Press, University of Copenhagen, 2008.

Nysten, Jes. "An Unrealized Lifelong Dream—Dreyer's Jesus Film." Danish Film Institute Dreyer website. Accessed July 4, 2023. https://www.carlthdreyer.dk/en/carlth dreyer/about-dreyer/themes/unrealised-lifelong-dream-dreyers-jesus-film.

Peucker, Brigitte. *The Material Image: Art and the Real in Film.* Stanford, CA: Stanford University Press, 2007.

Pribram, E. Deidre. "Melodrama and the Aesthetics of Emotion." In *Melodrama Unbound: Across History, Media, and National Cultures,* edited by Christine Gledhill and Linda Williams, 237–51. Film and Culture. New York: Columbia University Press, 2018.

Program for *Grevindens Ære.* Danish Film Institute Dreyer website. Accessed July 4, 2023. https://www.carlthdreyer.dk/carlthdreyer/filmene/grevindens-aere.

Program for *Mormonens Offer.* Danish Film Institute. Accessed July 3, 23. https://www .dfi.dk/viden-om-film/filmdatabasen/film/mormonens-offer#Materialer.

Program for *Vampyr.* Danish Film Institute Dreyer website. Accessed July 3, 2023. https://www.carlthdreyer.dk/carlthdreyer/filmene/vampyr.

Program for *Vampyrdanserinden.* Danish Film Institute. Accessed October 5, 2021. https://video.dfi.dk/filmdatabasen/20140/Vampyrdanserinden_20140_Filmprogram .pdf?_ga=2.2716720.1231899898.1633477019-1470532686.1633477019.

Rein, Sten. *Hjalmar Söderbergs Gertrud: Studier kring ett karleksdrama.* Stockholm: Bonniers, 1962.

Renoir, Jean. "Dreyer's Sin." In *Carl Th. Dreyer: Danish Film Director 1889–1968,* edited by Søren Dyssegaard, 41–45. Presentation Books, Ministry of Foreign Affairs, Copenhagen: Van Rasmussens Litografiske Trykkeri, 1969.

Rhodes, John David. "Art Cinema's Immaterial Labors." *Diacritics* 46, no. 4 (2018): 96–116.

Rifbjerg, Klaus. "Om Neergaard om Dreyer." *Vindrosen, Gyldendals Literære Magasin* 11 (1964): 65–68.

Rosenbaum, Jonathan. "Gertrud as Nonnarrative: The Desire for the Image." In *Placing Movies,* 105–16. Berkeley: University of California Press, 2020.

Rugg, Linda Haverty. "A Tradition of Torturing Women." In *A Companion to Nordic Cinema*, edited by Mette Hjort and Ursula Lindqvist, 351–69. Hoboken, NJ: John Wiley & Sons, 2016.

Sandberg, Mark B. *Living Pictures, Missing Persons: Mannequins, Museums and Modernity*. Princeton, NJ: Princeton University Press, 2005.

Sandberg, Mark B. "Mastering the House: Performative Inhabitation in Dreyer's *The Parson's Widow*." In *Northern Constellations: New Readings in Nordic Cinema*, edited by C. Claire Thomson, 23–42. Norwich, UK: Norvik Press, 2006.

Schamus, James. *Carl Theodor Dreyer's Gertrud: The Moving Word*. Seattle: University of Washington Press, 2008.

Schamus, James. "Dreyer's Textual Realism." In *Rites of Realism*, edited by Ivone Margulies, 315–24. Durham, NC: Duke University Press, 2020.

Schepelern, Peter. "Biograf-problemer—Refleksioner over den Psykobiografiske Metode I Martin Drouzys Dreyer Monografi." In *Sekvens Filmæstetik & Billedhistorie*, 123–48. Filmvidenskabelig årbog Institut for Film & Medievidenskab. Copenhagen: Copenhagen University Press, 1983.

Schepelern, Peter. "Danish Film History, 1910–1920." Accessed May 21, 2023. https://www.dfi.dk/en/english/danish-film-history/danish-film-history-1910-1920.

Schlüpmann, Heide. "Asta Nielsen and Female Narration: The Early Films." In *A Second Life: German Cinema's First Decades*, edited by Thomas Elsaesser with Michael Wedel, 118–22. Amsterdam: Amsterdam University Press, 1996.

Schlüpmann, Heide. *The Uncanny Gaze: The Drama of Early German Cinema*. Women and Film History International. Urbana: University of Illinois Press, 2010.

Schneider, Rebecca. *Performing Remains: Art and War in Times of Theatrical Reenactment*. Florence: Taylor and Francis, 2011.

Schrader, Paul. *Transcendental Style in Film*. 1972. Reprint, Berkeley: University of California Press, 2018.

Schröder, Stephen Michael. "Screenwriting for Nordisk, 1906–1918." In *100 Years of Nordisk Film*, edited by Lisbeth Richter Larsen and Dan Nissen, 96–113. Copenhagen: Danish Film Institute, 2006.

Sedgwick, Eve Kosofsky. *Touching Feeling: Affect, Pedagogy, Performativity*. Series Q. Durham, NC: Duke University Press, 2003.

Shambu, Girish. "For a New Cinephilia." *Film Quarterly* 72, no. 3 (March 1, 2019): 32–34.

Singer, Ben. *Melodrama and Modernity: Early Sensational Cinema and Its Contexts*. Film and Culture. New York: Columbia University Press, 2001.

Sirk, Douglas. *Sirk on Sirk: Interviews with Jon Halliday*. Cinema One 18. London: Secker and Warburg for the British Film Institute, 1971.

Sitney, P. Adams. "Moments of Revelation: Dreyer's Anachronistic Modernity." In *Modernist Montage: The Obscurity of Vision in Cinema and Literature*, 53–80. New York: Columbia University Press, 1990.

Snyder, Sharon L., and David T. Mitchell. *Cultural Locations of Disability*. Chicago: University of Chicago Press, 2006.

Sobchack, Vivian Carol. *Carnal Thoughts: Embodiment and Moving Image Culture*. Berkeley: University of California Press, 2004.

Soila, Tytti, Astrid Söderbergh-Widding, and Gunnar Iversen. *Nordic National Cinemas*. New York: Routledge, 1998.

Sørensen, Peer E. *Vor tids temperament: Studier I Herman Bangs forfatterskab*. Copenhagen: Gyldendal Press, 2009.

Thompson, Kristin. "Kristin Thompson on Variety (1925, dir. E. A. Dupont)." Video essay. Accessed July 2, 2023. https://www.youtube.com/watch?v=X4TovIvgoVI.

Thomsen, Bodil Marie. "On the Transmigration of Images: Flesh, Spirit and Haptic Vision in Dreyer's *Jeanne d'Arc* and von Trier's Golden Heart Trilogy." In *Northern Constellations: New Readings in Nordic Cinema*, edited by C. Claire Thomson, 43–57. Norwich, UK: Norvik Press, 2006.

Thomson, C. Claire. "The Slow Pace of the Era: Carl Th. Dreyer's Film Style." In *Slow Cinema*, edited by Tiago de Luca and Nuno Barrados Jorge, 47–58. Edinburgh: Edinburgh University Press, 2022.

Thomson, C. Claire, Isak Thorsen, and Pei-Sze Chow. *A History of Danish Cinema*. Edinburgh: Edinburgh University Press, 2021.

Thorsen, Christian Isak. "Isbjørnens anatomi: Nordisk Films Kompagni som erhvervsvirksomhed i perioden 1906–1928." PhD diss., Copenhagen University, 2009.

Thorsen, Isak. "Filmsfabrikken i Valby." In *Dansk film i krydsfeltet mellem samarbejde og konkurrence*, edited by Chris Mathieu and Jesper Strandgaard Pedersen, 93–111. Lund: Ariadne Förlag, 2009.

Thorsen, Isak. "Nordisk Films Kompagni 1906–1924: The Rise and Fall of the Polar Bear." In *100 Years of Nordisk Film*, edited by Lisbeth Richter Larsen and Dan Nissen, 52–71. Copenhagen: Danish Film Institute, 2006.

Thorsen, Isak. "Surviving a Crisis: Nordisk Films Kompagni as a World Player." In *A History of Danish Cinema*, edited by C. Claire Thomson, Isak Thorsen, and Pei-Sze Chow, 21–29. Edinburgh: Edinburgh University Press, 2021.

Truffaut, François. *The Films in My Life*. New York: Simon and Schuster, 1985.

Tybjerg, Casper. "The European Principle: Art and Border-Crossings in Carl Theodor Dreyer's Career." In *A History of Danish Cinema*, edited by C. Claire Thomson, Isak Thorsen, and Pei-Sze Chow, 41–50. Edinburgh: Edinburgh University Press, 2021.

Tybjerg, Casper. "Helvedesildens genskær: Allegori og frigørelsevilje i besættelsetidens film." *Kosmorama* 233 (Summer 2004): 93–115.

Tybjerg, Casper. "Searching for Art's Promised Land: Nordic Silent Cinema and the Swedish Example." In *A Companion to Nordic Cinema*, edited by Mette Hjort and Ursula Lindqvist, 271–90. Hoboken, NJ: John Wiley & Sons, 2016.

Tybjerg, Casper. "The Spy Who Loved Me: Benjamin Christensen and the Danish Silent Spy Melodrama." *Journal of Scandinavian Cinema* 9, no. 3 (2019): 253–76.

"Vampyr." Film Program at Danish Film Institute. The Program for Vampyr. Danish Film Institute Dreyer website. Accessed July 3, 2023. https://www.carlthdreyer.dk/carlthdreyer/filmene/vampyr.

Wahl, Jan B. *Carl Theodor Dreyer and Ordet: My Summer with the Danish Filmmaker*. Screen Classics. Lexington: University Press of Kentucky, 2012.

Wall-Romana, Christophe. *Jean Epstein*. Manchester: Manchester University Press, 2013.

Webber, Andrew. "Cut and Laced: Traumatism and Fetishism in Luis Buñuel's *Un Chien Andalou*." In *Projected Shadows: Psychoanalytic Reflections on the Representation of Loss in European Cinema*, edited by Andrea Sabbadini, 92–101. New York: Routledge, 2007.

Weber, Johannes. "'Doctor! I'm losing blood!' 'Nonsense! Your blood is right here': The Vampirism of Carl Theodor Dreyer's Film *Vampyr*." In *Vampires and Zombies*, edited by Dorothea Fischer-Hornung and Monika Meuller, 191–212. Jackson: University Press of Mississippi, 2016.

Williams, Linda. "Film Bodies: Gender, Genre, and Excess." *Film Quarterly* 44, no. 4 (1991): 2–13.

Williams, Linda. "Melodrama Revised." In *Refiguring American Film Genres: History and Theory*, edited by Nick Browne, 42–88. Berkeley: University of California Press, 2000.

Williams, Linda. *Playing the Race Card: Melodramas of Black and White from Uncle Tom to O. J. Simpson.* Princeton, NJ: Princeton University Press, 2001.

Williams, Linda. "'Something Else besides a Mother': 'Stella Dallas' and the Maternal Melodrama." In *Imitations of Life: A Reader on Film & Television Melodrama*, edited by Marcia Landy, 307–30. Detroit: Wayne State University Press, 1991.

Index

Note: Page numbers in *italics* refer to illustrations.

Aa Kühle, Kay van der, 179
The Abyss (Afgrunden) (film), 50, 194n42
"Acostatets første Offer" (script), 182
action film, melodrama and, 4, 14
actor(s): pressure on, Dreyer and, 11, 34, 43–44, 48, 65–69, 115, 186n33; spectatorial concern for, melodrama/corporeal spectacle and, 11, 66, 133. *See also specific names of actors*
affective spectacle: Dreyer's use of, 9. *See also* corporeal spectacle
Affron, Charles, 198n45
Afgrunden (The Abyss) (film), 50, 194n42
Aftonstjärnan (Söderberg), 164–65
All That Heaven Allows (film), 127
Den allvarsamma leken (Söderberg), 165
Almodóvar, Pedro, 5, 176
Almroth, Greta, 35
American cinema: early, use of makeup in, 197n20; melodrama in, Danish cinema compared to, 27–28, 106. *See also* Hollywood cinema
anagnorisis (recognition), melodramatic mode and, 184n8
Andrews, David, 6, 183n6, 185n15, 185n16
Anne Pedersdotter (Wiers-Jenssen), 98, 99
anxiety of influence, Bloom on, 84

archive(s)/archival research, 16–17; art melodrama as, 17; Dreyer's, nonlinearity of, 33, 40; Dreyer's, performative revisiting/reworking of, 18, 98, 170; Dreyer's affective engagement with, 16–17, 170, 176; Dreyer's self-archiving consciousness, 163; *Gertrud* and, 17, 18, 144, 146–47, 155, 156–62, 165–68, 170; as performance, 147, 155, 162–63, 170, 176, 205n35; pleasurable complexities of, author's first encounter with, xii; pleasures and pitfalls of, lace representing, 105; reading Dreyer's work and career as, 17–18, 176. *See also* research
Archive Fever (Derrida), 146–47, 156, 157, 160–61, 162
Artaud, Antonin, 42
art cinema: definitions of, 7, 185n15; and embodiment, 5–6; European, Dreyer's central status in, 8–9, 120, 175; and high culture, association of, 6; and ideology of personal expression, 185n22; "impurity" associated with, 5–6, 60, 183n5, 184n13; and melodrama, reconciliation in *Ordet* (film), 18, 120–21, 124, 137, 141–42; vs. melodrama, art melodrama as embodied performance of tensions between, 3–4, 174, 176; vs. melodrama, tradition of separating,

with, 99–100; camera placement/
movement in, 95, 112, 116; climactic
scene in, 110, *116*, 116–17; continuities
with early Nordisk scripts, 18, 24, 98,
102; corporeal spectacle in, 112–15, *113*;
critical reception of, 8, 101; as domestic melodrama, 105–6, 107; Dreyer's
attraction-repulsion to melodrama reflected in, 100–102, 116, 118–19; embodied inheritance in, 39–40, 110, 118;
emotional expressivity in, xiii, 83, 110;
ending of, 98–99, 115–17, 118; female
desire in, 95, 96, 102, 104, 107, 109–10,
117; formal innovation in, 9, 112, 118;
Herlofs-Marthe's character in, 111–13,
113, 114–15; immolation scene in, 34,
114–15, 196n6; "Kniplinger" script compared to, 98, 102, 104, 105–6, 107, 117;
lace in, function of, 95, 96, *96*, 105,
109–10, *111*, 117–18; latent tension in,
106; matriarchal character in, 195n56;
narrative ambiguity vs. melodramatic
subject matter of, 101; opening scene
in, 110–11; *Ordet* compared to, 127,
129; play inspiring, 98; plot of, 102–3;
production history of, 100, 186n33;
scrim scene in, 95, 96, *96*, 109; suffer-
ing/feminine suffering in, 112–15, *113*;
techniques of displacement in, 98; use
of sound in, 113, 114, 115; victimhood
and volition in, 79
deathbed scene(s): in "Chatollets Hemmelighed," 123, 138; and effigy culture,
138; in Nordisk films, 137–38; in
Ordet, 134–36
Delschaft, Maly, 58
Delusions (Söderberg), 166
De nåede færgen (*They Caught the Ferry*)
(film), 181
De Putti, Lya, 58
Derrida, Jacques, *Archive Fever*, 146–47,
156, 157, 160–61, 162
Der var engang (*Once Upon a Time*)
(film), 180
desire. *See* female desire
"De To Verdener" (script), 181

The Devil's Protegé (*Den Hvide Djævel*)
(film), 32, 47, 60, 180
Dickens, Charles, Danish adaptations
of, 193n32
Die Gezeichneten (*Love One Another*)
(film), 180
Dinesen, Robert, 22; Dreyer's scripts directed by, 128, 180, 181; in *The Vampire Dancer* (film), 77
disability: depiction in *Vampyr*, 90; as
representational device, in body
genres, 91
Doane, Mary Ann, 10, 189n48
"Döden Forener" (script), 179
Dødsridtet (*The Leap to Death*) (film), 179
Dogme 95 movement, melodramatic
sensibility in films of, 7
Doktor Glas (Söderberg), 165, 206n37
A Doll's House (Ibsen), 195n52; *Gertrud*
(film) compared to, 148; prototypical
"unknown woman" in, 153–54
domestic melodrama, 4; Dreyer's films
and, 10, 98, 105–6, 107, 143. *See also*
family melodrama
Doolittle, Hilde (H.D.), 13; response to
Jeanne d'Arc (film), 3, 12, 13, 129
Dreyer, Carl Th.: archive of, nonlinearity of, 33, 40; archive of, performative
revisiting/reworking of, 18, 98, 170;
attraction-repulsion to (Nordisk) melodrama, 16, 18, 28, 42, 48, 50, 53, 59,
98–99, 100–101, 116, 118–19, 120–21,
127, 146, 172, 175; career of, queer reading of, 18, 174–75; career of, standard
accounts of, 8, 24; central status in
European art cinema, 8–9, 120, 175;
charge of opposites in, 176–77; creative agency as director of art melodrama, 119; Dagmar Theater operated
by, 109, 145; and Danish film industry, pressure to save/develop, 40, 50–51,
99–100, 172, 193n33, 201n6; development as director, Danish cinema history and, 19, 31–32; friendship with
Neergaard, 145, 171, 173–74; great passion of, xi; insatiable artistic demands